RAINBOW WARRIOR

Also by The Sunday Times Insight Team
The Yom Kippur War
Ulster
Siege!
The Falklands War

Written and edited by
Robin Morgan and Brian Whitaker
In London
Rowena Webster, Roger Wilsher
In New Zealand
Robin Morgan, David Black, Antony Terry
In France
Brian Whitaker, Tim McGirk, Mark Hosenball,
Jean-Noel Fournier, Paul Prier
In Australia
Geraldine Brookes
On Rainbow Warrior
Paul Brown
Researcher
Caroline Robb

THE SUNDAY TIMES
INSIGHT
RAINBOW WARRIOR

The French attempt to sink Greenpeace

Hutchinson

London Melbourne Auckland Johannesburg

This edition first published in 1986 by Century Hutchinson Ltd
Brookmount House, 62–65 Chandos Place, London WC2N 4NW

Century Hutchinson Publishing Group (Australia) Pty Ltd
PO Box 496, 16–22 Church Street, Hawthorn, Melbourne, Victoria 3122

Century Hutchinson Group (NZ) Ltd
PO Box 40–086, 32–34 View Road, Glenfield, Auckland 10

Century Hutchinson Group (SA) Pty Ltd
PO Box 337, Bergvlei 2012, South Africa

Set in Linotron Ehrhardt by
Rowland Phototypesetting Limited
Bury St Edmunds, Suffolk

Printed and bound in Great Britain by
Anchor Brendon Limited, Tiptree, Essex

British Library Cataloguing in Publication Data
Rainbow warrior: the French attempt to sink
Greenpeace.
1. Rainbow Warrior *(Ship)* – History   2. Harbors
– New Zealand – Auckland – History – 20th century
I. Sunday Times Insight Team
363.1'23'09312'2   G530.R3/

ISBN 0 09 164360 0
ISBN 0 09 947720 3 Pbk

Contents

List of Illustrations

The *Rainbow Warrior* under full sail (*photo: Greenpeace/Fernando Pereira*)
The Rongelap exodus (*photo: Greenpeace/Fernando Pereira*)
The crew of the *Rainbow Warrior* (*photo: Greenpeace/Fernando Pereira*)
After the bomb in Auckland Harbour (*photo: Associated Press*)
Fernando Pereira (*photo: Greenpeace*)
David McTaggart (*photo: Gamma*)
McTaggart being beaten by French commandos (*photo: Greenpeace*)
Headquarters of the DGSE (*photo: Gamma*)
Dominique Prieur (*photo: Associated Press*)
Alain Mafart (*photo: Associated Press*)
Christine Cabon (*photo: Associated Press*)
Louis-Pierre Dillais (*photo: Agence France Presse*)
Eric Andreine (*photo: Agence France Presse*)
Jean-Michel Bartelo (*photo: Agence France Presse*)
Roland Verge (*photo: Agence France Presse*)
Restaurant visitors' book signed by the *Ouvéa* crew
The yacht *Ouvéa* (*photo: Sygma*)
The French submarine *Rubis* (*photo: Sipa*)
President Mitterrand and defence minister Charles Hernu (*photo: Sygma/Arnaud de Wildenberg*)
David Lange (*photo: Gamma*)
Laurent Fabius (*photo: Gamma*)
Pierre Lacoste (*photo: Sygma*)
Bernard Tricot (*photo: Sygma/Michel Philippot*)
The Tricot report (*photo: Gamma*)
Allan Galbraith (*photo: Sygma*)
The dove of peace (*photo: Greenpeace*)

PART ONE

Trail of the bombers

As she stopped talking, the old woman and the boy looked to the east and they saw a great rainbow flaming in the sky where a thunderstorm had passed.

'The rainbow is a sign from Him who is in all things,' said the old, wise one. 'It is a sign of the union of all peoples like one big family. Go to the mountaintop, child of my flesh, and learn to be a Warrior of the Rainbow, for it is only by spreading love and joy to others that hate in this world can be changed to understanding and kindness, and war and destruction shall end!'

from *Warriors of the Rainbow*,
William Willoya and Vinson Brown
(Naturegraph Publishers)

CHAPTER ONE

Marsden Wharf

AUCKLAND *July 10, 1985, 8.00 p.m.*

In the darkness, the hunched figure was barely noticeable. The waterfront buildings and seasonal drizzle obscured the lights of the city and hid his approach. His confidence bordered on arrogance, for this mission promised to be a pushover, barely stretching the skills he had mastered in a school where stealth, sabotage and assassination were high on the curriculum.

He was steering a grey Zodiac inflatable dinghy through Waitamata Harbour, the finger of Pacific Ocean which pokes into the east coast of New Zealand's North Island. The Zodiac had puttered across the harbour, past the container terminal, and into the port itself. Rounding King's Wharf, he silenced the engine and coasted the last few yards to the deserted dockside. He chained the dinghy to a rusty mooring and peeled off his Gulfstar weatherproof jacket to reveal a black wetsuit. From the well of the Zodiac he hoisted two white oxygen cylinders on to his back, strapped flippers to his feet and perched a face mask on his forehead. Silently he slipped over the side, reached back into the dinghy and pulled a large waterproof bundle into the water. He checked his wrist compass and dived.

On the other side of Marsden Wharf, the next dock along, Warren Sinclair sat stretched out on the bridge of the MV *Explorer*, a 140-tonne whitehulled vessel. He pulled the ring on a can of beer and fiddled with the tuning knob on his marine radio. Sinclair was tired. He had spent the day working on the boat, scraping, sanding and painting it to prepare it for the coming summer's tourist trips. Another month or two and the *Explorer* would be ready to take bookings. Sinclair was the relief skipper, living on board during the off season, earning an income until he could start the engines of his own boat, the *Inca*, to serve the same tourist trade. He had bought the *Inca* two years

9

earlier, realizing two popular Kiwi dreams – to own a boat and to be self-employed – after resigning his job as an engineer with Air New Zealand. For Sinclair, there was no comparison between the complex technology of a Boeing 747 and the simple attractions of his new profession, ferrying fishermen at forty-five dollars an hour to fish for snapper, shark and tuna. Lying at anchor, offering the odd tip on how to handle heavy tackle or land a thrashing marlin, was infinitely preferable to gulping kerosene fumes beneath whining Rolls-Royce engines on the hot tarmac of an airport.

It was midwinter in the city of sails which houses a fifth of New Zealand's population, and the *Explorer* was sprayed with a fine mist of rain. Alone on the bridge, eavesdropping on the radio traffic between passing ships, Sinclair was feeling mellow and warm. Short, stocky, and thirty-six years old, he enjoyed his own company. There was no wife to scold his absence. His time was his own after a laborious twelve-hour shift. It wasn't work, it was therapy.

People from the converted trawler berthed on the other side of Marsden Wharf were throwing a party and Sinclair was invited. But the hours had ticked by. Engrossed in his work, he had forgotten the invitation until, too late, he remembered the friendly gesture. By then he was too tired to get cleaned up. Instead he succumbed to the temptation of a solitary beer and the motion of the gently bobbing *Explorer*. But he did feel a little guilty about ignoring the invitation. The *Rainbow Warrior* had docked three days earlier and Sinclair liked the crew: no-nonsense, pragmatic people who busied themselves on board and obviously cared for their vessel. They were in sharp contrast to the usual crowd of itinerants who berthed at the wharves: American vacationers on floating gin palaces with stainless steel masts and polished teak decks. These gleaming yachts usually came to Marsden and Captain Cook wharves, together with the smaller merchant ships, while the high-walled Japanese roll-on roll-off vessels unloaded Toyotas, tractors and trailbikes at the bigger, busier King's and Queen's docks.

The *Warrior* was nearly three times the size of Sinclair's *Explorer*: a robust 417 tonnes, built in the Hall Russell shipyard at Aberdeen alongside warships for the Royal Navy. As the *Sir William Hardy* – named after a biologist and fisheries expert – it had served the British Ministry of Agriculture as a research vessel. Later, it had fished for cod in the North Sea.

Then Greenpeace bought it for £32,000 in 1978 and the veteran of the Cod Wars between Britain and Iceland found a new lease of life. It was the first really effective weapon in the Greenpeace armoury, carrying campaigns against the slaughter of whales or the dumping of nuclear waste to all corners of the world. In its first encounter under its new name, the *Rainbow Warrior*, it was pitted against an old foe, an Icelandic gunboat called the *Aegir*. The two vessels had fought many duels in the north Atlantic when Iceland had extended its territorial waters to preserve fish stocks for its own trawlers. The British government refused to accept the threat to its own deep sea fishing industry and sent Royal Navy frigates north to protect British trawlers. The result was a series of rammings, dented bows and scraped hulls. Many British trawlers had their nets sliced open by cables towed behind the Icelandic gunboats. In 1978 and 1979, with a crew of twenty Greenpeace volunteers, the *Warrior* took on the Icelandic whaling fleet in the north Atlantic and in September 1979 was arrested by the *Aegir*. Equipment worth £42,000 was confiscated. Early in 1980 the *Warrior* was again arrested, this time off the French port of Cherbourg while attempting to disrupt the transport of nuclear waste to a reprocessing plant.

Before long, the *Rainbow Warrior* scored a spectacular success, enhancing Greenpeace's growing reputation for daredevil action. In the spring of 1980 she sailed from Amsterdam to disrupt the activities of the Spanish whaling fleet. On arrival in June, she was again arrested and taken under escort to the military port of El Ferrol. The Spanish removed a thrust bearing from the propeller. They sealed the radio room, drained the fuel tanks and mounted a twenty-four-hour guard on the ship. The *Warrior* appeared to be immobilized indefinitely. The conservationists thought otherwise.

Five months later, on a chilly November night, the crew staggered down to the ship, apparently drunk and loaded with

11

bottles of wine. The guard turned a blind eye. They had furtively been plying him with drink for weeks. The only problem for Greenpeace was to pretend that one of the bags they were carrying was not heavy. The new thrust bearing seemed to weigh a ton.

The crew worked deftly to install the new part, playing Beatles records at full volume to try and muffle the noise of hammering. If they could only get the propeller working again then they could try a dash for freedom. Fuel was no problem. They had been smuggling it on board in wine bottles since June. And they had already turned the *Warrior* round to face the sea, using the pretext that they needed to paint her hull.

The Spanish guard thought he was dreaming when he saw the *Warrior* moving out of the harbour. A moment later he realized the escape was for real and sounded the alarm. The chase was on. Two Spanish gunboats raced after the ship. The Greenpeace crew members were aghast. The *Warrior* normally travelled at twelve knots. But now she was limping along at half the speed, restrained by seaweed that had grown on her hull as she sat in El Ferrol. They would never get away unless something incredible happened. It did. Just as the *Warrior* left the harbour a massive storm erupted around the pursuers and their prey. The sleek Spanish vessels were almost swamped and Greenpeace got away.

By 1981, the *Warrior* was under arrest yet again, held by the Canadian coastguard after an attempt to disrupt the annual and bloody cull of Nova Scotia seal pups. That summer she was back off the British coast to stop nuclear waste being dumped in the Atlantic. The crew had by now developed perilous tactics to impede the dumping. They raced inflatables alongside the ships and under the hoists used to dump the barrels overboard. The dumpers ignored them and dropped the containers, capsizing the Greenpeace inflatables and sending their crews flying into the icy water. It was inevitably a quixotic gesture, but Greenpeace had already mastered the art of publicizing its cause. Photographs of their apparently suicidal actions were snatched up by news-hungry picture editors and attracted many new members from all walks of life.

There were some who suspected that Greenpeace was part of a Warsaw Pact plot to undermine the West. Indeed, there are still many who remain convinced that its funds come directly from Moscow and the KGB, but Russia itself was Greenpeace's next target. In July 1983 the *Warrior* was to be found in the Bering Sea landing seven crew members on Soviet territory to document the illegal activities of Russian whalers.

Now the *Rainbow Warrior* was in the Pacific, and almost unrecognizable from her rusting, ice-clad trawling days. With conservation in mind, Greenpeace had replaced her old engines with new energy-efficient American diesels. Two masts had recently been added to carry sail in the hope of further savings on fuel. It was a conversion that attracted much attention among sailors and seamen in New Zealand, for the bulbous former trawler had been transformed into a graceful craft which commanded the admiration of all who saw her heeling under full sail.

PARIS *July 10, 1985, 8.30 a.m. local time*

There were others who showed a more furtive interest in the *Rainbow Warrior*. In a ten-storey glass and concrete office block on the boulevard Mortier a duty officer of the General Directorate for External Security (DGSE) waited by the telephone and watched the clattering telex machines. His office was below ground on one of the subterranean levels reserved for the department's more confidential activities. The building lies in the 20th arrondissement, next to a public swimming pool. For that reason the top security building has earned the nickname la Piscine in the French press. Those who work inside have their own euphemisms for the building; they call it la Boîte (the box) or la Crémerie (the dairy).

The DGSE has an Action Division with three main branches to carry out air, maritime and commando missions wherever the nation's interest or its government dictates. It is the secret service headquarters of a country that still regards itself as the world's prime source of culture and civilization, a superpower striving to maintain its position despite reduced circumstances. To that end the DGSE had despatched the frogman in the grey

13

Zodiac, who even now, ten hours ahead of Paris time, was checking his wrist compass. He dived silently below the surface and kicked his feet. It took him no more than a minute to cross to Marsden Wharf, where he surfaced briefly to check his bearings. The hull of the *Warrior* reared above him, backlit by the wharf security lamps. The muffled sound of gaiety on board would stifle any noise he might make.

He dived to six feet or so and stretched out his hand in search of the steel hull. He felt the outer skin of the stern curving tightly away from him, pushed himself deeper still and found the rudder and the blades of a propeller. He inched along the hull and selected a spot where the propeller shaft passed beneath the aft water ballast tank, just below the crew's sleeping quarters. Reaching into his diving bag he pulled out a cumbersome contraption and attached it to the hull.

Sliding between the wharf and the starboard hull, he kicked further along the length of the ship, took a second, identical package from his bag and pushed it up against the outer wall of the engine room. Each device weighed approximately thirty pounds, but built-in foam buoyancy blocks alleviated the strain on the diver's wrists. He kicked out once more, dived beneath the keel and surfaced for a second time to check his route back to the Zodiac.

MARSDEN WHARF *8.30 p.m.*

There was every reason to celebrate on board the *Rainbow Warrior* that night. The *Warrior*'s crew, together with New Zealand volunteers, had been busy patching up the wear and tear wrought by the Pacific. As the flagship of Greenpeace, it had spent recent months ferrying the inhabitants of Rongelap, a tiny Pacific atoll dusted with radiation from American nuclear tests, to a new uncontaminated island home.

By the end of the day the accumulated debris of weeks at sea had been swept away, the engineers were working on the marine diesels, the rigging had been expertly examined and cleaned. Rust streaks on the green hull and white wheelhouse had been scrubbed and touched up, and the garish rainbow that swept up and over the bows from port to starboard had been repainted.

14

Also on each bow was a dove of peace, and on the stern, pictures of whales. A banner slung across the bridge demanded a 'nuclear-free Pacific' in case the citizens of Auckland passing along nearby Quay Street needed any reminder of the superpowers' military interests in the region. Greenpeace was busying itself for another campaign – leading a protest armada of small boats to the French Polynesian atoll Moruroa, the Place of the Big Secret. It is well named, for France has regularly exploded atomic bombs there. This was to be the biggest protest yet against the nuclear tests. The *Warrior*'s recent arrival had been a major event in Auckland, where feelings against colonialism and military interference in the Pacific ran high. There had been a civic reception the night before and a Maori welcome for the crew.

Another reason for the party was that it was Steve Sawyer's twenty-ninth birthday. Sawyer was an international director of Greenpeace and the Moruroa campaign co-ordinator. A slim, bearded man, with thinning blond hair, he balanced the buccaneering spirit of Greenpeace with the cautious brain of a military strategist and the astute foresight of a cunning politician. In the open, often argumentative debates within the higher echelons of Greenpeace he spoke his mind and maintained the respect of friend and enemy alike. He had not fully recovered from a thirty-foot fall during the Rongelap exodus which had nearly killed him, but all that day, as volunteers cleaned and painted the ship, he held meetings to finalize the minutiae of peaceful protest. A conference in the untidy Greenpeace office in Courthouse Lane had already discussed the bare essentials of the *Rainbow Warrior*'s 1986 campaign itinerary. In the afternoon, however, Moruroa was on his mind.

A report published in 1984 had downplayed the effects of the nuclear testing there, but information assembled by Greenpeace suggested that the deep layers of rock hundreds of feet down were cracking, releasing radiation through the fissures into the sea. Sawyer wanted to discuss the Greenpeace reply to the report and the evidence that might be gathered to support their case once they reached Moruroa. They intended to take samples from neighbouring inhabited atolls to discover if the local populations were suffering higher than normal fatalities from cancer and radiation. Another meeting with the Canadian, Australian and New Zealand directors of Greenpeace followed before Sawyer was able to tackle the immediate subject: the coming campaign.

He was due to chair a meeting of the armada skippers on board the *Warrior*. The *Warrior*'s captain, Peter Willcox, and his two mates, Martin Gotje and Bene Hoffman, were already waiting. Also present were Chris Robinson of the ketch *Vega*, Richard Rae, the skipper of the *Klis II*, Russell Munro of the *Django*, Tony Still of the *Alliance* and Alastair Robinson of the *Varangian*.

Sawyer clambered down the ladder into the mess room, to be greeted by a far larger crowd. The crew, shorebased members and sympathizers were all assembled together with the international Greenpeace directors – they had not forgotten it was Sawyer's birthday. The relief cook, Margaret Mills, a fifty-five-year-old native New Zealander from Waiheke Island, was feeding the crew while the *Warrior* was in port. She had baked Sawyer a large chocolate cake for the surprise celebration.

He mumbled a few words of thanks and listened, embarrassed and a little impatient, as they sang 'Happy Birthday', for there was still much to do. A young Frenchman approached him, shook his hand and wished him well, both on his birthday and for the coming campaign. The thin, baby-faced young man introduced himself as François Verlon, a militant pacifist, and talked animatedly about his country's interference in the Pacific before taking his leave. 'I'm in a hurry,' he explained. 'I have to catch a plane to Tahiti.'

Sawyer, too, slipped away from the party to discuss the logistics of the Moruroa campaign with the skippers in the former fish hold, now converted to a library and theatre. There was much to discuss: the equipment which would be needed; the problems of rendezvous at sea when storms were likely to fragment the flotilla; the vital communications necessary to organize and protect each vessel when the French navy attempted to keep them from the atoll. Even personality clashes among crew members posed potentially disastrous problems if they were to spend weeks, if not months, cooped up in small boats under pressure from the elements and the French.

HOBSON'S BAY *Auckland, 9.00 p.m.*

A group of men at the Outboard Boating Club sat drinking beer, cracking jokes and discussing their common interest – the fuel-thirsty power boats dotted around Hobson's Bay in front of them. There had been a spate of thefts from the boat club and the members intended to catch the culprits. They had formed a vigilante group, though under strict instructions from the police that anyone caught tampering with the boats or attempting to steal them was not to be challenged. Detectives did not want bruised and bloodied suspects handed over to them. The club's vigilantes were simply to dial the emergency number and a squad car would arrive. The members organized two-man patrols in shifts while the others sat and waited with their beer.

Two events had already interrupted the tedium of their night vigil. Another, still to come, would shatter it completely. First there had been the sound of a siren from the hill behind them as a Blue Watch fire engine raced down the Strand and turned left on to Tamaki Drive, which snakes through the eastern suburbs to the downtown dock area. The fire engine was heading for the container terminal to tackle a chemical spillage on board an Australian merchant ship. At the boat club, more forgettable jokes were cracked and the siren was obliterated by the minor detonations of more beer cans. Then the second incident occurred. Mike Harris, an Auckland taxi driver and a boat club member for twelve years, recalls: 'We were all sitting about and then someone noticed this Zodiac dinghy pulled up on the causeway.' The attention that the Zodiac attracted is easily explained. It is a tough and expensive rubber craft rarely seen in New Zealand, much desired and much admired by the boating and yachting fraternity. The vigilantes began to squabble good-naturedly.

'If the owner doesn't come back in a hurry he won't have a boat to come back to,' said one.

17

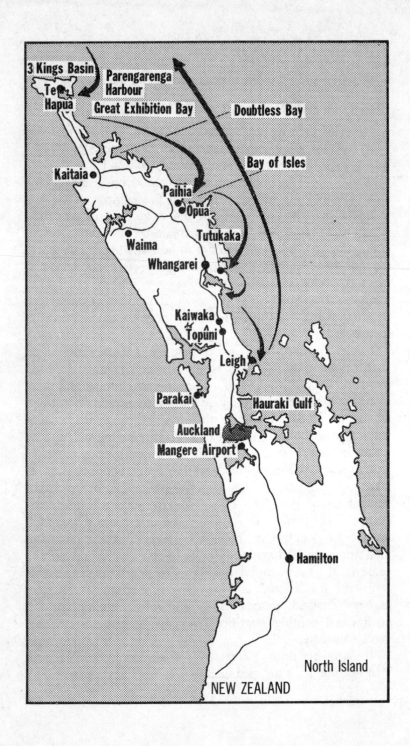

3 Kings Basin

Te Hapua

Parengarenga Harbour

Great Exhibition Bay

Doubtless Bay

Bay of Isles

Kaitaia

Paihia

Opua

Tutukaka

Waima

Whangarei

Kaiwaka

Topûni

Leigh

Parakai

Hauraki Gulf

Auckland

Mangere Airport

Hamilton

North Island

NEW ZEALAND

'Handy numbers, these Zodiacs. It's mine if the guy doesn't come back pronto,' said another.

'I'm opting out, mates,' said Harris. 'It's too big for me to carry. You can fight it out among yourselves.'

They agreed to warn the owner when he returned about the spate of thieving and vandalism. They were even willing to offer a temporary mooring at the boat club where the Zodiac would at least be safely guarded. Harris stood up, stretched and took his leave.

The two-man vigilante patrol returned to the boat house. They, too, had noticed the dinghy – and more besides. They had seen a man in a Gulfstar jacket steer the Zodiac under the Tamaki Drive bridge and into Hobson's Bay. He had followed the wall of the causeway to a set of concrete steps leading to the road above. Their suspicions had grown when he dragged the Zodiac up the embankment, climbed the steps and looked up and down Tamaki Drive. He seemed angry and hurried. Further up the road a Toyota camper van flashed its lights, started up and drove towards him. It pulled up by the steps, next to a telephone kiosk and a bus stop. A man got out and ran down the steps to help the first man unload the Zodiac and carry a large bundle to the rear of the van. The vigilantes moved closer. As the van sped past them in the direction of the city centre, one wrote down the registration number while the other rushed to the kiosk to call the police. They arrived eighteen minutes later but the camper van had gone.

It was still only 9.30 p.m. Before midnight, the beer-drinking but observant vigilantes, the partying Greenpeace members, the drowsing relief skipper on MV *Explorer* and the firemen of Blue Watch were to become bit-players in the opening act of a global drama, inextricably linked by a plot hatched 14,000 miles away and brought to fruition by the man in the grey Zodiac dinghy.

19

CHAPTER TWO

You can't sink a rainbow

'MIDNIGHT BLASTS RIP PEACE BOAT.' The headline in the *New Zealand Herald* next morning reflected official uncertainty about the explosions that tore two holes in the *Rainbow Warrior*. Was it sabotage or merely some kind of accident: gas cylinders, perhaps? The newspaper's first edition had just gone to press and Bert Nealon, the news editor, was climbing the stairs back to the newsroom when the shock wave from the first explosion hit the building at 11.38 p.m. He found his chief reporter, John Andrews, leaning out of a window and peering towards the docks just a few blocks away. Another reporter was already on the telephone, trying to squeeze the barest facts out of the police and fire services, when the second bomb exploded two minutes later.

It was one of those rare occasions in a journalist's life when he gets the opportunity to bawl 'Hold the front page' and can feel confident he is not ordering a wasteful and embarrassing halt to the printing presses. Staff at the *Herald* soon convinced themselves that the *Warrior* had been bombed. A 'gut feeling' told Nealon that exploding oxygen cylinders do not sink ships and that there was nothing else on the wharf to explain the event. Besides, Greenpeace had enemies throughout the globe – both political and corporate – and was a nuisance to many.

For other newspapers it wasn't a major story just yet. The world was still shocked by the Sikh terrorist bomb which had blown up an Air India jet 31,000 feet over the Atlantic, killing 329 passengers and crew. It was also enamoured still with young, blond Boris Becker who had just become the first German to win the men's singles championship at Wimbledon. The explosions that had sunk the *Rainbow Warrior* had taken place on the other side of the world and police were still looking for innocent explanations. In London, *The Times* carried a short, one-paragraph taster on the front page with a picture and a report inside. Sabotage was suspected, the newspaper said, but no one was certain.

Warren Sinclair, on the other hand, had no doubts at all. He was about to bed down in his bunk aboard the *Explorer* on the opposite side of the dock. He had just switched off his marine radio when a sudden wave lifted his boat and bumped it against the wharf. 'It wasn't a loud explosion, just a dull thud. You could feel it rather than hear it, and I knew it must have come from under the water.' The newspapers would later report explosions 'rocking' downtown Auckland; in fact there was only a subdued flash under the surface which boiled momentarily and then subsided.

The water had sandbagged the bombs and subdued the crack of detonation, concentrating the explosive force on the *Warrior* itself. The blasts burst through the steel hull, up through the lower decks, splintering metal and wood, and out into the night. Within four minutes the *Warrior* had settled on the bottom.

The *Warrior*'s relief cook, Margaret Mills, had found a quiet place and a typewriter to work on after the birthday cake had been cut. She was writing a play, and had completed the draft of the first act and put it in an envelope before slipping back to her cabin and climbing into her bunk. 'There had been some pretty noisy nights on board so I was sleeping deeply that night. The first bomb woke me but at first I thought someone had left a tap on. Then I realized something serious had happened – perhaps a ship had hit us. I dressed quickly and opened the cabin door. The corridor was filling fast with water and the ship's doctor, Andy Biedermann, was standing there. He said the ship was sinking and I turned to get my glasses but he said there was no time – we had to get off the ship.

'It seemed too unlikely. I thought, "Ships don't sink in port," and decided to humour him. I still thought someone had left a tap running or one of the water tanks was leaking. We splashed through the water and climbed up on deck and on to the wharf. Then the second bomb went off. It was only later that I discovered the second explosion had been directly below my

21

cabin. There was nothing left but a gaping hole where the floor had been.'

The ship's engineer, Davey Edwards, went to the engine room to investigate the first explosion. 'I opened the door and went down three steps. I was up to my knees in water. It was time to abandon ship.'

Sinclair ran out on to the deck of the *Explorer* and peered at the *Warrior* between two cargo sheds. He saw the ship settling fast at the stern, her twin masts keeling over the wharf. Her prow was held high by the mooring ropes keeping the white dove of peace and the rainbow painted on the port bow proud of the water. The crew members were milling around. Some had jumped on to the wharf; others had taken the quickest route to safety and leapt overboard. There was no panic, just dazed people in varying stages of undress. Sinclair dashed back into the wheelhouse, switched on his radio and put out a Mayday distress call to Auckland Marine Radio, the station at Musick Point which relays ship-to-shore calls.

At that time of night the control room on the ninth floor of the Auckland Central Police Headquarters was quiet. The bars had closed and the drunks were off the streets. The night-clubbers would not be setting off home until at least three in the morning, so apart from the usual crowd of young teenagers idling by the fast-food shops in Queen Street there was little to concern the police. Nevertheless, the twelve computer terminals in the control room were all manned. At four of them sat the operators who answered the emergency calls. They in turn relayed the calls through to one of two dispatchers for each of Auckland's four precincts. It is the dispatcher's job to locate the nearest available patrol car and send it to the scene.

The waterfront of Auckland Harbour falls within the busiest area, Central District, and the call that came in from Musick Point that night was routed through to the computer screen in front of Constable Andrew Gentry. Of the ten squad cars patrolling Central that night, Sergeant Geoff Holloway's was closest to the docks. The wharf police station, a small Victorian building on Quay Street just a hundred yards from the end of Marsden Wharf, had closed its doors at 11.00 p.m. and the duty officer was long gone. Holloway responded, but Gentry was unable to tell him much; just that there had been an explosion and the *Warrior* was sinking.

On occasions like this a panic button is pushed on Gentry's console. It alerts the control room supervisor by flashing details of the emergency and the response on to his screen in a quiet office in the corner. That night it was Senior Sergeant Tony Lee in charge. His first act was to open up the Special Operations room equipped with radios, telephone lines, telex machines and audio-visual aids for debriefing. The room is rarely needed, but Lee opened it all the same, for the *Warrior* explosions had the hallmarks of a growing crisis. Next he alerted Ron McNaught, the uniform inspector who would take control on the ground. Then he called Detective Inspector Bert Whyte from Criminal Investigations Bureau and Senior Sergeant Trevor Tozer who would fend off the inevitable – and often tiresome – calls from the media.

Back at Marsden Wharf, Sinclair found the *Warrior*'s American skipper, Peter Willcox, wandering along the dock. Willcox had been asleep in his bunk when the first bomb exploded below him. Pausing only to pull on a blue sweater he had rushed out of his cabin, naked from the waist down. 'He was a study of disbelief,' says Sinclair, 'that anything like this could be happening to him, to his boat – and in port, too. He was adamant that there had been nothing on board to cause the explosions. It had to be a bomb.'

Sinclair's first concern was to check if anyone was still on board. He and Willcox counted the crew and thought that three people were missing. 'There was no panic. Some people cried a little, others just sat on the wharf, while others busied themselves checking the boat and salvaging items of equipment.' Sinclair rushed back to the *Explorer* and got on the radio again. If people were missing, divers would be needed, and quickly too.

In fact it was the fire service which was first on the scene. Station officer Denis O'Donoghue and his crew had finished cleaning up the chemical spillage on board the Australian container ship and had only just returned from a false alarm at the primary school when they were called out to Marsden Wharf.

'When we got to the wharf we couldn't see anything because it was pitch black. We raced up the wharf on the wrong side, past the MV *Explorer*, and turned the corner at the top to come down the other side. We saw all these people. Some were standing, others were lying down and most had been in the water. Then we saw the boat. It was right down at the stern with only the funnel and the bridge showing. There were two blokes still on board, standing on the bridge, and they were making no effort to get off. They were pretty agitated because they thought some people were still trapped below. We put a ladder across and donned our breathing apparatus just in case. Three of us climbed on to the boat to talk to the men – Willcox, the skipper, and the engineer, Davey Edwards.

'There was hardly any light, just a dim street lamp or two, but the crew were remarkably calm. We normally have to deal with people who are really spaced out but these people were well in control. The skipper and the engineer had been trying to dive down through the radio shack to get to the crew's quarters.'

O'Donoghue and his men had been on the wharf just two minutes when the boss drove up in his red Colt, lights flashing and headlamps blazing. Divisional Fire Officer Trevor Sampson, forty-three, had arrived to take control. A lean man with close-cropped hair, he had been commended for bravery once and was addicted to jogging long before it became a global craze. He was not one to sleep while his men worked. He was also the kind who turned down promotions because they involved desk work.

He had finished his rounds of fire stations, checking on training and equipment, and watched the 9.30 p.m. news on television in the rest room. He had got a cup of coffee and settled down with a book in the armchair. Then the phone rang. He could have ignored it but he was gripped by curiosity. 'My first thought was that it must be another sauna war. Every now and again, a massage parlour boss decides to firebomb a competitor. We had three go up in one night, just like a pack of crackers.'

While driving to the docks he heard that the explosion was

24

at Marsden Wharf itself. 'You get a gut feeling after a few years in this job. I wondered what the hell there was down there to cause an explosion and then had a tingling feeling in my stomach and I knew some bugger must have had a pop at the *Rainbow Warrior*.'

Sampson found the wharf strangely quiet when he arrived. After a quick debriefing from the station officer he strode over to the *Warrior*'s skipper and asked: 'What were you doing to cause the explosions?'

'We weren't doing anything and there was nothing on board to cause them,' replied Willcox.

'Do you think someone has put bombs on board her?' Sampson asked. Willcox's nod spurred him to action. He shouted to O'Donoghue: 'Get everyone off the boat. There might be more. Get off in case it goes again.'

Sampson, along with other senior fire officers, had had some experience of explosives. A short course of instruction from the New Zealand army had taught him how to respond to just such an emergency. 'We put that training into effect immediately – we took bloody long steps out of there.' Within minutes the dock was cleared, just as Constable Holloway pulled up in his squad car.

'What's happened, do we know?' he asked Sampson.

'To be honest, mate, I think someone has blown the bloody thing up.'

'What do you want me to do?' asked Holloway, slightly confused by the enormity of the Divisional Fire Officer's statement. The question upset Sampson. He thought the answer should have been obvious, and rounded impatiently on the unfortunate constable.

'Go and get a bloody senior officer,' he bawled. Holloway snapped to attention, ran back to his squad car and radioed control.

O'Donoghue meanwhile had not been idle. Willcox thought three people were trapped. Firemen had lined the wharf and were tapping the part of the ship's hull still above water in the hope that anyone below might be trapped in an air pocket. But there were no replies. 'We decided right off that if they were

25

forward, then they stood a good chance of surviving in an air pocket. But if they were in the stern the chances were slim to say the least.' Eventually one missing crew member walked on to the wharf. Hanne Sorensen, an engineer from Denmark, had gone for a walk earlier and had returned to find out what the fuss was about. Another member, who had been overlooked in the head count, was found safe and well on the docks, leaving just one unaccounted for.

Greenpeace's Steve Sawyer had left the ship half an hour before the bombs exploded. He had gone to prepare for the next day's meeting of Greenpeace directors and continue the birthday celebration with his girlfriend and some other close friends at the Piha Surf Club an hour's drive away. They were sitting around the table chatting when the telephone rang. Sawyer wondered who could be calling at that time of night and checked his watch. It was 1.07 a.m. His first thought was that the caller must be Greenpeace headquarters back in England, twelve hours behind and forgetful of the time difference.

In fact it was Elaine Shaw, who helps run Greenpeace's Auckland office. She sounded shocked. 'Steve, the *Herald* just called me. There's been an explosion on the *Rainbow Warrior* and it's sunk in the harbour.' Sawyer made her swear on oath that it wasn't a joke, ran back to tell his friends, then returned to town. He found the *Warrior*'s crew sitting in the tiny dockside police station which had been reopened as an incident room and makeshift Greenpeace office. As he went in, a voice said: 'They blew up the boat and they've killed Fernando.'

Fernando Pereira, a Portuguese-born photographer, was a popular member of the crew. He had been assigned to cover a Greenpeace protest three years earlier and had been converted to the cause. His pictures of the Rongelap exodus had been relayed around the world. He had two children – a boy and a girl – and an estranged wife. He had settled in Amsterdam after fleeing Portugal to escape military service and now he was missing, trapped somewhere below.

Warren Sinclair was furious. A trained diver himself, he had volunteered, even insisted on getting his gear from the *Explorer*, to dive in search of Pereira. But the possibility that other bombs might be on board prompted Inspector McNaught, who had arrived to take charge, to forbid the attempt. He was waiting instead for the Auckland police force's own divers. It is a source of considerable bitterness within the force itself that the only professional police divers are based in the capital, Wellington, hundreds of miles to the south, where they can be of little use in an emergency. There are many who believe that Auckland, as the biggest port and probably the biggest sailing centre in New Zealand, should have its own professional team. Instead it relies on part-time volunteers from within its police force, men who dive for leisure when they can find the time.

Not surprisingly the volunteers are relatively inexperienced. When they arrived thirty minutes after the blast their first attempt to search the wreck was also their last. They had already squeezed into their wetsuits when their van drove on to the wharf. Two divers leapt into the dock and ducked below a boom which the harbour board had thrown around the sunken ship to prevent bilge oil and diesel from contaminating the harbour. When they surfaced on the other side of the boom to don their face masks and mouthpieces, they broke through a foul-smelling slick that clogged their gear and forced them, choking and coughing, to abandon the attempt.

Sinclair fumed and in the heat of the moment cursed the officers for their stupidity. Again he demanded to dive in the hope that Pereira might still be alive, but McNaught was adamant. He had decided to wait for naval experts from across the harbour.

Lieutenant Hugh Aiken, the staff diving officer of the Royal New Zealand Navy, had spent the day renovating the eighty-year-old weatherboard house he had bought behind the naval base at Devonport, across the water from Auckland. He was in bed with his wife Geraldine when he was woken at 1.10 a.m. His team of divers was already assembling and the police launch *Deodar* was on its way to collect them.

On the wharf he surveyed the wreck and examined plans of the *Warrior* hastily drawn by Willcox. Pereira had been sitting

27

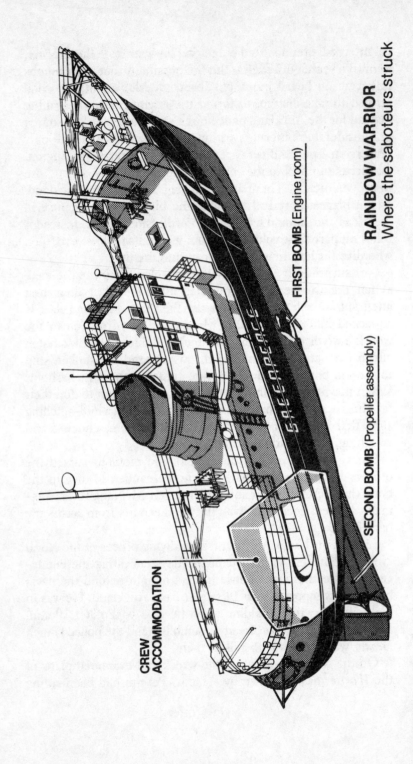

CREW ACCOMMODATION

SECOND BOMB (Propeller assembly)

FIRST BOMB (Engine room)

RAINBOW WARRIOR
Where the saboteurs struck

in the mess room with most of the others when the first bomb went off. Probably believing he had time to rescue his cameras and take some photographs before the ship sank, he had gone below and was caught by the second blast somewhere near the five cabins which were located just above the propeller shaft and rudder.

Leading divers Robert Schmidt and Moe Maurireie climbed gingerly on board, waded into the water on the sloping deck and dived through a hatch. Trailing a 25mm lifeline they fingered their way down through water muddied by silt and diesel oil. Schmidt searched the first cabin they came to, the starboard front cabin which Pereira occupied. He was not there. Maurireie found the photographer next door. He was wedged behind the door, face down, having stumbled into it by mistake in the dark. The second blast had knocked him out as the cabin filled with water. A post mortem examination would later register drowning as the cause of death.

The navy divers tied a rope round Pereira's lifeless form, pulled him into the gangway and signalled to their colleagues above – five short, sharp tugs to indicate they had found the body and one long pull to tell them to heave.

On the wharf there was no longer an emergency to cope with. A long, frustrating period of investigation was about to begin. Sampson had already ordered two other fire engines and the rescue wagon with cutting gear to return to base, but he asked O'Donoghue to hang around. The police and divers still needed the portable lights carried on the fire engines and the firemen might yet be required as the night wore on.

The crew of the *Warrior* had mostly gone. Chief engineer Davey Edwards explained later: 'We all went our different ways for the night. We needed to be alone, to try and gather our wits.' For many of the crew, one night was not enough to do that.

CHAPTER THREE

Four men and a boat

Four men, each a leader in his own right, received the news at different times, in different places and with varying reactions. In the days and weeks to come, each would be inextricably linked by the single act of violence in Auckland that night. Each would play a major role: victim, villain, avenger and investigator.

David McTaggart, the fifty-two-year-old Canadian-born chairman of Greenpeace, regarded by most as the buccaneering founding father of the modern ecological army, was too old and wise to be surprised by the body blow to his cause. He had been in bloody confrontations himself while campaigning in the past. His organization's enemies could do little to shake him, and, although earlier in the year he had been laid low by a virus for six weeks, he was at a Greenpeace board meeting in Bournemouth, England, when the call came from New Zealand. He showed no emotion, just picked up a pen, scribbled the details and announced the news to the meeting.

A softly-spoken, silver-haired man, his face betrays a desire for mischief. He talks the dialect of American campus culture in the 1960s despite his acquired British citizenship, liberally sprinkling conversations with 'hey, man' or 'lemme tell ya'. He sits at the head of an organization staffed by young, tough and committed people (many are middle-class and well-educated professionals) yet seems less concerned with the intellectual issues than with the challenge and confrontation they promise.

If anything he is an opportunist who has found a cause in which to exercise his talent and ego. It is doubtful whether any other figure in the Greenpeace movement could have welded the organization together from a fragmented cross-section of small, disorganized and argumentative groups. He established a firm financial base not unlike that of a multinational company.

Perhaps his greatest talent, however, is inveiglement. With remarkable cunning and considerable insight, he is able to embarrass nations with well-planned strategies and carefully laid traps, and inspire zest and enthusiasm among the slothful or disenchanted. It is a talent that works on all but his closest friends and advisers – and even they let their guards slip sometimes.

It is not surprising that McTaggart runs Greenpeace with entrepreneurial flair. Before he espoused the ecological cause, the construction business was the focus of his life. By the time McTaggart was in his mid-thirties, he was general manager and vice-president of Bear Valley Development Corporation, running a 400-acre ski resort in the mountains east of San Francisco. With his wife, Betty, and three children, McTaggart fitted more easily into the mould of the successful, hard-working family man than that of the world conservationist. But there were already signs that he was not as staid as first impressions would suggest. He had publicized the ski resort with a controversial poster of his wife skiing in the nude. Soon his capacity to shock would be channelled into a totally different cause: publicizing the horror of nuclear tests.

But it took a very different horror to draw McTaggart away from his business interests and into ecology. A propane gas explosion ripped apart his lodge in the Bear Valley Resort, and two of his employees were badly injured. Nobody was killed, and blame for the explosion did not lie at McTaggart's door, but McTaggart maintains it was then that his thirst for making money died. 'My drive for upward mobility had ended there that afternoon in the High Sierras,' he says.

Certainly his business confidence was severely bruised that day. Not long after the accident, McTaggart was offered – and accepted – $50,000 a year and a substantial stock option to become president of a venture capital company in New York. The cataclysm really came when, soon afterwards, McTaggart sued the propane company over the explosion. Friends assured McTaggart that the court hearing would be a walkover for him. They were wrong: his claim failed. The surprise outcome sent McTaggart into mental confusion. He did not know what had

31

become of his life; he could no longer bear the strain of high-pressure living. He was unable to turn to his wife for comfort – their marriage was on the rocks. So, with his emotions in turmoil, McTaggart left home, straightened out his business affairs, drove to San Francisco, got rid of his Mercedes, and took a plane to Tahiti.

It was the sort of escape from the rat-race that many people only dream of. The fact that McTaggart actually left his world behind, instead of just thinking about doing it, marked him out as a doer, someone willing to act. This active spirit was to become the hallmark of Greenpeace. But for the moment nobody knew that, least of all McTaggart. For the next six months he lived, rarely sober, on the island of Moorea, off Tahiti, drinking to ease his mental pain. Then one morning he awoke to find that his anguish was ebbing away. He did not want to live in oblivion any longer. Instead, he found he had an urge to do something. He wanted to go to sea.

He left Moorea for New Zealand. There he fell in love with – and purchased – a small sailing ketch, the *Vega*. It was not the only object of his affection at that time. Soon McTaggart had also fallen for a young New Zealand woman, Ann-Marie Horne.

President François Maurice Marie Mitterrand, Croix de Guerre, Officier Légion d'Honneur, wartime Resistance leader and now France's socialist head of state, was lunching at the fashionable Bonnoit restaurant near Grenoble when the bombs exploded in Auckland. He made a detour after leaving to greet competitors cycling in the Tour de France and wave to the spectators before returning to Paris.

In 1985, Mitterrand's beleaguered government was fast losing its grass-roots support; his former socialist colleagues viewed him with suspicion, believing him to be a bourgeois turncoat who, once in power, had deserted the left-wing ideals which had put him in the Elysée Palace. The fate of the *Rainbow Warrior* must have come as a great relief. For months now, his defence minister and the armed forces had been complaining that the Greenpeace protest armada could severely disrupt

32

France's 1985 nuclear test programme. In particular the refinement of the French neutron bomb – a device which leaves buildings, roads, and vehicles untouched while killing all inside them – was threatened. For a moment it seemed that one of the many problems facing the French president, albeit minor in comparison with other political headaches, had been solved.

Mitterrand has been a reserved loner since childhood. He was born in Jarnac in the undulating Cognac country of western France in 1916. His father was station master at Angoulême, on the route south to Spain, then manager of a successful vinegar works. François inherited his ambition – and a love of long, solitary walks – from his father. His sister describes him as obstinate, and a bad loser. He studied law and political science in Paris but joined the army at the outbreak of war and was captured by the Nazis. Three times he managed to escape, joined the Resistance and married Danielle Gouze who nursed the wounded.

By the time Paris was liberated he was a powerful figure. He became one of de Gaulle's youngest ministers, although the general distrusted him and thought him a closet Communist. By 1969 he had begun rebuilding the French Socialist Party, which had just been humiliated in the elections, taking a minuscule six per cent of the vote. By May 10, 1981, his task was complete. The socialists were the biggest and most powerful party in France and he was president.

Mitterrand has maintained a dictatorial control of his government. It is rumoured that when his ministers travel to his country retreat in the Landes they walk behind him in single file on his long strolls. He illustrated his dominance with a series of sweeping legislative changes: abolition of the death penalty, university reform, industrial democracy, leasehold reform and the abolition of military tribunals. He had promised a wind of change and shocked many with the scale of it.

His policies soon began to alienate both left and right. Even his ministers turned on him when he began to stage vitally important meetings to discuss policy and action without inviting his prime minister or finance minister. The party became embroiled in internecine feuding; the franc was devalued three times; there were violent demonstrations in the streets and factories; fifty-eight French paratroopers were killed in Beirut. Later Mitterrand would admit with uncharacteristic frankness, 'We dreamt a little in 1981. I didn't have the experience to see we were wrong.' In essence, a man famed for his long-term strategies was now living with hand-to-mouth policies. His popularity had plunged from over seventy per cent in the opinion polls to less than forty per cent. His problems were mounting week by week and the socialists had entered the phase of greatest unpopularity: the run-up to an election year. Though Mitterrand is safe until 1988, the socialists have been given little hope of success in the March 1986 parliamentary election.

Greenpeace must have been a minor irritation to Mitterrand, but the military was deeply agitated. If Mitterrand or his generals thought that with the sinking of the *Rainbow Warrior* the Greenpeace ghost had been laid to rest, they were in for a surprise: soon it would return to haunt them.

David Lange, New Zealand's portly prime minister, had been woken before breakfast at his residence in Wellington with the news of the bombing. Immediately he asked for an early briefing from his Commissioner of Police, Ken Thompson, and ordered a security conference for later in the day.

Around the table sat Lange himself, Commissioner Thompson, Air Marshal David Ewan Jamieson (chief of the defence staff), Frank O'Flynn (defence minister) and Bernard Hillier (director of New Zealand's External Intelligence Bureau). It was a short and relatively unproductive meeting. The police had a few tenuous leads. Airports and harbours were being watched. Interpol had been contacted in the hope that it might have some intelligence which would explain the bombing. A statement was prepared which would fill the gap until more was known.

'The police will be given every resource to investigate the sinking,' Lange promised. No effort would be spared.

The prime minister's passionate reaction to the bombing was undoubtedly heartfelt but – like most politicians – he could not ignore the opportunity to increase his stature among voters with

34

a shopping list of suggestions which he knew would curry considerable favour. In carefully chosen words he talked of replacing the *Warrior* with a frigate from the Royal New Zealand Navy to lead the protest armada to Moruroa. He promised to establish a fund to help Pereira's dependants and offered a reward for information leading to the arrest of the bombers. To each promise he added caveats explaining why it might be impossible.

It has been said that the Falklands War enhanced Margaret Thatcher's reputation as a strong and resourceful leader at a time when her popularity was flagging. Certainly the conflict in the south Atlantic helped win the landslide 1983 election for the Conservative Party and became known as Thatcher's Falklands Factor. Likewise, the sinking of the *Rainbow Warrior* was proving to be Lange's lifejacket at a time when the nation was growing increasingly discontented with his strange mix of socialist and monetarist policies which had set inflation raging. Unemployment had begun rising towards the politically fatal twenty per cent and the mortgage rate, that other great ingredient of electoral success or failure, was nudging twenty-five per cent.

David Lange, at forty-three, is New Zealand's youngest prime minister ever and only the fourth Labour leader to hold power in the country's history. His rise has been swift and he has established a remarkable reputation for tough-talking honesty and strong moral beliefs.

He graduated in law from Otahuhu College, Auckland University, and travelled to London, where he met two of the three great influences on his life and career. Working in the accounts department of a city insurance company he rented a bed-sitting room for five pounds a week on his salary of six hundred pounds. It was during this lonely period of his life that he walked into a west London mission and encountered 'the most lucid sermon I'd ever heard'. The speaker was Dr Donald Soper (now Lord Soper), Britain's premier Methodist and one of the great orators of parliament, whose interests and deep knowledge range from a hatred of cruel sports and nuclear power to a powerful grasp of economics. Lange was hooked. He spent less and less time in his lonely bed-sit and more and more time at the mission with Lord Soper. He salvaged newspapers from dustbins and devoured the foreign news pages. He also fell in love with a young volunteer at the mission, Naomi Crampton, from Nottingham. They married and returned to New Zealand.

Back in Auckland, Lange practised law in much the same way that the third great influence on his life, his father, Roy, practised medicine. Roy turned his back on rich consultancies and private practice to care for poor people whom he charged just three shillings for surgery visits and five shillings for home calls. The son turned his back on a lucrative career at the bar to seek out those who could not afford adequate representation in the courts.

His arrival in politics in 1977 as MP for Mangere, the airport suburb of Auckland, was described by one commentator as 'the arrival of a show-stealing fat man at the circus'. Lange was a dishevelled and mountainous twenty-two-stone figure with a permanent cloud of tobacco smoke around his head. He appeared to be one of the few young politicians who would not be intimidated by the bullying leader of the right-wing National party, Sir Robert Muldoon.

Success in his new-found calling required a dramatic change of image. Lange underwent surgery to reduce his weight to fourteen stones. He also quit smoking and soon emerged as the likely leader of the next Labour government. He had only been in politics six years when he was elected leader of the opposition in February 1983, and a little over a year later he swept Muldoon from power, taking on the roles of foreign minister and head of intelligence in addition to the prime minister's office.

Victory was ensured through Lange's apparently unbudgeable moral stance as he campaigned against nuclear arms. He had promised the electorate a new style of government that took the citizen into its confidence. He pledged to make New Zealand's voice known and respected throughout the world, to steer the country out of its south Pacific cul-de-sac and into the fast lane of international affairs.

It only took a matter of months. He banned American ships carrying nuclear arms from New Zealand's ports. While insisting on his allegiance to the western alliance, he attacked French,

American and Russian interests in the Pacific and savaged New Zealand's most famous asset, the All Blacks rugby football team, for its proposed tour of South Africa. New Zealand was suddenly appearing on the world stage, but Lange's obvious intellect and leadership did little to solve the growing economic crisis. By early 1985 he was using his rhetorical skills to sweeten the bitter financial pill being swallowed by the nation. 'I tell you now that we are not going to get an economic recovery this year or next, but economic recovery there will be.'

Lange employed those skills when the *Rainbow Warrior* sank. The economic crisis was quickly forgotten as a huge sense of injustice and a demand for retribution gripped the nation. New Zealand generally regarded Greenpeace with affection, but its pride had been injured besides and its hackles were up. Terrorism had arrived, the nation's old-fashioned equilibrium had been upset, and someone must pay. Lange himself carried the torch at the head of the hue and cry.

It was a lasting desire for revenge. In the months to come, when it looked as if the perpetrators might evade justice and Lange's Rainbow Factor had faded in the glare of ever-present economic discomfort, the prime minister himself would become a target, carrying the heavy burden of suspicion that a discontented band of followers can impose on its leadership.

Thursday July 11 was a day of immense activity. It was a time to draw breath, to examine the scene in the cold light of day. Auckland's top detective, Superintendent Allan Galbraith, had been called in to take charge. A native of Scotland, he had been a cadet police officer and done national service in the Scots Guards before emigrating to New Zealand. He had risen quickly through the ranks to head the national drugs squad in Wellington, and had been sent on a year's secondment to Thailand, a major source of narcotics smuggled into New Zealand. He had been in Auckland just a few months when he landed the biggest case any Kiwi cop had ever handled – the hunt for the *Rainbow Warrior* bombers.

Once the silt had settled again in Auckland Harbour, Lieutenant Hugh Aiken's divers went down once more to survey the damage. Sunlight now penetrated almost to the seabed. For the first time there was official confirmation from experts. The *Rainbow Warrior*'s hull was ruptured in two places. The holes gaped six feet by nine wide and the shattered, jagged edges curled inwards. Only explosive devices attached to the outside of the hull or fired at it could have inflicted such damage. But who had done it? Why? And where were they now?

Galbraith began to assemble his team immediately, switching the incident room from Special Operations on the ninth floor of Central HQ to the more spacious squad room on the third. There is no such thing as a murder squad in New Zealand, which has a national police force rather than forces recruited and employed on a local or regional basis. Galbraith began to call on Lange's promised resources, installing detectives from all over the country in his incident room. At the height of the investigation he was to have seventy officers working full time. They would collect more than 400 statements and 1,000 exhibits, travelling all over the world to build their case. But there were more immediate problems.

Unlike the chiefs of more sophisticated forces in Europe and America, Galbraith did not have access to computers. Instead he relied on old-fashioned methods, box-filing the paperwork as it mounted. For that he called on the services of Sergeant Glenda Hughes, a New Zealand shotputting champion with a photographic memory. She specialized in running the filing systems of large-scale investigations and was reputed to have total recall of any fact from the statements handed to her, even telephone numbers. She could reel off times and car registration numbers, apparently without a second's thought. She debriefed detectives as they reported back to the incident room and liaised with Galbraith daily. Soon she had built up a system of forty-eight box files.

The investigation was split into branches, one each for such areas as exhibits, witnesses, suspects, scene of crime, forensic evidence. In charge of each was a senior sergeant leading a team of detectives.

One of the fastest-filling baskets was the Nutters' Tray. Into that went the 'eyewitness report' from a pilot who, 1,000 feet above Auckland Harbour in his light plane on the night of the bombing, swore that he could pick out the hunched man in the Zodiac dinghy as it rounded King's Wharf. He even picked out a mugshot, identifying the face by a distinctive mole on the left cheek. Even when it was pointed out to him that the bombing took place in darkness, he stuck to his story. Another 'witness' insisted that four men had walked unannounced into his home one day and asked him to build them a bomb. As the investigation progressed, officers would flick through the Nutters' Tray in search of some light relief from the increasingly complex investigation. By midday on Thursday July 11 there were still precious few clues to follow, but the dour, methodical Galbraith was not deterred.

The vacuum left by the midnight bombing and the lack of hard answers to the questions raised prompted speculative articles in the New Zealand press. One newspaper carried a long piece by two political reporters predicting that the tidal wave of international terrorism had finally reached the shores of New Zealand. They suggested links with a series of terrorist bombings in Europe by anarchist groups attacking American air bases in Germany. But the article tailed off, not unnaturally, without revealing why anti-American bombers would attack such an unlikely target as the *Rainbow Warrior*. The *Auckland Star* carried an opinion piece that summed up the quizzical reaction of New Zealand's population: 'A mad bomber – or bombers – has struck again, this time in the heart of Auckland. With an irrationality that is impossible to fathom they have struck at crusaders whose tactics have always been non-violent.' The author explained his predicament and came close to answering the question he himself had posed. 'We are still innocents to international terrorism . . . this act remains incomprehensible to most if not all of us. It is still hard for New Zealanders to imagine an individual deranged enough to act like this, or a terrorist group or state-backed sabotage squad dedicated to such acts.'

Someone had to break the ice, and it was not long in happening. Greenpeace's London director, Bryn Jones, listed the powerful enemies made by the organization and opted for French involvement. Independent Television News in Britain broadcast his suspicions and soon the world's press was seeking confirmation.

In New Zealand the French embassy in Wellington was besieged by reporters demanding a statement. 'In no way was France involved,' protested spokesman Charles Montan. 'The French government does not deal with opponents in such ways.' Perhaps he was badly informed or simply being smug but he added: 'France was not worried by the anti-Moruroa campaign.'

Suspicion was then pointed at Canada, where Greenpeace had clashed with government-hired hunters who culled the Nova Scotia seal pups. 'It is beyond belief that Canada was in any way involved in the bombing,' said an angry High Commissioner, James Ganderton. Then it was the turn of Britain, where Greenpeace had campaigned against nuclear waste dumping. 'The suggestion is beyond the realms of fantasy,' said a spokesman.

Reporters continued their rounds. The Soviet Union took its place in the list of potential defendants, having suffered at the hands of anti-whaling campaigners. 'The Russian people support Greenpeace and wish to express their sympathies. We are surprised that Greenpeace might consider Soviet involvement,' commented Sergeo Buranov at the Russian embassy in New Zealand. The Japanese response to accusations was characteristically polite: 'We are deeply saddened by the bombing. Japan has a strong anti-nuclear movement and a strong belief in freedom of speech. This terrorist attack threatens them both,' said Hiroshi Sato, the embassy's political officer.

The newspapers were running out of people to blame when their attention was suddenly focused on the tenuous leads being pursued by Galbraith's detectives. The police wanted to interview the young *Frenchman* who had been on board the *Warrior* on the night of the bombing; a merchant ship had left the harbour shortly after the bombing flying the *French* flag; and a mysterious Zodiac dinghy abandoned at Hobson's Bay was of *French* manufacture. When they were checked out, the first two seemed to lead nowhere. But the third marked the start of a trail that would lead to the doors of the Elysée Palace itself.

CHAPTER FOUR

The odd couple

Auckland's international airport in the suburb of Mangere is like any other serving a large city – miles from the centre of town and hell to reach in the morning rush hour. So it was quite understandable when detective sergeants Terry Batchelor and Neil Morris switched on their siren. They had good cause to curse, for there was heavy traffic as they headed south towards the airport, and they half expected to find themselves in hot water when they returned to the Central Police Head-quarters.

When Superintendent Galbraith first heard that two people who might throw some light on the bombing were about to catch a plane out of New Zealand, he ordered the two senior sergeants to pick them up. They had piled into the lift with three colleagues and rushed out to the car pool to find their vehicle hemmed in by another. Desperate to reach the airport before the aircraft left, they had commandeered the nearest vehicle – a new Ford Falcon, recently delivered to carry the police force's top brass. The Chinese car cleaner had just finished polishing it and Batchelor had snatched the keys from his hand. A quick scuffle had ensued as the cleaner tried to retrieve them. 'What you do? What you do?' he demanded. Batchelor had little time to explain. He jumped into the driver's seat and roared off, leaving the irate cleaner holding his head in his hands and screaming: 'That bosses' car! That bosses' car!'

The detectives debated whether to pick up the radio and order the plane to be delayed, but it was still only 9.00 a.m. and Air New Zealand Flight 27, bound for Singapore and London, would not start boarding until 10.20. It was Friday, July 12, nearly thirty-six hours after the bombing.

When the owner of the expensive Zodiac dinghy found at

Hobson's Bay failed to return and collect it, the police checked the registration number of the van that had picked him up on Tamaki Drive. The white Toyota Hiace, LB 8945, was owned by Newman's, one of New Zealand's biggest travel and car rental firms. It had been hired from their downtown Auckland office by a French-speaking Swiss couple on honeymoon and they had promised to return it to the Wellington branch. The police had been looking for the couple, Alain and Sophie Turenge, on all routes south; they had checked ferries connecting the two islands of New Zealand in case the Turenges had changed their minds. There was also an officer awaiting their return at Newman's Wellington office. But now the couple had suddenly reappeared at Auckland airport. They had called into Newman's depot there, demanding a refund on the grounds that a sick relative forced their early return to Europe. They hoped to get standby tickets on Flight 27 if only Newman's would hurry and process their claim.

Had it not been for a stroke of good luck, the police might have missed their opportunity to speak to the Turenges. By chance, one of Newman's receptionists, Becky Hayter, had been moved from the downtown branch to the airport. It was she who had rented the camper van to the couple in the first place, and the police had since telephoned her at home to arrange an interview about her Swiss customers. She could hardly believe her eyes when she arrived for work at 8.30 that Friday morning. 'The couple were waiting in reception. M. Turenge explained that they wanted to return the van early and had estimated they deserved a refund of one hundred and thirty dollars. I was surprised to see them so soon after the call from the police but I didn't do anything at first. I thought that as they were here, the police must have seen them already and that everything had been cleared up. But I mentioned who they were to another girl, Claire Gilbert, and she decided to call the police to double check.'

The police asked them to make excuses and stall the Turenges until detectives arrived. So the women said they had to check the exact amount of the refund – just a formality, paperwork really, they explained. But twenty minutes passed, and still the police had not arrived. And the Turenges were growing suspicious.

'She was very nervous. She kept jumping up and going to the toilet and drinking coffee,' recalls Kelly Hogan, a receptionist in her first week at Newman's. 'I asked them both how their holiday had been. He said it was fine and she, in the same breath, said it was awful.'

Soon the women had to think up another excuse to calm the nervous Mme Turenge. The refund of $NZ130 was being prepared now, they said, but none of the directors had arrived yet to sign the cheque. It struck the receptionists that the couple had little to do with one another. They seemed remote, aloof even, rarely exchanging more than a word or two – they must have had an argument.

By now the women at Newman's were running out of excuses, and beginning to get tired of the charade. Then the plain clothes detectives pulled up outside. The Turenges, sitting with their backs to the window, did not notice Sergeant Batchelor stride up to the desk and whisper: 'Where are they?' By now totally engrossed in the drama, Kelly Hogan rolled her eyes to the left to indicate the couple sitting directly behind him. Batchelor turned on his heels, followed by Morris, and walked out of the door. Seconds later they returned with half a dozen other officers.

Batchelor walked up to the couple and asked their names. Alain Turenge stood up immediately and asked why he wanted to know. Batchelor responded by flashing his police warrant card and suggested the subject might be better discussed back at the station. The Turenges showed no obvious signs of surprise; he turned to her and they spoke in French for a moment, then he protested that they had no time because they were due to catch an early flight out. For an experienced officer like Batchelor, such encounters were normal. There was rarely need to get aggressive, for he had learned that the polite approach usually created less fuss and completed the task in half the time.

'Don't worry,' he told the Turenges. 'We just want to ask you a few questions. As soon as you've satisfied us we'll have you on that plane in plenty of time.' The couple stood up and

44

followed the two detectives out to the waiting cars. Batchelor took the husband's arm and steered him to the first vehicle while Morris indicated the second car to Mme Turenge.

'She became very agitated, refusing to be separated from her husband. We had to explain that there was nothing for her to worry about, that the cars would be one behind the other and she would be able to see her husband all the time, but she was not too pleased.'

The convoy of police cars drove back to the city centre and into the car park at the rear of the Vincent Street headquarters. The couple were taken up to the third floor squad room where Superintendent Allan Galbraith waited. They were not immediately interviewed, just left together in a side room while the detectives conferred. Galbraith decided that Batchelor should tackle M. Turenge and Morris should deal with the wife. It was a deliberate decision. If the Swiss couple knew anything at all, the husband had already shown he would be a tough nut to crack. His wife appeared to be jumpy, was certainly under stress and might be more forthcoming.

There was little to choose between Batchelor and Morris in terms of years or experience. Both were senior, street-wise detectives with long records of service. Terry Batchelor was a British immigrant born in Loughborough in Leicestershire thirty-eight years earlier. He had gone to New Zealand with his parents at the age of six, joined the police force straight from school and now had a wife and three growing children of his own. Of the two, he was the more reserved, a cool-headed patient man. They had reported, late, for duty on the morning of July 11 to find the Senior Sergeant of Staff, better known as the Chief Detective, drumming up a squad to investigate the bombing. 'He was slumped at his desk looking a little withered, battered by recent staff demands and the prospect of a massive inquiry to weaken him still further,' Batchelor recalls.

The 'Chief' gave a jubilant whoop at the sight of the two senior detectives suddenly appearing to solve his manpower shortage and sent them to see Galbraith. 'Don't worry,' he told them. 'You'll only be needed for a couple of days.'

There was always a chance that Mme Turenge might develop

45

an affection for Morris. If a film is ever made of the *Rainbow Warrior* saga, then the director could do worse than cast Burt Reynolds in Morris's role. At thirty-five, he is still unmarried – probably because of his fondness for women. He is a dapper, mustachioed man, whom his more irreverent friends might describe as a Lothario. In the weeks to come, after Galbraith had decided that these two officers alone should deal with the Turenges, Morris and Mme Turenge forged a friendship of sorts.

But for now, the problem was the night of July 10. The couple were adamant that they did not know the man from the dinghy whom they had picked up in Tamaki Drive. He had waved them down as they approached and had asked for their help. All he needed was a lift and they obliged. They knew his name was Peter and he was a fisherman, but that was all. They were in a hurry to leave the country because a close relative, Uncle Emille, had been taken seriously ill. They had not particularly enjoyed their holiday and could not wait to get home.

Frank MacLean is one of those jovial Australians who shoots from the lip and makes no apologies for his lack of discretion or tact. He speaks his mind and if it hurts or offends, then so be it. That is one of the reasons why he has not progressed in the customs service which he joined after settling in New Zealand and marrying a Maori. His title, Senior Customs Officer, does not denote seniority; it simply recognizes his length of service. But MacLean is undoubtedly good at his job. He lives and works in Whangarei, the biggest self-styled city north of Auckland. The new oil refinery being built along the coast has transformed the once-sleepy town over the past ten years but the boom is coming to an end. The growth of urban sprawl is being checked, the refinery is almost complete – and when that happens many jobs will disappear. Though Whangarei still bears the hallmarks of prosperity, with new office blocks rising between the single-storey clapperboard shops on the main street, it has now chiefly reverted to its previous role, that of New Zealand's northernmost official port of entry. It serves the sailors who cruise the Pacific and flee south to the Antipodes to escape the hurricane season.

MacLean lives in an untidy bungalow on a small plot of overgrown garden on Lovett Avenue, two miles north of the town. On the day after the bombing, Thursday July 11, he was away in Auckland on a customs training course and staying in the Royal International Hotel. 'I read in the morning paper that there had been an attack on the *Rainbow Warrior* and that police wanted to interview a Frenchman who had visited the ship a few hours before the bomb went off. "By Jesus," I thought, "I bet the *Ouvéa*'s got something to do with it."'

The *Ouvéa* was a thirty-eight-foot sloop crewed by four Frenchmen who had aroused his suspicions when the vessel had docked in late June. MacLean had boarded the *Ouvéa* to check for contraband and to deal with the immigration formalities. He had found nothing to justify turning the boat upside down and searching the bilges for drugs or the keel for secret consignments in specially hollowed-out sections. Nevertheless there were nagging inconsistencies which aroused his interest and maintained it now.

It was probably a long shot, he thought, as he drove home from Auckland on the afternoon of July 11. All the same, he would mention it to his boss, Bruce Cooper. Cooper, the collector of customs for Whangarei, was understandably sceptical. A handsome, intelligent man with fair hair and a moustache, he was young to occupy such an important position – younger than most of the men who worked for him – yet had obviously earned promotion by merit. He is the type of keen-witted individual who considers every move he makes, and he did so now when MacLean raised the possibility that the *Ouvéa* might be connected with the *Warrior*'s sinking.

Cooper's jurisdiction follows the east coast north from Whangarei to the tip of New Zealand at Cape Reinga and back down the west coast, a distance of some 250 miles. With scores of yachts sailing up and down the coastline to any one of a hundred bays, and a handful of customs officers, he had precious few resources to waste on the hunch of one officer. All it amounted to was the fact that the *Ouvéa*'s crew did not resemble, in the

47

slightest detail, the stereotyped yachting folk normally welcomed to New Zealand's shores by the customs men. The usual visitors were either sleek, rich men in designer clothes with fastidious vessels and blondes on the deck, or ocean-going hoboes in weather-beaten, often home-built, boats. But the *Ouvéa*'s crew possessed an uncommonly military bearing that did not sit easily in either of these two categories.

The fact that three of them had new, uncreased and unmarked French passports had been an interesting, even unusual, coincidence. One was supposed to be a photographer yet there was no camera on board and MacLean suspected the man was lying when he said he never brought his equipment on holiday. With hindsight, MacLean recalls other warning signs: the boat had the spotless cleanliness of a vessel ready to sail, rather than one that had just crossed the south Pacific. There were no personal effects, no photographs, no books near the bunks. And, most important, the *Ouvéa* had come in winter, a strange time for French holidaymakers to visit.

Experience had taught MacLean's boss that in ninety-nine point nine per cent of cases there was an innocent explanation for such inconsistencies. But experience had also taught him that it pays to be cautious before the event rather than wise after it. He did not object when MacLean suggested calling Gus Lindstrom, a detective sergeant at Whangarei police station. MacLean fixed a meeting for Friday afternoon and took the *Ouvéa*'s immigration papers, customs declarations and yacht details with him. The detective listened to MacLean's suspicions and shared Cooper's scepticism. But he knew that Superintendent Galbraith in Auckland was putting together a team of officers to investigate what could turn out to be the biggest case ever in New Zealand. Galbraith had telexed all stations asking for details of anything out of the ordinary. Officers were queuing up to get in on the team and this might be Lindstrom's lucky break. He called Auckland.

For fourteen hours, barring breaks to stretch their legs in the squad room, Sophie and Alain Turenge were questioned

48

separately in two small offices with pastel-painted walls and just a table and four chairs for furnishings. There were always at least two officers present when they were questioned, and at frequent intervals detectives would step outside to compare notes and confer with Galbraith. Time and again they asked the Turenges to describe their movements on the night of the bombing. They were puzzled that the couple could not recall where they had dropped off the fisherman called Peter or how long he had been with them. They were unable to recount their route while he was in the camper van and made one crucial – and repeated – mistake. Alain Turenge insisted that 'Peter' had sat in the front of the van with him. Sophie Turenge said he had sat in the back of the van and that *she* had been in the front passenger seat.

There were of course other oddities. The couple had French driving licences and Swiss passports, which made them Swiss residents of France. The passports had apparently been issued by the Swiss consulate at Lyon in central France and the licences issued in Paris. The driving licences had wildly differing numbers yet both had been issued on the same day, May 28, 1984. Galbraith and his detectives felt it too coincidental that a husband and wife, he thirty-three and she thirty-six, should either pass their test or be granted new licences at the same time and not be given approximately consecutive numbers.

Details of their passports had been telexed to Interpol's office in Berne, Switzerland, for checking. At first glance they seemed genuine enough. The couple both appeared to have been born in Lancy, near Geneva, but it was now Friday lunchtime in Switzerland and Galbraith expected little information from there until after the weekend. In fact, Interpol's legal officer, Joseph Herrmann, was already processing Auckland's request. Officers had begun to search electoral rolls, telephone directories and any other register they could find to establish the bona fides of the Turenge couple.

For Galbraith, time was running short. There was a limit to how long he could hold the Turenges on the strength of a discrepancy in their alibis. So, shortly after midnight, the police told them they were free to go, though they would have to be

49

seen briefly the next morning. The police promised to ensure they caught the next available flight out of New Zealand, for it seemed that their Uncle Emille was getting sicker by the hour. Indeed the police sounded almost apologetic. They insisted on booking the couple into a motel and picking up the bill: it was the least they could do after imposing on the Turenges. They drove the couple in an unmarked police car to the motel two miles away, arranged a comfortable – if lacklustre – room and promised to return their passports in the morning. Little did the couple know, as they settled in for the night, that the police had chosen the motel, in Auckland's Herne Bay suburb, for a particular reason: they had bugged one of its bedrooms.

Galbraith did not need an Hercule Poirot to explain the emerging series of coincidences. Everywhere his detectives turned, a French connection of sorts seemed to enter the investigation. They had already recovered a dinghy of French manufacture which might just be connected with the bombing. He had a French-speaking couple of dubious nationality helping with inquiries. A strange Frenchman had visited the *Warrior* uninvited on the night of the bombing. And now Gus Lindstrom from Whangarei had phoned about a suspicious yacht called the *Ouvéa* which was crewed by four Frenchmen. The French presence was uncommonly frequent considering there are only 600 French expatriates in New Zealand. Galbraith had already sent detectives north to interview the customs officer MacLean and had ordered a trace on the yacht, *Ouvéa*, which had sailed from New Zealand the day before the bombing. It seemed that Galbraith was on the verge of a breakthrough.

Now his team of detectives, swollen to over sixty, had something to get their teeth into and they set about the task with relish. Motels, hotels and car rental companies were visited, copies of bills and receipts collected and statements taken from all those who had come into contact with the Turenges. A search of the camper van had already uncovered a puzzling find: a file of receipts from motels for rooms, from restaurants and supermarkets for food and from garages for petrol. The couple had carefully preserved all their bills, though for what reason Galbraith could only guess. It was possible they were over-zealous souvenir collectors who treasured every memory of a holiday and kept them for reminders. But some of the motel bills added up to surprisingly high totals. One that should have registered $NZ35 for a night amounted to $NZ350. Closer inspection revealed that the receipt had been doctored. Some-one was travelling on an expense account and operating a primitive and well-worn fiddle.

Some of the hotel bills also showed expensive telephone calls to Paris. In New Zealand, international calls are routed through the exchange where numbers are recorded, the cost estimated and both figures referred back to the motel for billing. Yet when Galbraith's detectives attempted to redial the number, supposedly sick Uncle Emille's home, they were told that the number did not exist or had not yet been allocated to a subscriber. One telephone call to Paris convinced Galbraith more than anything else that the Turenges were involved in the *Warrior* bombing, or something very serious, right up to their necks.

The couple had stayed in the Gold Star motel in Auckland on the night after the bombing and before their arrest. The proprietors, Bill and Christine Garrett, had noticed that Alain Turenge had spent some time in the camper van listening to the radio, even though there was one in his room. He had later rejoined his wife and called Paris 846 8790 at 8.30 p.m., which cost $NZ8.90. It was a number the couple had called on previous occasions during their holiday. When detectives asked French police to check the number they were told it did not exist. Yet the charge for the call from the Gold Star was on the bill, so there must have been a connection. Galbraith picked up the telephone himself and dialled the number. It rang for a few seconds and was answered. Galbraith slammed down the re-ceiver without speaking. The French police were lying.

Later, inquiries would show that numbers are often lent to the French security services before they are allocated to private subscribers. They are used for a few weeks and then discarded. This number was one of them. When the intelligence agency

51

later abandoned the number, it was given to an Arab in Paris who grew increasingly annoyed by calls from the press asking to speak to the 'head spy'.

But for now Unit 7 at the Gold Star motel had revealed other interesting objects. Stuffed into the waste bin outside were four towels and a pair of jeans that still had plenty of wear left in them. The only reason for dumping them appeared to be thick mud on each of them. Why the Turenges did not wash them out in the bath, hand them in to reception to launder or simply leave them for the maid to find baffled Galbraith further. He certainly did not believe their story that they knew nothing of the towels and that the maid must have accidentally put them in their bin.

Senior Sergeant Terry Batchelor was already sure of Alain Turenge's guilt. Instinct had convinced him long before the evidence began to accumulate. But the interrogation had been so fruitless that Batchelor had let his guard slip and insulted his charge. 'Monsieur, I think you are a very sloppy spy.' He regretted it instantly – an unprofessional act, a weakness displayed to the enemy. The Frenchman had sat in the tiny interview room fielding the detective's questions. To each Turenge would shrug his shoulders, cock his head to one side and exhale through pouting lips. 'I showered him with questions and he dodged, blocked and countered with a skill that marked him as a professional,' says Batchelor. Even then, after a weekend of dramatic revelations that confirmed the suspect's guilt, the repeated pattern of baited traps laid by Batchelor failed to produce the smallest nibble. No matter how much the police already knew, Turenge was not going to make it easy for them.

Next door, Sophie Turenge had already cracked, up to a point. Perhaps it was the easy charm of Senior Sergeant Morris or simply fear that led her, after initial displays of bravado, to weaken. At first she had mirrored her partner's contempt for the police officers but, as it slowly dawned on her that the detectives were no fools, her nerves began to fray. She stuck to the well-rehearsed story – indeed it never changed, even when they later appeared in court to face murder charges – but at odd moments she slipped up, perhaps through panic or pride.

52

'Check us out in Paris. Then you will find out who we really are and you will have to let us go,' she told Morris in one instant of confusion. It did not matter that both adhered to the simple line that they were on honeymoon, had picked up a fisherman and given him a lift: outside in the squad room the evidence was mounting faster than the deskhands could analyse it.

First there had been the discovery of the outboard motor, a blue Yamaha, almost new, dumped on the bed of Hobson's Bay just a few yards from the abandoned Zodiac. No Kiwi boatman who had accidentally dropped such a valuable engine would have left it to rust; he would have donned scuba gear or found someone else to do so and retrieved it within minutes. Then, just across the bay where the currents deposit litter and scum on the shoreline, a resident whose garden backs on to the water had spotted the white oxygen cylinder bobbing against the rocks. It had French markings and he had called the police. Another would be found later, more than two miles away where another current had slowly carried the buoyant, half-full cylinder. Both were remarkable for their rarity in the Pacific, or indeed anywhere else. They were manufactured near Nice on the Côte d'Azur, for one customer only: the French armed services, and the special forces in particular. The jeans and towels found in the rubbish bin at the Gold Star motel had been sent for analysis to discover if the mud matched that of Waitamata Harbour. The camper van had revealed another intriguing find: a label bearing the motif 'Plastimo', a brand name used on weatherproof clothing, sailing accessories and dinghies, was found screwed into a ball of tampon wrappers, yet there was nothing in the Turenges' belongings which could have carried the label.

The Turenges in particular had proved a rich source to tap. During Friday's interviews, all conversations had been tape-recorded until a French-speaking policeman could be found. When he eventually arrived, there were already several cassettes to translate. But first Galbraith told him to sit in the interview room, when, during breaks in the cross-examination, the Turenges were allowed to sit together. In no circumstances was the young French-speaking police cadet to show that he understood the short, unfriendly exchanges between the two.

53

The conversations that took place were surprisingly frank. The Turenge couple stupidly assumed they could not be understood. 'Be like a mountain, do not move an inch,' Alain would order his 'wife'.

She was much more concerned with the future. 'If they send us to prison, will they still pay our salaries and pensions in Paris?' she asked Alain. It was these exchanges that proved the most telling in the early hours of interrogation. For not once did the supposed honeymooners display any warmth or affection for each other. There was no loving reassurance, no display of concern as each was led away for questioning. Indeed, there appeared to be no love lost between them.

Their arrogance continued. During the day they had been allowed one telephone call. Sophie Turenge dialled the same number in Paris that they had tried from the Gold Star motel the evening before and would dial again when she was closeted in their bugged room that night. She was, she claimed, getting up-to-date reports on Uncle Emille's health.

The police had wasted no time in following the Turenges' trail around New Zealand from the carefully preserved and clumsily doctored motel receipts. They were already beginning to build up a picture of a very odd couple indeed. 'Foreigners stick out a mile in New Zealand,' says Batchelor, 'especially in winter and especially if they are camping. Being French and holidaying in New Zealand in winter made them stick out like sore thumbs. It is a friendly place, particularly out in the country. They don't get many foreigners and they want to pass the time of day with visitors, they want to know where you come from and where you are going. But the Turenges were remembered wherever they went: typically French, downright bloody rude.

'They were supposed to be married but never made any effort to appear so. Even if a couple are fighting like cat and dog, there are some manifestations of involvement. Even if you hate each other's guts, you still touch or smile occasionally, but not these two – they didn't even try. They behaved like total strangers with each other. They never referred to each other when making decisions like which room they might occupy, or whether the

54

other might like a cup of tea as well. Even people bound by mutual hatred share something – and they were supposed to be on honeymoon.'

Morris adds: 'We both got the overriding impression that he was a soldier and she was along for the ride. She didn't seem to come to terms with what was going on. She didn't want to. She was just there to provide cover for him and nothing else, and he had no time for her whatsoever.' They were indeed an odd couple. He was tall, handsome and arrogant, but jovial and relaxed under pressure. She was cold, waspish and fragile with a sadness in her eyes. Though both were obviously well educated, they were a poor match and were definitely not on honeymoon.

It all helped Galbraith, but not much. He still had no hard evidence to link the Turenges to the bombing. Indeed, he had nothing to hold them on other than suspicion. They had spent a quiet night at the motel and the bugging devices recorded little. The next morning, while under surveillance, the Turenges were seen leaving their motel. They headed downtown immediately to the Air New Zealand office and tried to change their bookings for the missed flight to the next available flight out of New Zealand. Alain Turenge protested when told there would be a delay in changing the tickets and immediately produced a wad of dollars and insisted on buying two new tickets to save time. It was not, mused the watching detectives, the actions of an innocent couple who had just twenty-four hours previously waited around for a refund of $NZ130 on their camper van.

Galbraith was growing impatient. He had still not heard from Interpol in Berne and had called on New Zealand immigration officials to give the passports a thorough examination. There was nothing specifically untoward but they were suspicious, he was told. Something was not quite right. Galbraith was looking for holding charges, anything to delay the Turenges, and immigration offences seemed the best hope. His hunch proved correct. Joseph Herrmann's men in Berne had worked overtime checking their registers and finally came up trumps on Saturday evening. The passports looked genuine enough, but the people, Alain and Sophie Turenge, did not exist – so the passports must be phoney. The telex from Switzerland chattered shortly after lunch on Sunday in Central Police Headquarters, giving Galbraith the holding charges he needed. In using false passports to enter the country, the couple had made false declarations on the immigration cards they completed shortly before landing at Mangere airport. They had therefore entered New Zealand illegally. Galbraith dispatched Batchelor and Morris to pick up the Turenges once more – though this time without the shining Ford Falcon which had been returned to exclusive duty with the top brass.

CHAPTER FIVE

Hunting the Ouvéa

The *Ouvéa* had made remarkably good time in rough weather, ploughing through high seas and thirty-knot winds. A French-built First 38 sloop, single-masted with mainsail and jib, she was more than adequate for a long voyage, though the four men on board cannot have enjoyed it. The yacht had cleared customs in Whangarei's Town Basin shortly after 9.30 a.m. on July 9 – the day before the *Rainbow Warrior* bombing – motored out past the Marsden Point oil refinery and picked up a ten-knot south-easterly. It was a fair wind to push the vessel north-west to Norfolk Island, an outcrop of Australia half way to the *Ouvéa*'s home port, Noumea in French New Caledonia.

It was a cloudy morning, with a few light showers, but the weather was deteriorating as a cold front pushed up from the Antarctic. By noon the wind had begun to shift, though there were still plenty of safe havens indenting the New Zealand coastline a few miles off the *Ouvéa*'s port bow, should her crew decide to run for cover. The showers were increasing both in duration and in intensity. As midnight approached, the tail wind shifted almost a hundred degrees, accelerated to twenty knots and flew into the faces of the four Frenchmen on board. By noon the next day, Wednesday July 10, it was blowing thirty knots from the north-east and the yacht was making little headway. The skipper, Raymond Velche, had expected as much from the forecasts and had filled the *Ouvéa*'s tanks with diesel. He started the engine to augment the sails and maintain progress. It was not the act of a sailing purist – a move to be considered by true yachtsmen only in an emergency, or if in a desperate hurry. Velche was motivated by the latter need.

Even with the hatches battened down, it was cold and damp on board the *Ouvéa*. The decks were awash and the bunks

57

sodden. In such seas it can take half an hour to make a hot drink; twice as long to prepare a simple meal on a galley stove. But at least the *Ouvéa* was equipped with one of the latest navigation aids, which picked up radio pulses from orbiting satellites and computed the messages into longitude and latitude so that the crew members were always aware of their position.

Velche remained on deck most of the time, for he was the only experienced sailor among them. His two closest comrades, Eric Audrenc and Jean-Michel Berthelo, had only rudimentary skills where canvas was concerned, though their knowledge of powered craft was considerable. All three were tall, lean, fit men with short neat hairstyles and manners to match their laconic looks. The fourth man on board was so unlike his crewmates that he might almost have been a paying passenger. He was Dr Xavier Maniguet, shorter and more fashionably groomed, handsome, lively and above all garrulous. He loved to talk about himself, to impress his three companions with his wit, his culture and his exploits as a seasoned traveller and self-styled amateur adventurer. He had a sordid pastime of showing friends, even strangers, video recordings of his conquests between the sheets and boasted of the quality of his lovemaking. If it had not been for the fact that he was also quite jovial, he might well have been tossed overboard. In the confined space of a small yacht on a long and uncomfortable journey, his presence was immensely irritating.

Guzzling diesel from the tanks, the *Ouvéa* motored into Norfolk Island on July 13 in the evening. She had torn a sail in the gusting headwinds whipping across the Three Kings Basin, yet had still managed the journey from New Zealand in good time.

From the air, Norfolk Island presents its tranquil face: grassy hills, pine-clad meadows, grazing horses. But from the sea the picture is far more forbidding. Fringed by reefs, the solitary island's looming cliffs and ragged, rocky inlets seem to fend off ocean voyagers. Captain James Cook had a lot of trouble finding a place to put ashore when he discovered the uninhabited outcrop in 1774. The island's rich history is marred by maritime mishaps. In the early 1880s, when the brutality of the convict settlement there earned the place the name 'hell-hole of the Pacific', supply ships were often delayed or damaged by the treacherous seas around the island. Later, when Norfolk was settled by the descendants of the *Bounty* mutineers, the little colony's survival was often put at risk by its inability to get reliable sea transport to trade its farm produce.

The island, some 1,000 miles north-east of Sydney, is an Australian territory which has had a measure of self-government since 1979. About 1,800 people live there year-round, but a stream of Australian tourists is drawn by the balmy climate and extraordinary natural beauty. Despite those attractions, however, Norfolk Island has never become a common port of call for Pacific yachtsmen. It has no harbour, and it is famous for sudden, violent wind shifts that churn calm waters into crashing surf, drag up anchors and dash boats on to the rocks. Yachts that do stop there generally stay only long enough to take on a few provisions. There are two choices of mooring on the five-by-three-mile island. To the south is Kingston Bay, the heart of Norfolk's sparse settlement, still dotted with the ruins of convict-built jails and barracks. To the north is Cascade Pier, where a concrete jetty pierces rough surf at the foot of forbidding grass-topped cliffs.

The *Ouvéa* visited Norfolk Island twice: once on its way to New Zealand, and again on its way back. On both occasions the *Ouvéa*'s crew chose secluded Cascade as its mooring place. There are no coast-watchers on these cliffs. The nearest farm-house is almost a mile away, tucked behind the cliffs in a sheltered valley. Few people seem to have noticed the *Ouvéa* when it made its first call at the island, shortly after midday on June 17 – three weeks before the *Warrior* bombing. Lori Meincke, receptionist at a small hotel on the island's main street, booked Maniguet into a single room that afternoon. He asked if all the crew could use the room's shower, although only two of them proposed to sleep there since the others had to stay with the boat. The next day, Meincke stood by as Velche made a brief call to a Paris number (288 8266). The *Ouvéa* sailed from Norfolk on the morning of June 19, having raised little interest on the island.

The second visit, after the bombing, was a different matter. When the *Ouvéa* next put in at Cascade, the crewmen did not seem to care what happened to the boat. They moored it perilously close to the rocky shoreline and left it there unattended through the night. All four took comfortable beds at the South Pacific Hotel, the biggest and flashiest on the island.

Early on Sunday morning, July 14, Duncan Sanderson was getting ready to take his own boat out for a sail when somebody told him that a foreign yacht had put in overnight at Cascade. Sanderson, an avid yachtsman with a bushy nautical-style beard, keeps his own twenty-foot keel craft on a trailer at Kingston Bay, but he never misses an opportunity to look at visiting boats. He and his son, Miles, thirteen, drove across the island to see the *Ouvéa*. All four crewmen were on board, struggling to change a ripped Genoa. Sanderson offered to give them a hand and ended up having tea and biscuits on board.

'They asked me if I wanted to go to Noumea with them to replace the doctor, who said he was leaving by plane the next afternoon to get back to his practice.' Maniguet, it seemed, had had enough. The rough weather had killed any interest he might have had in ocean cruising. Sanderson, who runs a busy duty-free jewellery store in the island's tourist centre, somewhat reluctantly declined. The prospect was appealing, but who would look after the shop? After they had chatted for about an hour, Sanderson realized that the boat had not cleared customs. Norfolk Island has its own customs and immigration laws which, for visitors, are perfunctory. People who do not intend to stay for more than a month are not usually required to present passports. Nevertheless, Sanderson was concerned about the crew's indifference, and he persuaded them to follow him back into town to find the customs officials.

Tracking them down was not easy. Sanderson had to drive to the island's airport, where he finally found some customs officers at work in the freight shed. The officers recognized the crew members from their previous visit and seemed in no hurry to deal with them. 'They told the guys to meet them in their office in town two hours later,' Sanderson recalls. As far as he knows, customs never set foot on the boat.

The crewmen went on to their hotel, where they proceeded to make themselves highly conspicuous. 'This is a geriatrics' resort,' says Sally Morrison, twenty, a wispy-haired blonde waitress. 'You get anyone young here, you notice them.' The *Ouvéa* crew members made themselves particularly noticeable by their insistent advances to the hotel's female staff. 'They were completely blatant about it,' Sally Morrison says, asking waitresses to go dancing, to have drinks, to come to their rooms. The young women, most of them New Zealanders on working holidays, joked about the Frenchmen's persistence, weighing up whether Maniguet's 'amazing piercing blue eyes' were enough of an asset to offset his habit of wearing too much aftershave.

That weekend, Morrison got a call from her father, a New Zealand member of parliament. He told her that the whole country was in an uproar over the Greenpeace affair. 'Next time I was serving the Frenchmen in the restaurant I had a joke with Steve, the barman, about how these guys were probably the bombers,' she says. But the crew certainly did not act like terrorists who had just ended a man's life. They swam in the hotel pool, rocketed around the island in a rental car, drank red wine in a dimly-lit hangout named the Driftwood Bar, played squash and generally behaved like tourists.

On Monday afternoon, Velche drove Maniguet to the airport to catch the daily service to Sydney, where the doctor planned to make a Paris-via-Singapore connection. On his way back into town, Velche stopped at a travel agency to make onward reservations from Noumea for the rest of the crew. There did not seem to be any special hurry to get back to France. Velche booked three seats on a flight from Noumea to Paris on July 26. He asked the travel agent to arrange a stopover of a day or two in Singapore. 'Do you want low, medium or high cost accommodation?' she asked. 'The best available,' was Velche's reply.

But the *Ouvéa* crew members never got to enjoy their luxurious Singapore sojourn. Just a little before 5.00 p.m. Senior Sergeant Paul MacIntosh of the Australian Federal Police got a call from Wellington saying that a Royal New Zealand Air Force Caribou would arrive on the island at about 7.15 that night bringing detectives to interrogate the crew of the *Ouvéa*. MacIntosh was stunned. He had been struggling to keep up with the *Rainbow Warrior* affair, despite the island's chronic shortage of newspapers. In winter, planes flying to Norfolk often have to take on extra fuel in case bad weather forces a diversion to Fiji or New Zealand, and newspapers are the first items to get left behind in an effort to save weight. Suddenly the news-starved sergeant found himself part of the story. 'You don't expect to get caught up in international incidents here,' says MacIntosh, who had served ten months on the island on secondment from Australia, and had found the job fairly undemanding. There is little crime on Norfolk: cars and houses are left unlocked, violence is unheard of. MacIntosh's only excitement had been the arrest of some local youths on a marijuana-growing charge.

He and his two assistants started calling the island's hotels, trying to track down the *Ouvéa* crew. Meanwhile, the island's Australian-appointed administrator, an ex-naval commodore named John Matthew, was urgently telexing the Australian minister of territories, seeking advice on how to handle the incident. The administrator was already looking for ways to extricate peaceful Norfolk Island from involvement with terrorists. In a confidential telex he asked the minister to consider sending a naval unit to pick up the yacht on the high seas rather than risk a confrontation on the island. The Australian territories department shot back a telex instructing the administrator to offer the New Zealand police all possible assistance within legal and safety limits.

Meanwhile MacIntosh had reached Mark Propert, manager of the South Pacific Hotel, who told him that he had three French guests right in front of him, drinking in the bar.

Many islanders noticed as the big New Zealand air force plane rumbled on to the airport tarmac just after dusk. Islanders can usually set their watches by the comings and goings of the few scheduled flights, and this arrival raised eyebrows. On board were seven New Zealand police, including forensic experts. There was also a legal officer and a French interpreter.

At 7.45 p.m. the police team met with the administrator. They told him that questioning of the Turenges pointed to a strong connection with the *Ouvéa* and its crew. The administrator said that under the island's law the crew could be detained for questioning on suspicion that the boat carried explosives. At that point, New Zealand police had not issued warrants for the arrest of the four Frenchmen.

MacIntosh took the New Zealand team to the South Pacific Hotel, where they checked in and held a strategy meeting. Word was starting to get around the hotel staff that something big was up. Some staff were apprehensive, fearing a shoot-out. But when the police finally made their move, the confrontation was without drama. At 10.00 p.m. they knocked on the crewmen's door, introduced themselves as detectives, and went inside. Through the undrawn curtains, hotel staff watched as the interrogation went on through the night. Part of the time, the Frenchmen lay sprawled on their beds as the police fired questions at them.

By morning, as some of the haggard police officers emerged for breakfast, it was clear that the interrogation was not getting far. The suspects, one officer confided, were too professional to give anything away. The only slip-up came when Velche and Berthelo claimed they had not been in Auckland. Police confronted them with the fact that they had been seen there in a rented car. The two backpedalled rapidly. They said yes, come to think of it, they had been in Auckland, but neither of them could remember details of the trip.

Hoping to break down their carefully constructed stories in individual interrogations, the police split the three crewmen up, even taking one of them down to the awesome old precincts of the island's convict quarters. But with only one skilled interpreter, the questioners found themselves constantly running into language barriers. At one point, someone sent out to the local school for a French-English dictionary.

While the police struggled to extract enough evidence from the crewmen to justify the issue of a warrant, the forensic specialists were combing the *Ouvéa* itself. John Pearson, a local yachtsman, had been sound asleep on Monday night when a policeman arrived at his door. Pearson does not have a phone and his first thought when he opened the door was that something had happened to one of his family. The officer quickly reassured him. What was needed was an experienced sailor to help mind the *Ouvéa* in case one of Norfolk's notorious wind shifts tore it loose in the night, before the forensic team could examine it at daybreak. 'We might be dealing with international terrorists,' the policeman warned. Pearson said nothing, but as he dressed hastily he thought, 'My God, what am I getting myself into?'

Down at the jetty, the two men pushed an orange dinghy into the dark water. They could just make out the *Ouvéa*'s white hull gleaming dully in the blackness. On board, Pearson looked on as the policeman began to shuffle through the crew's belongings. Among them was a colour snapshot of Audrenc and Berthelo. Both were wearing diving gear. Berthelo had a red woollen cap.

At daybreak the forensic team started going over the boat. In its bilges they found traces of substances they thought might be explosives. Despite the lack of progress in questioning the suspects, that convinced some members of the police team that they had the bombers.

But as the day wore on, the prospect of an arrest slipped slowly from their grasp. Matthew, the local administrator, was concerned that the island might get embroiled in a humiliating international incident if it continued to hold the Frenchmen without charging them. He advised the New Zealand authorities that they would have to issue a warrant by 2.00 p.m. if they wanted the suspects held in custody any longer. That put the police in a dilemma. Although they had asked Interpol to conduct urgent checks on the Frenchmen's identity documents, there was little hope of getting any word on that score within twenty-four hours. The smooth-talking spies had been able to bat away all their interrogators' allegations. The substances on the boat could not be positively identified as explosives with the gear the police had on hand.

MacIntosh, for one, was not clear in his own mind whether the Frenchmen were bombers or not. 'At the end of the day, I would not have put money on it one way or the other,' he says. 'If you get into an international incident you have to dot every i and cross every t. There's a reasonable standard you have to meet. You have to ask yourself, "What would a reasonable man do?" It's not reasonable to hold someone on and on if you don't have anything on him.'

With Matthew's deadline approaching and the Frenchmen now angrily demanding to be allowed to sail on, New Zealand detective Senior Sergeant Denby got on the phone to Galbraith. The two talked for some time, going over details of the interrogation, what they had and what they did not have. Finally, Galbraith told Denby that he had better let the Frenchmen go.

Just before 8.00 p.m. the New Zealand police gave the Frenchmen back their passports. Velche, cool as ever, paid the hotel bill and reminded the police that he had a rental car to return. The police called Joy Evans, manager of the rental company, at her home number, to ask if she would mind opening up again to settle Velche's account. Her son went down and unlocked for Velche, who bought $166.40 worth of diesel fuel. Evans was struck by the large amount, since it was half as much again as the crew had originally bought to cover the greater distance from Norfolk to New Zealand. Wherever the sailors were going next, they suddenly wanted to get there in a hurry.

Norfolk Islanders like to say that their island measures five miles by three minutes. News of the Frenchmen's release certainly spread quickly. By the time they got to Cascade, a small crowd had gathered to watch their departure. The last anyone saw of the *Ouvéa* was its navigational lights skipping quickly away across the dark ocean.

A few hours earlier, Xavier Maniguet had also skipped away, slipping effortlessly through the fingers of Australian and New Zealand police in Sydney. When Maniguet had arrived on East-West Airlines' daily service to Sydney from Norfolk Island, officers of the Australian Federal Police had been waiting for him. 'I came back down to earth with a bang,' says Maniguet, who had hoped to continue his journey to Singapore. An airline employee had approached him first, asked his name and informed the doctor that he could not, after all, make the connection to Singapore. 'I'm sorry, but you cannot leave the country.' The Australian police officers told him to await the arrival of two New Zealand detectives and suggested he book into the Southern Cross Hotel in downtown Sydney.

'I was flabbergasted. I tried to find out what was going on, but no one would tell me. I went to the hotel, switched on the television and the news came on. It said the *Ouvéa* was suspected of complicity in the bombing of the *Rainbow Warrior* and that I was being sought. Me? A terrorist? I could not believe my ears.'

Much alarmed, Maniguet tried to reach the French consulate, but found it already closed for the day. In his fifth-floor room in the Southern Cross Hotel, a comfortable establishment in a slightly seedy but centrally located part of the city, Maniguet pondered his predicament. Unbeknown to him, the police had already made arrangements to book into the room next door, and had discussed with each other the pros and cons of bugging it.

Anxious and a little apprehensive, Maniguet took off for a walk through the city's main shopping district. He went into a cinema on Pitt Street where David Lean's epic film *A Passage to India* was showing. But Maniguet had little opportunity to enjoy the experience. Before the interval he was approached by four police officers, two from New Zealand and two from Australia. They had not needed to search for him. He had been under surveillance since leaving the airport.

'They interrogated me the whole night, from 9.00 p.m. to 6.00 a.m., and I hid nothing from them,' Maniguet now claims. Certainly his story was plausible, a display of injured innocence, a tale of probity fallen prey – by accident or design – to the whims of fate. He had, he insisted, become embroiled in an incident that concerned neither himself nor his colleagues on board the *Ouvéa*. Some strong circumstantial evidence existed which could link the *Ouvéa* and its crew to the bombing, but such supposition was pure fantasy, he argued. The press, of course, was to blame. It had inflated the *Ouvéa*'s importance out of all proportion. As Maniguet recounted his story to the detectives he grew confident: it was good, very good, and he would soon be on his way after convincing them of his innocence.

66

They would apologize and leave, thanking him for helping them to eliminate this tenuous lead from their burgeoning inquiry.

Typically, Maniguet was too obsessed with his own talents to consider those of the officers. He might have been believed if he had not over-acted his protests of innocence, if he had been more tight-lipped. His story was well prepared, but the man who loved the sound of his own voice could not ignore an opportunity to over-embellish. The detectives came away with a story that seemed to fit all the known facts . . . and the strong conviction that Maniguet was a liar.

'I am a traveller, a specialist in tropical diseases,' he had protested to the detectives. 'I am also a reserve officer in the marines, a pilot instructor at the Dieppe Flying Club and experienced in parachuting and sub-aqua diving. I am financially well off and can do as I please but I am not a terrorist. Indeed I have followed Greenpeace's campaigns sympathetically. I did not wait for them to organize and fight for ecology. I joined the Society for the Protection of Nature ten years ago.' Maniguet had decided to start at the beginning and it was his role in the dialogue rather than the detectives' questions which made the interview last nine hours.

He claimed that he had decided early in 1985 to take a few months off work and travel. He flew a little, played around and eventually at a dinner party in Paris perked up at a friend's suggestion that he try ocean cruising in a yacht. The thought of diving in the Pacific, off Fiji perhaps, appealed to him immensely. Soon afterwards, other friends put him in touch with a Paris travel agency specializing in yacht charters and they booked him on a fifty-day charter on board the *Ouvéa*, berthed in Noumea, with a crew of three. He flew in on June 11 to meet his fellow vacationers. 'I was introduced to Raymond Velche who said he was the skipper. We went straight to the harbour where I met the other two members. I was shouldering three-quarters of the cost, about twelve thousand New Zealand dollars, but it was only later that I realized that it is normal practice on such charters for the skipper or helmsman to go free and the cost to be split between the rest on board.

'They were men of my age, about thirty-five to forty years old, athletic, approachable but blunt and, on the whole, not very sociable.' Maniguet insisted that he had learnt little about his companions during their five weeks together. One man was from Paris, he said, the others from Marseilles and Toulouse.

'We talked about everything and nothing, and quite often about the sea and beautiful girls. In fact I became the centre of conversation. My passion for flying sharpened their curiosity – typical of people who have never touched the controls of a plane. They were always on at me to tell them about flying and in the end the roles were reversed. I was there to learn how to sail and I was teaching them how to fly. I eventually had to insist that I was instructed in what I had come to learn.'

It was Velche, the skipper, who decided the itinerary for the fifty-day charter, a fact that annoyed him, Maniguet complained, because he was bearing the brunt of the cost. First they would sail south to New Zealand, leaving the Pacific storms behind them, and return north via Fiji later when the weather mellowed. The *Ouvéa* had sailed on June 13 – coincidentally the day the *Rainbow Warrior* had set sail for Auckland from Majuro – and the voyage south was memorably bad. Maniguet and other members of the crew were so violently seasick that on occasions some of them doubted if they would make it. It was then that the doctor decided he would find more civilized transport for the return leg.

He went into some detail about the *Ouvéa*'s arrival and stay in various marinas and bays on the east coast of New Zealand's North Island before berthing in Whangarei. He talked of a short sightseeing trip to the South Island and boasted about his sexual prowess, managing to make love to eight women in seven days. His account of his philandering was taken for idle exaggeration by the detectives, though they would later discover that, as far as female company was concerned, the *Ouvéa*'s visit had in fact been an astounding success.

Maniguet said that the day before the yacht left Whangarei he told his crewmates that he would not be sailing back with them. The skipper, Velche, was celebrating his birthday that night (two days early because they would be at sea on the actual day) in a Whangarei restaurant when Maniguet informed him of his intentions.

'I'd had enough. The storms had put me right off. I'd seen enough of the Pacific and of its paradise landscapes. The others were very angry. They claimed there would not be enough of them to get the boat back to Noumea. I found that surprising, as I had been of little use to them on the way out, but I ended up agreeing to sail back with them.'

It was on arrival at Norfolk Island on July 13 that Maniguet recalls hearing of the *Rainbow Warrior* bombing for the first time. 'I had heard on the radio that President Reagan had a tumour. I thought it was cancer. Being a doctor I wanted to read as much as possible about it and I went ashore to buy newspapers. There I saw a photograph of the ship sunk in Auckland Harbour. I told the others about it but they didn't seem very interested. They made no comment except one jibe about "not shedding any tears for Greenpeace".' (Maniguet has since said that he first heard the news on the radio while the *Ouvéa* was off the North Cape of New Zealand on the way to Norfolk Island.)

The coup de grâce, or so Maniguet thought, was his closing statement. He reasoned that if the *Ouvéa* crew had in some way implicated itself, he might yet save himself. After all, he was travelling on genuine papers and the other crewmen, according to the police, were not. He therefore decided to introduce the possibility that he might have been a gullible adventurer taken in by conniving terrorists. 'I want to forget this entire story and not be pestered any more. I am staggered that I have been mixed up involuntarily in this dreadful spy story where I have played, so it seems, the role of the baddie. It's not very funny. I am absolutely shocked that I might have travelled on a bed of bombs. Did they deliver the explosives to Auckland during my sightseeing tour? I know nothing and I don't want to say anything more or accuse anyone of anything without any proof. I have been the victim of my own naivety and imprudence.'

He was certainly the victim of his own imprudence. The detectives had noticed something else when they introduced themselves to Maniguet during the movie. He was not alone in the cinema. Unbeknown to the doctor, his fellow viewers were also being interviewed by police officers.

Pierre Roussel, an expatriate French businessman, claimed that he had not particularly wanted to go to the pictures that night, but his wife had demanded that he take her to see *A Passage to India*. The couple had quite a rush to make it to the cinema in time. They had just taken their seats when, by chance, Maniguet entered the cinema. He noticed the empty place they had left on the aisle, and sat down alongside them.

His luck – if luck it was – was extraordinary. Against all odds in a city with such a small French community, he had chosen a seat next to a couple who were speaking together in French. And not just any French speakers. Roussel is a former trade commissioner and recently elected delegate to the Conseil Supérieur des Français à l'Etranger – an organization that advises the French senate on expatriate affairs. His work with that organization takes him frequently to France, where he puts the views of French expatriates in the south Pacific basin. Generally their views are conservative; most are in favour of nuclear testing and against independence for French colonies.

Maniguet apparently had introduced himself to Roussel, explaining that he was in trouble with the police and concerned that they might take him away to be interrogated without the consulate, or anyone else, knowing about it. Roussel assured him that he would help. Then the police had arrived and taken Maniguet to Federal Police Headquarters in Redfern where they questioned him closely.

Despite the assurances of Maniguet and Roussel, the police were unimpressed. It was too much to expect the detectives to believe that the meeting had been a coincidence. Then there were the inconsistencies in Maniguet's story. He had, he insisted, cut short his sailing holiday because he was weary of seasickness. Yet he had already told others that he was returning home because of pressing commercial problems in Paris. He had also said that he had to be at the bedside of a sick aunt. When this was recounted over the telephone to Superintendent Galbraith in Auckland, the detective was struck by the sudden poor health enjoyed by relatives of French vacationers in New

70

Zealand. The Turenge couple's sick Uncle Emille was already a standing joke in his squad room.

The detectives paid a second visit to Maniguet but it was a frustrating episode. They knew the prime suspects were slipping from their grasp. Had they been apprehended in New Zealand there might have been some way of detaining them: an unpaid parking ticket, or some other flimsy excuse until statements could be checked. But for now Galbraith's hands were tied. There was, as yet, no hard evidence to put before an Australian judge and request either detention or deportation. The situation could quickly become a diplomatic embarrassment. Like Velche, Berthelo and Audrenc, Maniguet would have to be allowed to leave the country.

Every hour brought new leads, fresh suspicions, but the absence of incriminating evidence persisted. The Southern Cross Hotel received a call for Maniguet from a woman in Noumea. The caller's message, to ring her back from 'a neutral phone', was tantalizingly suspicious, but again a competent lawyer could tear holes in any case based on such circumstantial evidence. Finally, the police told Maniguet he was free to make his Singapore connection. As he waited in the bar for his taxi to arrive, the policeman who had been tailing him sat down with him for a friendly drink. The gesture, however, was not entirely social. As Maniguet left the bar, the barman reached to pick up his empty glass. 'Don't touch that!' hissed the policeman, who then revealed that he was a fingerprint expert.

The Lockheed P3 Orion of the Royal New Zealand Air Force rumbled on to the tarmac of Whenuapai air base north of Auckland and awaited clearance for take-off. Its four turbo-prop engines lifted it over Hauraki Gulf to 20,000 feet and it turned north. The plane belongs to Number 5 Offensive Operations Squadron, its principal task being to patrol and defend New Zealand's 200-mile-wide fringe of Pacific Ocean. To that end it had recently been refitted with new radars that could scan both sea and sky from high altitude. It has a range of 2,000 miles and its radars can see up to 400 miles farther. It performs several surveillance functions, specifically to detect surface war-ships and aircraft. But such is the sophistication of the Orion's radars, it can search the skies for nuclear missiles in flight and pinpoint their likely impact point, or find a small boat wallowing in heavy seas.

It was for the latter task that Galbraith had approached the RNZAF and requested the help of its aircraft and crew. The *Ouvéa* had sailed from Norfolk Island on July 15 and it would be days before the forensic tests on the substances found in the bilges were complete. The yacht had taken on a large amount of fuel and was now heading north again, to the French Pacific territory of New Caledonia, a cigar-shaped island at the tip of the sprawling archipelago which has its roots in Asia and forms Indonesia, Borneo and New Guinea as it curves around Aus-tralia and into the Pacific. It was expected to berth in the southern port of Noumea, where its journey had begun in the Noumea Yacht Charters boatyard managed by Roger Chatelain.

But now it was missing. Radio contact had been made with the yacht by a New Zealand journalist on Thursday, July 18, when the *Ouvéa* gave its position as one hundred miles north of Norfolk Island, and the three remaining Frenchmen denied any involvement in the bombing. Three days later, on July 21, at 6.20 a.m., an Australian journalist on assignment in Noumea radioed the *Ouvéa*, apparently just fifty miles south of New Caledonia, sailing in heavy weather and making slow progress. The crew could of course have sailed into Noumea within two days, but the charter company had been told the *Ouvéa* would berth on the 24th at the earliest, so perhaps they planned a leisurely final fling around the southern coast of New Caledonia.

They were obviously in no hurry, for waiting in Noumea were three New Zealand detectives. The outcome of forensic tests on the samples and articles taken from the yacht in Norfolk Island was known, the press had reported that traces of plastic explosives had been discovered, and Galbraith now had enough evidence to seek their extradition once they arrived in French territory. Like the Turenges, the crew had also entered New Zealand carrying false passports identified by Interpol. The superintendent was ready to issue arrest warrants.

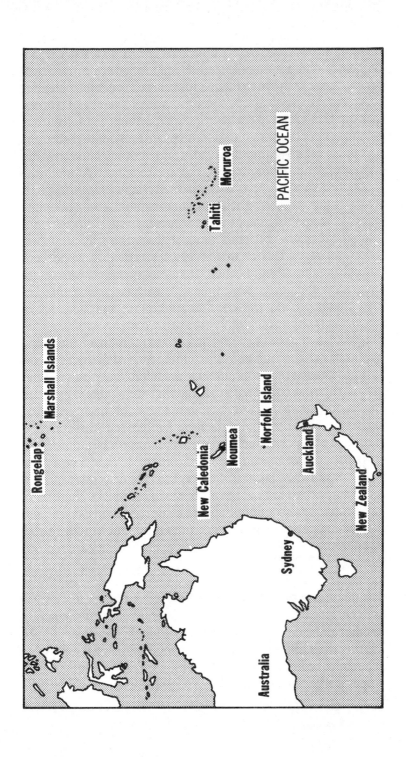

PACIFIC OCEAN

Moruroa

Tahiti

Marshall Islands

Rongelap

New Caledonia

Noumea

Norfolk Island

Auckland

New Zealand

Sydney

Australia

It had been a massive gamble on Galbraith's part. Perhaps with luck and some considerable political pressure he might have persuaded the Australian authorities to order the detention of the *Ouvéa* crew and Maniguet in Norfolk Island and Sydney. Instead he had played it by the book, letting them go in the belief that the latter could easily be picked up in Singapore and the others on arrival in New Caledonia. But by Thursday, July 25, the yacht was forty-eight hours overdue and Galbraith was worried. The Orion's first flight that afternoon was a direct result of his concern. It flew a search pattern for six hours, so close to New Caledonia that it violated French airspace and brought an angry rebuke from the authorities there. It was becoming increasingly obvious to Galbraith that the French were decidedly uncooperative. Requests for an air-sea search from New Caledonia were met with courteous inaction. The *Ouvéa* might still arrive, said the authorities, and there was as yet no evidence to suggest it was in distress.

It was obvious to the three Frenchmen on board the *Ouvéa* that their present freedom, due largely to legal protocol, would be short-lived if they stuck to their intended itinerary. They had listened to the news bulletins on the radio, they knew that Maniguet had been questioned at length, and they were aware that three New Zealand detectives had arrived in Noumea to continue the discussions curtailed on Norfolk Island. Despite their protestations of innocence the chase was on. The Orions were up and searching. If they kept to schedule there was the possibility of arrest or a major diplomatic scandal if the French authorities openly refused New Zealand's request for help. There was only one alternative: the *Ouvéa* and its crew had to disappear.

It is not uncommon for armies, navies and air forces to exaggerate the efficacy of their weapons. It helps keep the potential enemy confused, promotes morale at home and, as a sideline, attracts overseas buyers. Generally the claims for the speed or range of a missile, or the agility of a jet fighter or firepower of a main battle tank, remain classified information, with ball-park

74

figures quoted to muddle the opposition. But France has always built good submarines and the *Rubis* is no exception. Its nuclear reactor generates 48 megawatts which in turn provide 64,000 horsepower. Even supposing it loses 10% of its power in friction, heat loss, and so forth, and another 15% to run support systems on board, the reactor still supplies 45,000 shaft horsepower to propel the submarine through the water.

The *Rubis* is also rather small compared with British and American submarines, which are two or three times the size but generate only a third of the power. One reason is that France has made remarkable leaps forward in reactor technology, enabling it to build small craft around powerful reactors. Another is simple philosophy. A submarine is virtually useless if it can be easily detected, and the best method of detection is by the noise it emits. Britain and America build big submarines with plenty of muffling material to hide the noise. The French attack the problem by eliminating it altogether. The *Rubis*'s drag co-efficient is equally impressive, better than that of any submarine built elsewhere. The result is a small, fast and very quiet vessel built for speed underwater. It's reasonably sluggish on the surface, averaging no more than 15 to 20 knots, but submerged it is a thoroughbred. With little effort it can maintain 40 knots, accelerating to 46 knots when necessary – fast enough to outrun most torpedoes, any depth-charging destroyer and all but the finest hunter-killers of the Soviet navy. Such figures would normally be of interest only to the obsessed militarist, submariner or foe, but now, two weeks after the bombing of the *Rainbow Warrior*, Auckland detectives were flicking through the reference books to calculate speeds, times, distances and probabilities. The Royal New Zealand Navy has no submarines, and therefore no expert submariners to help them.

The question facing detectives and the Orion aircraft hunting the *Ouvéa* was crucial: did the *Rubis* pick up the crew off New Caledonia and steam more than 3,000 nautical miles at full speed to Papeete in French-held Tahiti?

No one seems in any doubt. All accounts so far suggest that that is precisely what happened. The *Rubis* homed in on a directional beacon aboard the *Ouvéa* and the unfortunate sloop was scuttled in the deep ocean by its three-man crew, who then donned diving gear and jumped overboard. In a routine 'pick-up' practised scores of times in the Mediterranean, they plunged to thirty feet, where the *Rubis* waited at periscope depth, and entered its sleek hull through the escape hatches. The *Rubis* had sailed from Noumea on July 4, the *Ouvéa* crew had sailed from Norfolk Island on July 15, the *Ouvéa* had disappeared and the *Rubis* arrived at Papeete on July 22 – plenty of time to do the journey even at half speed.

The theory has its drawbacks, however. On July 17 a shore-to-ship telephone call seeking the *Ouvéa* had been transmitted and answered by Velche. He answered a similar call on July 21, giving the *Ouvéa*'s position as fifty miles south of New Caledonia. If that was true and the yacht was scuttled after that last contact shortly after 6.00 a.m., not even the *Rubis* could have made it to Papeete by the next day. That would have required the unimaginable speed of over eighty knots.

The second theory is that the *Rubis* could have rendezvoused with the *Ouvéa* much earlier, within a couple of days of the yacht's leaving Norfolk Island on July 15. It had listened to the HF radio transmissions, heard the requests from prying journalists for the *Ouvéa* to respond and had carried out a successful con. With an aerial erected at periscope depth, it might have been possible to convince shorebased listeners that the radio transmissions from Velche were from the *Ouvéa* when in fact he was on board the *Rubis*. The *Rubis*'s military communications equipment would have had little problem replying to transmissions from Noumea marine radio. Noumea radio certainly had the range to reach as far as Tahiti and even beyond, to the Americas. But would the *Rubis* even bother to listen to commercial radio traffic? The only possible motive for the charade would be to give the *Rubis* time to clear the western Pacific where the New Zealand air force Orions were patrolling. But why bother? A submarine in such a vast ocean is undetectable unless it is on the surface, and the *Rubis* is built for deep water speed.

There is also a third theory. This one lacks both complexity and conspiracy and is therefore the most likely. The *Ouvéa* was indeed fifty miles off New Caledonia on July 21. The crew sailed close in to the rocky, sparsely populated south coast, scuttled the yacht and used the outboard motor and dinghy on board to get them ashore. A contact picked them up and took them to Noumea where, reverting to their real identities and carrying military passports, they simply jumped aboard a military transport plane out of the Pacific, easily avoiding the traceable formalities of customs and immigration. Their membership of an elite military school ensured that protection. There would have been no need to divert an expensive and strategically vital nuclear submarine from its patrol to pick them up and no need to risk the threat of careless talk among its complement of sixty-six officers and crew when just a handful of officials ashore could mask their departure with ease.

PART TWO
The Salvation Navy

CHAPTER SIX

Lunch with the admiral

For David McTaggart it began where the *Rainbow Warrior* ended – in Auckland Harbour. The year was 1972 and his thirty-eight-foot kauri-built ketch, the *Vega*, was moored at a jetty, preparing to sail for France's nuclear testing ground at Moruroa. There was no shortage of helpers. Some were New Zealand supporters of the Campaign for Nuclear Disarmament. But most, like McTaggart himself, were sailors who thought it outrageous that France should carry out atomic tests which – contrary to international law – involved cordoning off 100,000 square miles of ocean that lay in the path of the fallout. Armed with a letter drawn up by the Department of Law at Auckland University, McTaggart planned to enter the forbidden area, proclaim his legal rights, and stay there. No civilian had ever sailed into a nuclear testing zone before. Whether the French would respond by abandoning their tests, dragging him away, or blowing him to smithereens was anybody's guess. But someone somewhere in New Zealand was determined to stop him going.

He was working below deck when the *Vega* began to rock as five pairs of heavy feet jumped aboard, bringing a search warrant. Within moments, all the drawers and lockers were open, and McTaggart's belongings, so carefully stowed in preparation for the three-month voyage, lay scattered on the cabin floor. Suddenly there was a triumphant cry from one of the policemen. He had found a revolver. McTaggart protested that it was normal for cruising yachts to carry one for protection, and anyway he had a permit. The police did not heed him but decided to take the weapon for further investigation. Then they found the watches. While in Fiji the previous summer, McTaggart had tried to put his savings – $2,500 – in a bank, only to find that the banks would not accept American dollars.

So he used the money to buy the next best thing to hard currency: 104 duty-free watches. On arriving in New Zealand he had not declared them to customs and had put most of them in a bank's safe deposit box, leaving just seven on board for use as presents. These were what the police had now found.

Faced with a court case that threatened to stop him sailing to Moruroa, McTaggart found a solicitor who offered to arrange a deal with the police. He would have to own up to the remaining watches in the Auckland bank but if he did so the police would not press their case so vigorously.

The court room was full – especially the press benches. 'David Fraser McTaggart, you are charged with unlawfully smuggling into New Zealand . . .' He pleaded guilty as arranged and the solicitor rose to explain that his client was an honest man and a victim of problems with foreign currency. The magistrate flicked through his papers and pronounced sentence: 800 New Zealand dollars in fines or 120 days in jail if the fines were not paid immediately. McTaggart was stunned. So was everyone else who had been party to the backstage plea-bargaining, not least the prosecuting solicitor who jumped up to plead for McTaggart to be given time to pay. 'Denied!' said the magistrate, and turned to his next case. McTaggart had no money and was summarily bundled off to the cells. So much for Moruroa, he thought.

For hours he lay on his cell bed. Outside, day had turned into night. Suddenly, with a rattling of keys, the cell door swung open. His solicitor had evidently been working overtime and now a clerk appeared carrying a cheque and a paper for McTaggart to sign in order to be released. It was strictly against regulations to release prisoners after eight o'clock in the evening but now – just before midnight – the guards were ignoring the rules to set him free. 'Go get 'em, lad, and good luck,' said the guard as McTaggart walked out through the door.

Back at the *Vega*, work had been continuing under Nigel Ingram, an Englishman who was to join McTaggart as navigator on the voyage. Ingram had studied at Oxford, graduating in mathematics and philosophy, and had later served as a lieutenant in the Royal Navy. Though only twenty-six, he was a more experienced sailor than McTaggart, having spent the last few years skippering racing yachts in the south Pacific. McTaggart had met him on the docks painting a ketch, and had taken an instant liking to him. He had a cool head and seemed ideally suited for the trip.

Besides Ingram, McTaggart had recruited three others to act as crew. First there was Ben Metcalfe, then chairman of Greenpeace, a Canadian like McTaggart, who had more or less recruited himself. At fifty-one, he was by far the oldest, though he claimed on the telephone from Vancouver to be as fit as a thirty-five-year-old. He said he had looked after the radio on the first Greenpeace voyage – against American nuclear tests off Alaska – and suggested that since Greenpeace was putting up some of the money for the Moruroa trip, perhaps he should come along as the organization's representative.

The second member was Gene Horne, a New Zealander and jack-of-all-trades. It was he who had first shown McTaggart a newspaper report about Greenpeace and its objection to nuclear testing on Moruroa. Though deeply conservative, Horne found the French activities there distinctly annoying. Finally, there was Roger Haddleton, six feet tall, powerfully built and a rugger enthusiast. He had spent six years in the Royal Navy, finishing as a leading hand.

The preparations were almost finished, for if the *Vega* did not sail within a couple of days she would be unlikely to reach Moruroa before the tests started. But McTaggart and Ingram had reckoned without their next unwelcome visitor, Mr Turner, an inspector from the marine department. Such was Turner's diligence, or perhaps the importance of his mission, that he called to see them on Anzac Day, a public holiday in New Zealand. The news he brought was that the *Vega*, in common with all New Zealand yachts, would have to undergo a thorough safety check. She would have to be taken out of the water for up to a week while two marine surveyors examined every inch of her. McTaggart protested that the *Vega* was not a New Zealand yacht. He had bought her in New Zealand, certainly, but she was registered as a Canadian yacht and flew the Canadian flag – which meant that she did not need to be checked by the New Zealand authorities. The inspector was sceptical at first but went away, apparently satisfied, when McTaggart showed him papers to prove the point.

Turner returned to the attack a few hours later. 'You have changed the name of your boat,' he said, pointing to the side where Ingram had painted 'Greenpeace III' in large letters.

McTaggart took Turner round to the stern, where the name *Vega* could still be clearly seen. 'Greenpeace Three is not the yacht's name,' he explained. 'It's the codename for our voyage.' Turner fumed quietly and went away for a second time.

Next day it was the turn of the police to visit the *Vega*. An officer said they wanted to ask McTaggart about the revolver found during the raid on the boat. There was a problem about some forms that had not been filled in. Would he be kind enough to turn up at the police station at 11.00 a.m. tomorrow? McTaggart found the choice of 11.00 a.m. interesting. Whether by coincidence or not, this was the time when the *Vega* was due to sail. He thought for a moment, then agreed to go along to the police station next day. But it was a promise he had no intention of keeping. He was now determined to leave that same day, before the authorities could cause any more trouble. The interest that New Zealand officialdom had been taking in McTaggart and the *Vega* was plainly no accident. There had been rumblings in the press about the damage McTaggart's voyage might do to New Zealand's butter sales to France.

They started the *Vega*'s engine and moved her, ready to load the rest of the supplies. Suddenly Gene Horne, the New Zealander, arrived on the quayside looking anxious. 'I can't go,' he said. The immigration department had told him his application for a passport was the last in a queue of 900 and it would not be ready in time. McTaggart was determined not to postpone the start of the voyage, so he began searching desperately for a replacement crew member. He remembered Grant Davidson, an eager young man who had never been to sea but who said he was a good cook. Davidson had another advantage: dual Australian and New Zealand nationality. This meant that if any harm came to the *Vega*'s occupants the French risked damaging their relations with the governments of the four countries represented on the boat: Australia, Canada, New Zealand and Britain. Several frantic phone calls later, Davidson got McTaggart's message and hurried to the docks. As night fell, the *Vega* cleared customs and slipped out of Auckland Harbour, bound for Mururoa.

Metcalfe quickly became a problem on board. A broadcaster and theatre critic by profession, he was expensively dressed, in sharp contrast to the untidiness of the rest of the crew. With a huge body and carefully trimmed beard, he was a flamboyant character who almost immediately clashed with McTaggart. Despite his earlier assurances about his skill with a radio transmitter, he failed to make the *Vega*'s radio work – until Ingram pointed out that he had forgotten to switch it on. When the *Vega* landed at Rarotonga, halfway to Mururoa, Metcalfe left the others on the boat and went to stay in a hotel. McTaggart decided it was impossible to let him complete the voyage and was on the point of breaking the news to him when Metcalfe announced that he had urgent business in Peru and would be leaving on the next plane. McTaggart thought this excuse sounded unlikely but was glad to see the back of him. He was less happy about the next crew member to depart. All the crew had developed a tropical fever but Roger Haddleton was struck particularly hard. When the time came to leave Rarotonga, he could still barely eat. McTaggart delayed sailing for one more day. When Haddleton still showed little sign of recovery they arranged to have him flown back to New Zealand. The remaining three – McTaggart, Ingram and Davidson – then sailed without him.

For thirty days and nights since leaving Auckland they had battled against high winds and rough seas. Then, on the evening of June 1, after a journey of 3,500 miles, they crossed the invisible cordon around Mururoa and popped the cork on a bottle of champagne. Their plan now was to draw close to Mururoa and station the *Vega* about twenty miles downwind of the atoll, in the immediate path of any fallout. With luck, that would force the French to postpone their nuclear tests. The problem was to stay close enough to Moruroa to cause a nuisance but at the same time to avoid straying inside the twelve-mile territorial limit where the French would have the legal power to arrest them.

They raised their radar reflector to let the French know they had arrived, and hove to. 'Heaving to,' says McTaggart, 'was slow torture. At no time could we relax because our bodies were constantly working to counteract the motion of the yacht. Imagine that you're sitting in a very small room with a very low ceiling and that it's rolling back and forth all day. At every movement you feel a pulling weight as your body shifts one way, then the other. Lower your arm limply on a table and it will move back and forth with the room itself. You have to live with the motion, eat and sleep with it. There's no escape, no place to find a steady footing for even a minute. It wears the nerves, making bad moods even worse and shortening tempers.'

By June 10 the winds had eased and the *Vega*'s crew saw the first signs of activity around Moruroa. First they heard two muffled explosions, like heavy guns in the distance. Next a plane passed by to the north, followed by two more. They were preparing for supper when a military helicopter approached them directly and circled the *Vega* twice at little more than mast height, stippling the water with the down-draught from its rotor blades. Then, without so much as a wave from the pilot, it was gone.

That evening McTaggart tuned his marine radio to the 2182 frequency in the hope of sending out a message, but as usual it seemed that nobody was listening. At the time he blamed the lack of response partly on atmospheric conditions and partly on his transmitter's low power. What he did not know was that the French were jamming his transmissions. As an experiment, McTaggart switched to the emergency frequency. 'All ships . . . all ships . . . this is Greenpeace Three. Do you receive? Over.'

There was a pause. Then the reply came back. 'Greenpeace. Greenpeace. Greenpeace. This is FAYM. Do you receive? Do you receive?'

'This is Greenpeace Three. Receive you faintly. We have been twenty miles off Moruroa for the last ten days. Have food enough for five weeks. All well. Request you advise New Zealand. Please acknowledge.'

'Roger. Roger. Roger.'

'This is Greenpeace Three. This is Greenpeace Three. Reception very weak. Request you call us at 2025 hours tomorrow. Acknowledge.'

'Roger. Roger.'

The conversation ended. McTaggart remembers his feeling of relief as he climbed into his bunk that night happier than he had been in weeks. 'All we could think about was the radio call. We doubted that even our short message had got through properly, but another human voice saying "Roger. Roger. Roger" was more than music. It felt as though we had joined the human race again.'

In the days that followed, the *Vega*'s crew would get to know that friendly voice better. He would tell them his name was Mueller, radio operator on a Belgian ship, the *Astrid*, near the island of Tubai, 800 miles away. And each day McTaggart would run the *Vega*'s engines for a short while to recharge his batteries in preparation for calling Mueller with messages to be relayed to the outside world. With Mueller around, McTaggart felt safe.

He would have felt a great deal less safe if he had known the truth. For Mueller did not exist. In fact the *Vega*'s crew had been talking to a radio operator aboard the French cruiser *De Grasse* which was lurking over the horizon just out of sight.

After supper on June 16, McTaggart stood on the *Vega*'s deck, staring into the sunset over Moruroa. There was still no sign of ships, but a small black dot in the sky caught his attention. At first he thought it must be another helicopter, but it did not move. He went below for the binoculars. Then he saw that it was a balloon – the balloon used to suspend a bomb over the atoll before exploding it. The crew stared at each other in fright and remembered the words of a scientist back in Auckland: 'When you can see the balloon you are too close.'

Despite their fears, no one suggested retreating. At dawn next day, they hoisted the *Vega*'s sails and moved in closer. In the early morning light the balloon was bone-white, a bit like an old-fashioned dirigible, with a huge fin at the back. As the day wore on and the light improved, they could just make out another object hanging below the balloon: the bomb itself.

By now the French were taking a much closer interest in the *Vega*. All the way to Moruroa the *Vega* had tried to mislead the French by radioing false position reports. However, once the *Vega* arrived inside the forbidden zone around Moruroa they were able to locate her and track her with radar. But she was a wooden boat and radar could very easily lose her in bad weather. For this reason, two minesweepers, *La Bayonnaise* and *La Paimpolaise*, had been brought specially from New Caledonia to tail her. Both stayed out of sight until June 18, when the *Vega*'s crew suddenly noticed *La Bayonnaise* about a mile off their port side. They hoisted their sails to try and take a closer look but *La Bayonnaise* kept its distance.

Further away they noticed a much larger ship painted brilliant white instead of the usual naval grey. She had antennae above her funnel, a huge radar dish near the bow and a box-like building towards the stern. McTaggart took some photographs with his long-range lens. Later, he discovered that the mystery vessel was not French but American – the Victory ship *Wheeling*. 'This was my initiation into the complex world of nuclear intrigue,' he says. 'As a signatory to the partial nuclear test ban treaty, the United States was not supposed to be involved with atmospheric tests. Yet here was an American instrumentation ship well within the French cordon, obviously with the approval of the French authorities. We had stumbled across proof that American and French officials were co-ordinating their activities so that the US could collect data from atmospheric tests that it had promised not to conduct itself.'

On June 21 they were awakened by the sound of a megaphone from *La Bayonnaise*. 'Greenpeace Three! We have a letter for you.' The French launched an inflatable and three men came across. The message was a formal warning in English and French that the nuclear tests were about to start and that the *Vega* was in the danger area. McTaggart signalled that he had a reply, and the inflatable returned. He handed over the letter drawn up at Auckland University, asserting his legal right to stay put. The French replied with another warning, this time from Admiral Christian Claverie, commander of the nuclear test force.

By dawn next day the warnings became more physical. 'There's a huge bloody ship coming in on us,' Davidson shouted as he woke the others. It was the cruiser *De Grasse* hurtling past them.

'It took up half the sky,' says McTaggart. Fifty yards ahead of them it slowed abruptly and swung round. A collision was imminent. Just in time, Ingram started the engine and swung the *Vega* hard to port, missing the cruiser by only ten yards. The *De Grasse* then sailed away as *La Bayonnaise* and another minesweeper, *L'Hippopotame*, closed in, one passing the *Vega* fifteen yards away to starboard and the other by the same distance to port. These tactics continued for an hour, with the *Vega* frequently sandwiched in the dangerous eddies between the two vessels. 'They had broken the most basic law of the seas, which is not to block the path of another vessel under sail,' McTaggart says. 'We could see the captains leaning over the decks giving orders to the helmsmen – who were too close to see us – and we could only pray they would not make an error.'

June 26 dawned with a heavy grey sky. At 9.40 a.m. a twin-engined plane dived out of the thick clouds and roared over the boat, little more than a hundred feet above the waves. Meanwhile the two minesweepers appeared and shuttled back and forth close to the *Vega*, revving their engines. The plane climbed, turned and swooped again. In all it made seven low passes over the *Vega*. After that, McTaggart says, 'the plane seemed to go completely bananas, flying in tight figures of eight directly overhead. The sound of the waves was completely lost. We had to shout at each other to be heard. There was only the high-pitched whine and clatter of the plane, the deep rumble of the ships' diesels.' Suddenly, at 11.00 a.m., the plane vanished into the clouds and the minesweepers retreated.

The reason for this bizarre activity remained a mystery until, three days later, McTaggart heard on Radio Australia that the French had tested their first bomb (actually only the trigger mechanism, but radioactive none the less) on June 26 – the day of the noise torture. Then he realized that the harassment by ship and plane had been designed to mask the sound of the blast. Apart from feeling disappointed at having failed to stop the bomb, the *Vega*'s crew listened in horror as the radio newsreader went on to say that their boat had peacefully left the testing area on June 21 – which was nine days ago. By now they were convinced that the French were paving the way to dispose of the *Vega* in an 'accident'.

La Paimpolaise, the second minesweeper brought specially from New Caledonia, had now taken over the task of shadowing the *Vega*. In the early hours of the following morning she moved nearer, circled the *Vega*, then closed in on the starboard quarter. The *Vega* swung away in an effort to avoid a collision, but it was too late. The minesweeper crashed into her. The two vessels were locked together with the *Vega*'s rigging caught on *La Paimpolaise*'s bow. As the wooden yacht was dragged along, creaking and groaning, Ingram seized a knife and hacked at the rigging to free her.

The French were in the wrong; of that there was no doubt. They had broken the rules of navigation at sea and caused the collision. The *Vega* was not sinking, but she was leaking badly and was in no condition to hazard the 1,600-mile voyage to the nearest neutral port, let alone back to New Zealand. McTaggart catalogued the damage: the bobstay hull fitting was leaking; the bowsprit end fitting was twisted; the masthead fitting was severely damaged; the main boom topping lift was broken; there was hull damage on the starboard side; the starboard mainmast backstay was too weak to support the mast; the spreaders on the mizzen mast were badly buckled; the mizzen masthead fitting was bent; the mizzen mast was snapped; deck beams were broken; the starboard chainplate was strained; and the radio aerial was damaged.

McTaggart had every right to sue the French, and decided to stake his claim on the spot, hoisting his F flag, a red diamond on a white background, which in international seafaring code means, 'I am disabled, please communicate with me.' *La Paimpolaise* showed no response and the *Vega*'s crew began to wonder whether it would abandon them to their fate. They lit a red distress flare, then waited. Nothing. They lit another. At last *La Paimpolaise* began to move towards them.

The French lowered an inflatable and two men climbed in. As it approached they could make out the uniform of the man in front; he was the minesweeper's captain. 'I'm sorry, I'm sorry,' he said as he stepped gingerly aboard the *Vega*. 'What do you wish me to do?'

'We want the collision reported and our position reported to our governments and we want to be escorted to a port for repairs, but we want to hear it confirmed on New Zealand Broadcasting Corporation or Radio Australia that we are under way.'

'I do not think the admiral will permit a cable to be sent out about this.'

'Well, that's what we want. If a cable is not sent, we will radio a Mayday that will bring out air-sea rescue . . . the New Zealand air force. We dare not turn ourselves over to you until our governments know where we are.'

The captain glanced at the *Vega*'s radio aerial dangling use-lessly from the mast. He must have realized that McTaggart was bluffing, for there was no way they could have sent a Mayday call. But he said nothing and returned to his ship.

McTaggart, despite having the law on his side, was well aware that the French held all the cards. The *Vega* was powerless to communicate with the outside world, and if the French wanted to ensure that news of this embarrassing incident never leaked out the *Vega* and all aboard her could simply be made to disappear. Still, the French had had plenty of opportunities to sink the *Vega* earlier, and they had not done so. A more immedi-ate problem for McTaggart was the fact that the *Vega* was drifting where he did not want her to go. Although she was then twenty-two miles off Moruroa, the wind was blowing her inexorably towards the atoll. She was too fragile to tack against the wind, so all the French had to do was wait. Before long the wind would push her over the twelve-mile limit into territorial waters – and then they could arrest her. McTaggart wondered whether the French had thought of this too.

If the thought did occur to them, they decided to ignore it. An hour later the captain was back, this time inviting McTaggart to go with him on board *La Paimpolaise*. From there he could communicate with the admiral. Seated in the captain's chair McTaggart scribbled a note to the admiral, repeating his earlier demands. While the message was being sent, the captain and two officers sat down with McTaggart for a meal of wine, beef, sausages, sauerkraut, pickled beetroot, apples, cheese and coffee. 'I should have enjoyed it,' McTaggart recalls, 'but I was too tense and the food seemed almost nauseatingly rich.'

The admiral's reply, when it came, was far from cheering. On no account would the French relay the message for broadcasting. However, if McTaggart signed a written request to enter Moruroa for repairs, the boat would be fixed and they would be allowed to leave. McTaggart and his crew now faced a dilemma. Without a message telling the world where they were, how could they be safe in Moruroa? On the other hand, if they waited much longer, the *Vega* would undoubtedly be arrested for drifting into territorial waters without permission. The argument was clinched when Ingram climbed aloft to check the mainmast's fittings; they were severely weakened and it was plain that any attempt to sail away would not get them very far. Reluctantly, they decided to accept French help on Moruroa.

As they drew nearer to the atoll they could see that what had at first looked like a dead landscape actually had a few shrubs and palm trees as well as a cluster of low buildings. But these were dwarfed by the grey hulk of the cruiser *De Grasse* and other warships. There were also several passenger liners, apparently converted to provide accommodation for the military, and – most surprising of all – dozens of small pleasure boats for the French navy to relax in.

In their darker moments, McTaggart and his crew had imagined Moruroa as a black hole into which they and their craft might vanish for ever. At best, they had thought, they could expect to spend their time on the island in some squalid prison cell. But they had underestimated the subtlety of the French.

The three naval men who had boarded the *Vega* for the journey into Moruroa were constantly smiling; one of them, a young officer, seemed almost overcome with admiration for the bearded, barefoot sailors who had come halfway across the Pacific. 'We are proud to have the honour of towing you in,' he said. 'I think you are the first foreign ship ever to enter Moruroa.' From the *De Grasse* there came a whistled salute as they passed, and the small pleasure craft circled the procession as it entered the harbour. Many of the occupants seemed genuinely pleased to see the *Vega*. It was a hot Sunday morning and the holiday atmosphere on Moruroa left McTaggart and his crew bemused. They had expected to be dragged to the atoll in ignominy but here they were being welcomed almost like heroes.

As soon as they had landed, the French started repairing the *Vega*. McTaggart and Ingram were in the middle of explaining, with a mixture of diagrams and sign language, what repairs needed to be done when Captain Rochebrochard from *La Paimpolaise* appeared and announced: 'The admiral requests that you and your crew join him for lunch.'

Admiral Claverie had a house on a clean part of the beach about a mile away from the harbour. He was informally dressed in lightweight fatigues and wire-rimmed sunglasses; a man in his mid-fifties with a firm handshake who struck McTaggart as a kindly sort of patriarch. Captain Rochebrochard acted as interpreter. 'The admiral wishes to know if you would like to go for a swim.'

'No thanks . . . we've had our fill of salt water for a while.'

The admiral repeated his invitation. 'He says the water is very clean,' Rochebrochard explained.

It was then that McTaggart noticed a figure lurking behind a palm tree and realized that the admiral's hospitality was not all it seemed. The man behind the tree was a photographer armed with a telephoto lens. Suddenly everything became clear: the invitation was a ruse, a propaganda stunt devised by the French. The plan was to get pictures of the nuclear protesters swimming in the 'harmless' waters of Moruroa and release them to the world's press. If it had succeeded, Greenpeace would never have been able to live it down.

93

Fortunately for the *Vega*'s crew, they had spotted the trick just in time. But what followed was almost equally embarrassing. After weeks of tinned and dried food, the admiral's offer of lunch had been irresistible. A table had been prepared beneath the palm trees and decked out with roast beef, pizzas, salad, potatoes, bread, cheese, and vast quantities of wine. Admiral Claverie motioned McTaggart and Ingram to sit on either side of him. The admiral's chief of staff, a commander, a major and three experts on the medical effects of radioactivity joined them for the meal.

The admiral talked amiably about his life at sea and the wonderful girls he had met in the nightclubs of Auckland. McTaggart, who shared his admiration for New Zealand women, was beginning to like him. 'He talked on,' says McTaggart, 'leaving me with the distinct feeling that I was the first person he could talk openly with in a long time.' All the while, the visitors' glasses were constantly topped up with wine. The admiral himself drank only a little, and what he did drink was mixed with ample quantities of water.

McTaggart asked the admiral if he knew why the *Vega* had sailed to Moruroa. Yes, said the admiral, adding a touch of flattery: 'It is the first constructive protest we have come up against.' He agreed that France had no legal right to cordon off part of the Pacific, but she had done so to protect people from fallout – because she valued human life above human rights.

McTaggart protested. 'But the bomb is designed to destroy human life.'

The admiral thought for a moment. 'Yes. Things could have been different and I could have been sitting in your seat.' Whatever the effects of nuclear weapons, the admiral insisted that he personally was a good Catholic, a family man, and had no intention of harming anybody.

The conversation was leading nowhere – which was precisely where the admiral intended it to lead. It did not really matter what was said, so long as the dinner-table chat appeared amicable until the French photographers, snapping away at a discreet distance, had completed their task.

The meal ended with the admiral wishing the *Vega*'s crew

'bon voyage'. McTaggart said goodbye and just in time restrained himself from adding, 'Thank you.' Claverie, he realized, had not become commander of the nuclear test site by accident. 'If there was one expression he might have uttered which would have summed up the secret look in his eye, it would have been: "Son, you've been had."'

Forty-eight hours after landing, the *Vega*, hastily patched up but still leaking a hundred gallons of water a day, was peremptorily towed out to sea. It was not long before her crew picked up a news broadcast from Radio Australia. McTaggart remembers the moment with bitterness. 'The report stated simply that a faulty manoeuvre on our part had led to us crashing into a minesweeper. The French had generously responded to our plea for help, and the crew had joined the admiral of the nuclear fleet for wine and lunch under swaying palms. A note of humorous contempt crept into the announcer's voice: wasn't it all a bit of a lark?'

There was worse to come when the crew landed and found that the picture of their lunch had been published in many newspapers around the world. 'With the brilliant flourish of a single carefully-staged photograph, the French just about completely negated the effect of the *Vega*'s first journey to Moruroa,' McTaggart says. For him, it was a painful lesson – but one he would not forget. Never again would he let the French beat him at the public relations game.

CHAPTER SEVEN

Beaten but unbowed

David McTaggart desperately wanted to settle the score. So when the French announced a new series of tests at Moruroa in 1973, McTaggart announced that he planned another voyage to oppose it. Friends, relatives and even Greenpeace all thought it was pointless for him to go back. Despite niggling doubts at the back of his own mind, McTaggart set about raising funds for the voyage. One morning a letter arrived offering him $5,000 to change his mind. The letter came from the French government, who said they would pay the money in compensation for damage to the *Vega* – on condition that his second voyage was called off. McTaggart was furious. If the French thought they could shut him up with money then they could think again. 'Perhaps more than any other single thing, that confirmed in my mind the decision to get rolling,' he says.

The *Vega* left Auckland Harbour on July 9, 1973. McTaggart and Nigel Ingram were the only two crew members from the previous trip. The others on the boat were their girlfriends, Ann-Marie Horne and Mary Lornie. After the collision the previous year which had almost sunk the *Vega*, McTaggart thought the French would be less likely to use violent tactics if they knew that women were aboard.

For Ann-Marie and Mary, the voyage was to be their first taste of adventure at sea. But it was not their first involvement in opposing nuclear tests. Both women had been part of the back-up team which had prepared the *Vega* for Moruroa in 1972.

McTaggart was particularly anxious to have Ann-Marie on board. He had fallen head over heels for her. She was the daughter of Gene Horne, the friend who had planned to sail with McTaggart on his first voyage but then had to drop out at

the last minute because of passport problems. The age difference between the couple was considerable: McTaggart was
then thirty-nine, she was a nineteen-year-old student, studying
English at Waikato University. But they were well suited to each
other in some ways. Ann-Marie was as stubborn and headstrong
as her lover. Unlike McTaggart, however, she was also religious.
The day the *Vega* sailed, she invited an Anglican vicar down to
the harbour to pray for their safe-keeping and for an end to the
'senselessness of nuclear testing'.

Mary Lornie, a Kiwi legal executive, was different. McTaggart remembers that she was openly contemptuous of Ann-
Marie's faith that God would protect them. Mary was more
practical and physically stronger than the slender Ann-Marie.

All four had been looking forward to the trip, though their
enthusiasm was tinged with trepidation at the reception they
might get. They had a frustrating wait before they could even
test the reaction of the French. The weather was foul. For
thirteen days the *Vega* lay at anchor in Urquhart's Bay just off
the New Zealand coast. They could not go back on land because
they had already cleared customs. But whenever they tried to
head out to sea, the *Vega* was tossed about so furiously that they
were forced to turn back.

Suddenly, on July 22, the protesters' luck changed. The wind
swung round and began blowing in the perfect direction to take
the *Vega* straight to Moruroa. That same day, 3,000 miles away
on the atoll, the French detonated the first atomic bomb of the
1973 series. Their relief at being able to start testing without
being hampered by protest boats was great. For the moment,
the French thought that the good fortune lay with them.

Meanwhile, the *Vega* was hurrying along at eight knots, sometimes hitting nine. Within ten days, she had reached the halfway
mark. Spirits on board were high – until they heard some news
on the radio that swamped them, suddenly, like a tidal wave.
The second test at Moruroa had taken place and the French
were not saying whether there would be any more explosions.
McTaggart was crestfallen. Possibly they were too late.

The mood on board remained subdued. Then, just a couple
of days before they were due to reach the forbidden area around

Moruroa, Ingram picked up another radio news report saying that a further test was expected within days. Suddenly the crew was bristling with excitement again. The *Vega* would soon be there to upset French plans once more. On the night of August 12, they crossed the cordon line and hoisted their radar reflector to let the French navy know that they had arrived. Miraculously, the little ketch had covered 3,000 miles in twenty-one days.

Next morning, the *Vega* was only thirty-five miles from the atoll. The atmosphere on board was tense. McTaggart remembers: 'I started to feel jittery – I suspected it would not be long before the confrontation came.' On board the French minesweeper *La Dunkerquoise* the atmosphere was nerve-tingling too. The *Vega* had arrived on the very day that an atomic explosion was scheduled. The protesters could not be allowed to jeopardize the nuclear testing programme for long. Action would have to be taken immediately. At midday, McTaggart spotted *La Dunkerquoise* approaching at full speed. She circled behind the *Vega*'s stern and stopped a quarter of a mile away. McTaggart watched closely. He saw an inflatable being dropped over the side and four men jumping into it. They sped to the *Vega*'s side. Quickly, the *Vega*'s crew jumped into action. McTaggart grabbed their movie camera, Ann-Marie took the Nikon and Ingram snatched up a document prepared for them – as in 1972 – by the University of Auckland declaring their rights of passage in international waters, sealed in an envelope along with a letter declaring the crew's intention to stay put.

One of the men in the inflatable, a lieutenant, proffered an envelope. Ingram took it and handed over his envelope in return. The inflatable raced off. But the encounter was not over yet. An officer on *La Dunkerquoise* shouted something to the men as their dinghy was pulling in to the minesweeper's side. The inflatable spun round and headed back to the *Vega*. As it came near, McTaggart saw that the lieutenant was madly waving the envelope they had given him. He realized the French were refusing to accept the Greenpeace document.

The previous year the French had tripped up by accepting a similar document. This had enabled the Canadian government to state that McTaggart had formally notified the French of his right to sail in international waters. The French did not intend to get ensnared in that trap again. But neither would McTaggart take the envelope back. The lieutenant reached over and put the envelope on the *Vega*'s deck. McTaggart tossed it back. Back and forth the unwanted envelope flew between the *Vega* and the inflatable. Finally, the angry lieutenant threw it into the water and headed back to *La Dunkerquoise*. Only then did McTaggart open the envelope that the French had given him. The warning was the same as the previous year, with the addition of news that the exclusion zone was now legal under French law (though not under international law). McTaggart was unimpressed. He was in international waters and was going to fight to keep those waters free.

The *Vega* continued on course for Moruroa, with *La Dunkerquoise* trailing about three miles behind. The weather turned stormy but eventually, on the morning of August 15, the *Vega* reached the spot – due west of the mouth of Moruroa lagoon and fourteen miles from the atoll – that Ingram reckoned was the best place to wait. They sat there nervously, wondering what would happen. Several other protest boats had ventured out towards Moruroa earlier in 1973 but only the *Vega* had got this far.

At 3.00 p.m. they decided to head a little closer to the atoll, to sit just one mile beyond the twelve-mile territorial limit. As soon as they started to move, *La Dunkerquoise* came speeding towards the *Vega* on a collision course. The women screamed. Ingram and McTaggart gasped. They were all petrified. Less than a hundred yards from the *Vega*, the minesweeper veered away. Then it charged again and did not pull over until it was about fifty yards from the *Vega*'s side. McTaggart's nerves were in shreds. He felt no better when, shortly afterwards, he spotted, through binoculars, a small boat coming towards them from the direction of Moruroa. What the hell was happening now? Ingram had an answer. 'I think we're going to be boarded,' he said.

The small boat joined *La Dunkerquoise* and an approaching tug, *L'Hippopotame*, which had nearly run the *Vega* down the previous year while in service as a minesweeper. All three closed in on the little *Vega* and her anxious crew. As they drew nearer, McTaggart spotted an inflatable with people on it being towed behind *La Dunkerquoise*. The boarding party was on its way. McTaggart tried desperately to move the *Vega* out of their path, cranking the diesel harder and harder to work up some speed. But his attempt to make a swift getaway was in vain. The sailors on the inflatable grabbed the *Vega*'s safety rail and climbed on board.

'This is private property,' McTaggart said. 'You can't come aboard.' Thud. The first truncheon came down on the back of McTaggart's head. Thud. The next caught him across the shoulders. Thud. A blow landed on the back of his neck; then on his head; on his spine; on his shoulder blade; in the kidneys. Thud, thud, thud. The blows came with such rapidity that McTaggart felt he was being hit simultaneously everywhere. He was pinned down, unable to move. He could hear the women screaming as he was bundled out of the *Vega* into the inflatable. And still the blows came, thud, thud, thud. Something smashed into McTaggart's right eye. Pain racked his body and then, he remembers, 'everything went black'.

Next it was Ingram's turn. He felt the first blow on his head and briefly lost consciousness. He awoke to find he was being kicked in the stomach, groin and ribs until finally he heard a voice yelling, 'Ça suffice! Ça suffice!' (That's enough!)

After that the men rushed for Mary who had been filming throughout the whole ordeal. They wrenched the movie camera from her and threw it overboard. Ann-Marie, who had been taking pictures on the Nikon, knew that she had to stop them from getting that. Her pictures were now the only hope of proving to the world that this nightmare had taken place. She raced for the forward hatch, dived into the cabin she shared with McTaggart and locked the flimsy door. Where could she hide the camera? Suddenly she had an idea. She jammed it through a cubby hole and pushed it up into a cranny inside the structure of the boat. Just as she finished, the door was wrenched open and the boarding party raced in to drag Ann-Marie back on deck. She saw McTaggart in the inflatable and screamed desperately. But it was too late. Three sailors were back in the inflatable, pulling away from the *Vega*, with one man steering and the other two holding McTaggart down.

The remaining members of the boarding party stayed on the *Vega*. They turned her round and set off towards Moruroa. Ingram was put into the bunk in the main cabin. The women were ordered to huddle together on the port side of the deck until evening, when they were allowed to go below. It was then that Ann-Marie noticed the strap of the Nikon sticking out of its hiding place. The French were bound to notice it eventually too. She signalled to one of the guards that she wanted to take a bucket into the side cabin, as if to relieve herself. Closing the door behind her, she quickly shoved the strap back into the interior, then forced herself to do something in the pail.

Back on *La Dunkerquoise*, McTaggart's wounds were under scrutiny. The French were clearly worried about his injuries, particularly the damage to his eye. But, despite the pain he endured, he gained some comfort from the predicament the French had landed themselves in. 'The feeling I had was not so much that I was a prisoner but that, in the bloody process of seizing me, they had bound themselves to me, they had made themselves prisoners of *my* fate.'

When *La Dunkerquoise* arrived at Moruroa, McTaggart immediately made his needs known. 'Get me a decent doctor. Somebody who knows something about eyes.' The French said they would fly him to hospital in Tahiti. But when he asked to make a telephone call to Canada before leaving they refused permission. So McTaggart in turn refused to comply with their plans. Of course he wanted to save his eye. But he also knew that the French wanted to save it too, or they would be in even deeper trouble internationally. He relished the thought. 'I simply knew that they had overdone it and now I had the power to cause them a lot of trouble. Moreover, they all knew it too.'

In the end, McTaggart was persuaded to leave for treatment because, the French insisted, they were unable to make the telephone connection after eight o'clock at night. So with the promise that he could make a phone call as soon as they landed at the airport in Tahiti, McTaggart was taken off *La Dunkerquoise* and ushered into an ambulance. It was the middle of the night when he reached Tahiti. The call to Canada seemed to have been forgotten by the French, so McTaggart reminded them, insisting that he would not accept medication until the promise had been fulfilled. When a nurse approached him with a hypodermic syringe he jumped off the operating table and marched down the corridor. The hospital then swore to arrange the call if he would lie down in a bedroom while they were arranging it. Another attempt was made to give him an injection, but to no avail. The hospital authorities began to wonder if McTaggart was mad. He seemed to be enjoying running rings around them. Did he not care about his sight? Finally, at 7.00 a.m., they came in to say that his brother Drew was on the phone. McTaggart told his brother to send a telegram to the Canadian prime minister, Pierre Trudeau, asking him to secure the release of everyone who had been on the *Vega*. Drew tried to talk sense into his brother. 'Let them treat you right away. For God's sake, don't push it any longer,' he begged. McTaggart put the phone down and was wheeled, unprotesting, into the operating theatre.

On Moruroa, meanwhile, Ingram was trying to talk sense into the officials watching over himself and the women. 'We want to see David McTaggart in hospital,' Ingram insisted. That was impossible, the officials said. Instead the three of them were to be flown to the tiny south Pacific island of Hao, 300 miles away. Ingram, Ann-Marie and Mary all had one other concern: before they left the *Vega*, they had to get the film from the hidden camera. Five minutes before they were due to head for Hao they still did not have the film. Then, for just a moment, their guards all left the boat. Here was their chance. Ingram slammed the cabin hatchway shut and locked himself and the women below deck. Ann-Marie hastily found the camera and took the film from it. But where could they put it so that it would not be found?

There was a knock on the hatch. Ingram shouted back in French: 'We're just getting some personal belongings. Give us a few minutes and we'll be there.' What could they do? There was only one thing possible. Ingram took the film canister, pulled down his pants and tried to insert it into his anus. He could not manage it. Ann-Marie immediately realized what he was trying to do. Biting her lip, she took the film from him and inserted it, painfully, into her vagina. Then the trio unlocked the hatch and headed up the stairs to be taken away.

Soon news of the drama on board the *Vega* spread around the world. When the women were released from Hao, they flew back to New Zealand. Ingram headed for Vancouver. There he passed the film to Drew McTaggart, who handed it over to Greenpeace. Ann-Marie had done well. Thirteen pictures came out. The two best were picked up by wire services and published in at least twenty countries – excluding France. There the official story remained unchanged. David had slipped on the *Vega*'s deck and banged his eye on one of the cleats used to fix ropes.

McTaggart felt lousy when he arrived back in Vancouver twelve days after the boarding. Bombarded with photographers' flashguns and reporters' questions until his eye was agony and his head spun, he retired to hospital for tests. The doctors declared that his eye had healed but his vision was impaired. And there was always a risk that his sight could suddenly deteriorate. If McTaggart did not want to risk going completely blind in the damaged eye, he would always have to be able to get specialized help within fourteen hours. That would be impossible out at sea. If he wanted to preserve his sight, he could not go long-distance sailing again.

But if McTaggart's vision was diminished, his desire to get back at France was not. At first he hoped that the Canadian government would take his case to the world court. Soon he realized that what his government really wanted was to forget the whole affair. Good political and economic relations between France and Canada were too precious to risk for the sake of one man. A letter from the government's external affairs department reached him at the hospital. It explained that the government had commissioned a legal opinion on McTaggart's situation from a professor at Grenoble University in France. The report concluded that McTaggart could sue in the French courts but added: 'His chances of success are practically non-existent.' The Canadian government did not think that fighting for McTaggart was worth the expected cost – about $600,000. McTaggart felt sick. How could his own country abandon him after he had risked his life to safeguard the freedom of the sea? But the Canadian government's reluctance made McTaggart all the more determined to get back at the French. He would fight for justice – even if the battle was now going to be a lonely one.

In one important respect, France gave way before the battle had really begun. On November 1, the Canadian newspapers reported that France was to replace its annual atmospheric tests at Moruroa with tests underground. But for McTaggart the move made not one iota of difference to his complaint. He suspected that the French government was lying. And, even if it was telling the truth, France was still testing its nuclear bombs at the expense of south Pacific islanders. McTaggart was indignant at the implication that this concession would be enough for him. 'Quit now? It seemed that everything that had gone before had only succeeded in giving me this one real opportunity to strike at the heart of the beast.'

On leaving hospital, McTaggart went to live just off the coast of British Columbia in Buccaneer Bay while he thought about what to do next. It was a nostalgic step for him. McTaggart's family had had a summer camp there. 'It was like a second home to me,' he said. Before he began his legal onslaught on the French, McTaggart had one other matter to pursue. He wanted to get the *Vega* back. As it happened, he did not have to wait too long for news of his ketch. Three days after the announcement that French nuclear testing was going underground, McTaggart received another letter. The French would let him collect the *Vega* from Tahiti on condition that he sailed her away immediately. The snag was McTaggart's health. His doctors were adamant that he must not attempt the voyage.

Finally, after a month of heated negotiations and a flood of protest letters to the Canadian government, a compromise was reached. The Canadian government would pay the $12,000 cost of having the *Vega* shipped to Canada on a freighter. McTaggart accepted the arrangement on condition that Canada would claim reimbursement by France for the expense. So, early in December, McTaggart was able to fly to Tahiti, take delivery of the *Vega* and arrange for her transportation home.

Back in Vancouver, McTaggart mortgaged the *Vega* in order to buy a small cabin in Buccaneer Bay for himself and Ann-Marie, who had come from New Zealand to be with him. With the *Vega* home and a roof over his head, McTaggart then concentrated on trying to get the Canadian government to 'espouse' his case. Espousal involves one government putting pressure on another to settle a dispute through a kind of international arbitration board. However, this can only be done when the complainant has exhausted all other local legal remedies. Canada was not willing to go to the world court, but possibly the government could be persuaded to help McTaggart do so. McTaggart also turned to Greenpeace for help with his case. But, he says, the prospect of a costly legal action did not attract them at all.

Already McTaggart was so deeply involved with his case that, to him, it became the epicentre of the universe. He seemed to feel that this was his special mission in life, that he had been 'chosen' as the saviour of the seas and destroyer of the French. The obsession led this normally down-to-earth man to dwell philosophically on his plight. 'There did not seem to be any way to make sense out of what my life had become and the choices I now faced. There were moments when I felt it was all quite unfair – that no man's brain had ever been designed to cope with the ultimate kinds of questions that humanity now faced about its future survival on the planet,' he wrote. 'Few men had the opportunity that I now possessed: to set a precedent in international law which could apply at least one brake against the otherwise apparently unstoppable gallop towards some kind of nuclear holocaust.' While McTaggart basked in the glory of the impossible task that lay before him, Ann-Marie took a job as a dental assistant in Vancouver to make ends meet.

Meanwhile, in the offices of the Canadian government in Ottawa, decisions were being made about McTaggart's request for them to espouse his case. Eventually, at a meeting of the cabinet, the government decided to do as he had asked.

McTaggart was thrilled. This looked like the big break he had not dared to hope for. He snapped out of his depressed, philosophical frame of mind, got ready for action and waited. But nothing happened.

Why were the Canadians being so slow? Much of their sloth was to do with the country's own involvement in the nuclear industry. Canada had developed the sophisticated CANDU nuclear reactor and was trying to sell it worldwide. She also wanted to export uranium – which was where France came in. France aspired to become a nuclear world power, but did not have the natural resources – particularly uranium – to achieve her ambition. McTaggart viewed the developing nuclear partnership between the two countries with disgust. If he had known the truth about Canada and France, his disgust would have turned to horrified disbelief. The two countries had been joined in a price-fixing cartel to drive up the world price of uranium since 1972 – a month before McTaggart decided to make his first Moruroa trip.

After weeks of silence, McTaggart began to feel edgy. His lawyer said that time was running out. Within two months it would be too late to continue with the case over the collision in 1972. McTaggart wrote to Ottawa to find out what was causing the delay. But the legal experts at the external affairs department said there was no urgency; a thirty-year limitation period applied. Then, a month later, McTaggart received an anonymous telephone call from Vancouver. A mysterious voice told him, in urgent tones, that the government lawyers were wrong. The two-year limitation period definitely applied. Unless he acted within a month, his case would go down the drain. McTaggart was furious. Either the government lawyers had been mistaken or else they had been deliberately misleading him. But there was no time for anger; McTaggart had to act fast.

When his plane from Vancouver landed in Paris on May 31, McTaggart knew that he had to find a lawyer straight away. He wanted somebody old and experienced. But when he met Thierry Garby-Lacrouts, a lawyer in his mid-twenties, McTaggart changed his mind. The sudden shift in opinion just might have had something to do with the fact that the eager young

106

man was willing to give his services free. However, any doubts McTaggart might have had were soon dispelled as Garby-Lacrouts enthusiastically got to work sorting through all the files, affidavits and photographs that McTaggart had brought from home. Garby-Lacrouts went to court to serve a writ against the government of France, claiming $21,000 damages for the ramming and boarding of the *Vega*. After a month in Paris, McTaggart returned to Canada.

Back home, McTaggart continued to press his government to act. He also sweated and toiled to restore his beloved ketch. By late autumn the *Vega* was shipshape once more. But soon McTaggart realized that he could not afford to keep the boat. The only way to push his case through would be to have some money. So he sold the *Vega* and with the proceeds bought some waterfront property at Secret Cove, close to Buccaneer Bay. He reckoned that if he could build a roadway down to his new purchase, its value would multiply. (The *Vega* was later restored to Greenpeace for a nominal sum by a sympathetic owner.)

So by day McTaggart worked on the roadway. By night, he transformed himself from a labourer into an artist and made batik pictures – also for cash. Hard work helped to keep his mind from dwelling incessantly on the case. Six thousand miles away, in Paris, Garby-Lacrouts was channelling his energies into McTaggart's fight. His hard work was to pay dividends.

McTaggart's hands were shaking when, early in January 1975, he opened a telegram that had just been delivered to his home. What was happening to his case? Was it on or off? The news was good. A date had been set for the hearing – April 8 – and Garby-Lacrouts wanted McTaggart to go to Paris as soon as possible. There was a mountain of work to get through before the big day.

Garby-Lacrouts met McTaggart at Charles de Gaulle airport. From then until the hearing the two men were hardly ever apart. The work was even more draining than building roads. So much was at stake. According to French law, all evidence on both sides had to be submitted before the hearing. To add to the burden, many of McTaggart's documents were in English. These all had to be translated, with precision, into French.

107

Despite the fact that they were taking on the French government in its own courts, Garby-Lacrouts was confident. Ramming and boarding were indisputably illegal. What the young lawyer had to do, however, was to try and foresee the minor technicalities that the French government was likely to use in its efforts to wriggle out of the corner that McTaggart was putting it in.

April 8 arrived all too soon. In the court room, Garby-Lacrouts's youth seemed to his client to be more conspicuous than ever before. McTaggart could not remove a nagging doubt from his mind. Had he chosen the wrong man? Garby-Lacrouts spoke first. His voice sounded nervous and thin. He faltered. McTaggart's throat suddenly felt sore and dry. But Garby-Lacrouts quickly gained in confidence and soon he was holding the packed court room spellbound with his vivid description of McTaggart's ordeal at the hands of the French navy. When, after an hour and a half, Garby-Lacrouts finally sat down, McTaggart was a happier man. The young lawyer had done a magnificent job.

However, the worst part of the ordeal was yet to come. Jean Gallot, an old, experienced lawyer, rose to give his country's defence. McTaggart drew his breath and waited for an almighty blow that would scupper his case. But it never came. Gallot gave an unexciting, mediocre account of the encounters between the *Vega* and the French. All the punches he pulled had been predicted by Garby-Lacrouts.

Finally, it was the turn of the procurer, whom McTaggart's lawyer described as 'the voicebox of the government', to have his say. But instead of starting his speech, he marched down to where the three judges sat and conversed with them in whispers. McTaggart gave a heavy sigh. What was happening now? After a couple of minutes he got his reply, as the senior judge announced: 'The procurer has asked for a postponement before he can give his opinion.' He banged down his gavel. 'This case is therefore postponed until May 13.'

Five long weeks later, McTaggart and Garby-Lacrouts returned to court for the procurer's speech. McTaggart could not understand most of what the procurer said but he could tell by Garby-Lacrouts's face that things did not look too good. At the end of the speech, Garby-Lacrouts filled his client in. 'He has told the court that it is not competent to judge any part of the case and the only thing they can do is throw it out.' To McTaggart it seemed like the end of the road. His lawyer had already explained to him that whatever the procurer said was almost certain to colour the judges' 'opinion'. McTaggart went back to court alone to hear the judges' opinion on June 17. Garby-Lacrouts could not get the time off work. Anyway, he knew what the judges were going to say – or so he thought. However, he was in for a shock. Despite the opinion of the procurer, the court had decided not to dismiss the case entirely. The judges agreed that they were 'not competent' to deal with the charges arising out of the boarding of the *Vega*. But they would not throw the ramming charges out. Instead, the judges ruled that *La Paimpolaise*, the French minesweeper, had created a 'dangerous situation' at sea and had rammed the *Vega* deliberately. The government was instructed to pay out 2,000 francs for an independent marine surveyor to examine the boat so that full damages could be assessed and paid.

The court room was stunned, reporters were jubilant. The outcome was incredible. Only one person was miserable: McTaggart. He felt that the serious part of the case had been swept aside. The French had still got away with piracy. And no precedent had been set which would settle, once and for all, the question at the heart of McTaggart's action – who owned the sea? He remembers: 'To me it was all bullshit. It felt schizophrenic. It took almost everyone off the hook. It flinched away from the truth. It proved almost nothing. Or if it proved anything, it proved that what passed for justice was, at the very best, only half a loaf.'

It was not in McTaggart's nature to let things rest there. His task was not complete. So on January 18, 1976, he appealed against the decision. Even Garby-Lacrouts said that he had only the slightest chance of winning. McTaggart clung to the hope that the court might just find the courage to rule in his favour. But it did not. The government had said that the boarding was an 'exceptional case' and the court upheld that view.

Only at the end of the reading of the verdict did the procurer suddenly say something that left McTaggart amazed. 'It should not be denied that McTaggart may have helped to persuade the French government to decide to choose underground tests in place of atmospheric tests,' he said. 'It is very possible that McTaggart's attitude, reinforced by the reactions of certain countries and certain groups, caused the government of France to think again.'

CHAPTER EIGHT

Making waves

Lewes, in Sussex, is the sort of place a fast-rising American software company might choose to set up its European base: an old market town on the chalk hills, with narrow, steep streets and shops serving tea and cakes or selling hand-made pottery. Some would call it quaint, others would call it twee. Either way, it's clean, surrounded by countryside and has first-rate communications. London is sixty-two minutes' ride away, with trains every hour, and Gatwick airport, with flights worldwide, is only twenty-seven minutes away. Along the main street is a 1960s office block of the sort that would not be built there nowadays for fear of outraging local conservationists. It's set back from the road slightly, as if embarrassed to show its face. The first indication that this is not indeed the European headquarters of Consolidated Software Inc. comes in the lift: on the door someone has sprayed the letter A inside a circle – the trademark of a visiting anarchist. When one steps out into the office, the illusion returns. As befits an enterprise with an annual budget of ten million dollars, there are eight IBM computers for wordprocessing and electronic mail, photo-copiers, golfball typewriters, a facsimile transmission machine and a Nexus link to an outside database. But the illusion does not last long: piled up in a corner of the floor are rucksacks, kitbags and bits of wetsuits, and on the walls pictures of whales and rainbows. There are a dozen full-time staff here, mostly in their twenties or early thirties, and mostly speaking with North American accents. There are visitors too: earnest young Germans in gold-rimmed granny glasses, Scandinavian students wanting to help with the paperwork.

One of the smaller rooms at the back of the building looks untidier than the rest. No green screens here. Just books, a few easy chairs, piles of papers, photo albums and the reminders of an adventurous life. At the desk, in an open-neck shirt, sits David McTaggart, chairman of Greenpeace International.

It began in 1969. Flared jeans and LSD were the height of fashion. Flower power, though wilting a little, lived on in San Francisco. In Vietnam the war was raging more fiercely than ever, but opposition to the war was growing. France had put away its riot shields and tear gas and dismantled the barricades of May 1968, but elsewhere the campuses were in ferment. October 1 brought yet another demonstration, this time a few miles outside Vancouver in Canada. A crowd of around 7,000 protesters – mainly students plus a smattering of American draft-dodgers – converged on the Douglas border crossing that links western Canada with the United States. At 1.00 p.m. precisely, they stepped into the road and stayed there, closing the frontier. The focus of their attention was Amchitka Island, an American-owned hunk of rock 2,400 miles away in Alaska – and, more specifically, a 4,000-foot deep hole in that rock where the Americans were about to carry out a nuclear test.

News of the planned test had aroused anger and even fear along the west coast of Canada, for Amchitka lies only a few miles from a deep, earthquake-prone crack in the earth that curves round the ocean floor off Vancouver and emerges as the notorious San Andreas fault in California. Robert Hunter, a journalist on Vancouver's leading daily, the *Sun*, had voiced the fear a few weeks earlier: 'Scientists in Canada, the US, Japan and Hawaii have warned that there is a distinct danger that the test might set in motion earthquakes and tidal waves which could sweep from one end of the Pacific to the other.'

The frontier blockade was little more than a token gesture. The demonstrators left after listening to speeches, and two days later the Americans let off a one-megaton bomb at Amchitka. It neither leaked radiation nor caused tidal waves or earthquakes. But the test had obviously struck a deep chord; although the demonstration was small by the standards of the times, it was an extremely large one for Canada. No previous issue with

112

environmental and anti-war overtones had provoked such massive opposition there. What annoyed the protesters, though, was the fact that their action had failed to hit its target. The American news media had simply ignored it. One of the older participants was Jim Bohlen, then aged forty-three, an American missile and rockets engineer. He and his wife had both grown up in a Quaker community in Pennsylvania. 'We joined in non-violent action against nuclear weapons in the early 1960s,' he says. 'It was then that we learned the concept of non-violent civil disobedience.' Later, he had moved with his family to Vancouver so that his son could not be drafted to serve in Vietnam. He recalls his disappointment at the border blockade's lack of impact in the United States: 'We thought this was another example of the US government keeping information from the people. So we decided to start an organization, informing the public in a way that the media cannot ignore.'

Bohlen was a member of the Committee to Aid American War Objectors, as was his friend, Irving Stowe, a fifty-year-old Quaker and former Philadelphia lawyer, who had also moved to Vancouver when his son reached drafting age. Together with Paul Cote, a Canadian lawyer in his mid-twenties, they decided to carry the Amchitka protest forward and established the Don't Make a Wave Committee, so called after the threat of tidal waves caused by nuclear tests. The first few meetings led nowhere. Then, on the morning after one of these meetings, Bohlen's wife Marie said: 'Why the hell doesn't somebody sail a boat up there and park right next to the bomb? That's something everyone can understand.' By chance, a journalist phoned a few minutes afterwards to ask if any more protests were planned over Amchitka. Bohlen took the plunge. 'As a matter of fact we're going to sail a boat there,' he said.

The idea of sending a boat into a nuclear testing zone was not entirely new. The Quakers – who oppose war for religious reasons – had tried it twice before, and both times the boats had been seized long before reaching their goals. But the Don't Make a Wave Committee was well placed to try again. Paul Cote was an Olympic sailor and, through his family, had access to charter boats. Together with Bohlen, he began to search for a suitable vessel. Stowe, meanwhile, set about collecting donations from his fellow Quakers and persuaded Joni Mitchell to give a concert which raised $17,000.

Finding the right boat proved tricky. It had to be tough, capable of handling the seas around Amchitka at their most treacherous season: autumn (the time favoured by the Americans for their tests). More difficult still, it had to have an owner willing to risk his vessel against the might of American armed forces. Insurance was probably out of the question. At the very least, there was the danger of seizure, heavy fines and blacklisting for the skipper. Thirteen months after Bohlen first announced the plan, he found Captain John Cormack, owner of a rusting eighty-foot halibut seiner. Cormack had suffered several bad fishing seasons and was desperate for money. He agreed to a six-week charter of the vessel for $15,000. The boat, named the *Phyllis Cormack* after its owner's wife, was thirty years old with a top speed of only nine knots. Its barometer was corroded and the depth sounder had to be thumped to make it work.

By September 1971 the *Phyllis Cormack* was ready for Amchitka. As she left Vancouver Harbour under the eye of the television cameras, the crew hoisted a green sail decorated with peace and ecology symbols and bearing a new word – 'Greenpeace'. The origin of the name has given rise to some colourful (and probably apocryphal) tales in Greenpeace folklore. Jim Bohlen's explanation sounds more plausible than many. The founders, he says, soon realized that the 'Don't Make a Wave Committee' was too much of a mouthful. 'One night during a planning meeting at the Unitarian church in Vancouver, we were all sitting there trying to think up a really catchy name for us. Someone said, "It has to mention peace." Someone else said it had to mention "green" because of our conservation interest. Bill Darnell [who later joined the voyage] said, "The name is obvious. It has to be Greenpeace."'

Apart from Bohlen and the boat's owner, Cormack, there were ten people on the voyage. They included three journalists and a photographer whose main task was to record the events but whose presence might also deter the American navy from trying to sink the boat. The journey proved even tougher than expected. 'The vessel we were in was almost unseaworthy,' says Bohlen. And there were unpredictable hazards. Robert Hunter, one of the journalists, wrote later that a tape recorder on board had affected the compass.

'While we were grooving to the Moody Blues, the boat wandered ninety miles off course.'

In between grooving to the Moody Blues, Hunter was reading a book given to him by a man who said it would change his life. What the man did not know was that it would also have a profound effect on the embryo Greenpeace organization. The book was a collection of legends and prophecies of the North American Indians, including a 200-year-old prophecy by a Cree grandmother called Eyes of Fire. She foretold a time when birds would fall from the skies, fish would die in their streams, deer would drop in their tracks in the forest and the seas would be blackened – all because of the white man's greed. When that day came, Eyes of Fire warned, the Indians would have lost their spirit. But later they would rediscover it and begin to teach the white man to have reverence for the sacred earth. Then all races of the world would unite under the symbol of the rainbow and go forth to end the destruction and desecration. They would become Warriors of the Rainbow.

For the moment, though, they were warriors in a storm. As they sheltered in Akutan Bay, five days' sailing from the test site, an American coastguard ship arrested them for going ashore without reporting to customs. While that problem was being sorted out, arguments began among the crew. Several had taken time off work for the trip and had to return or lose their jobs. Others feared the boat might not survive the worsening weather. The amateur sailors headed for home, expecting to become the laughing-stock of Vancouver. But they were mistaken. Thousands of supporters, who had been following newspaper stories of their voyage, were waiting to greet them on the quayside.

In the meantime, unknown to the crew, Bohlen and Stowe had secretly been planning what the Pentagon would call 'second strike capability'. They had found another boat, a fast 154-foot former minesweeper. When they asked for volunteers to crew it, 400 people applied. The nuclear test was delayed while the US Supreme Court, in special session, heard last-minute pleas from environmentalists. The second Greenpeace boat raced towards Amchitka but was still 700 miles away when the Americans exploded their bomb, 240 times as powerful as the one that destroyed Hiroshima. For Greenpeace, it looked like failure. But within a few days an American government spokesman announced that there would be no more tests on Amchitka. In 1972 the testing-ground was officially abandoned 'for political and other reasons' and turned into a bird sanctuary.

Greenpeace had chalked up its first success. Not only that; its adversary had been the most powerful nation on earth, and Greenpeace had been the catalyst in persuading it to change its mind. What had begun with the old Quaker idea of 'bearing witness' had now turned into an extremely powerful weapon. There were several lessons in this which Greenpeace has since used to great effect. First, they discovered that the number of people involved in a protest did not really count. Thousands of people could march through the streets and fail to dent a government's armour. But put a handful of people in a small boat and the result could be very different. Their second discovery was that using a small number of people could be an advantage. It turned the issue into a David-and-Goliath struggle, where the public naturally tended to support the underdog. All that was needed then was to choose an imaginative course of action, to provide the public with an exciting and moving spectacle – and to ensure that the news media were there to report it.

In the wake of Amchitka – and David McTaggart's voyages to Moruroa – Greenpeace entered a chrysalis phase from which it emerged in 1975, not as a single-issue campaigner against nuclear tests, but as a full-scale environmental strike force.

Paul Spong was a New Zealander in his early thirties who had graduated in psychology from the University of California in Los Angeles and then moved to Vancouver. He worked for a time in the city aquarium, studying a captive killer whale

(Orcinus orca), but got the sack when he said publicly that the whale 'wanted to be free'. Later he set up a whale-watching station off Hanson Island and asked Greenpeace to join him in campaigning to end the mass killing of whales. There was already a measure of public support for the move. Whales are much admired on the west coast of Canada and the USA, and the Russians and Japanese looked like causing their extinction. An international commission had imposed quotas on catches and banned the killing of young whales, but the Russians were ignoring the quotas.

Greenpeace crews set sail in the *Phyllis Cormack* (now repaired and fitted with a new engine) and the *Vega*. They also took with them a number of inflatable Zodiac dinghies. McTaggart had first seen them used by the French off Moruroa – they were in fact a French invention – and had noted their usefulness. Without them, the French commandos would not have been able to board the *Vega*. They were easily launched from a larger ship and capable of high speeds – up to thirty knots in a calm sea. They were also highly manoeuvrable and extremely safe. Even if overturned, they would still float. When someone pointed out that Jacques Cousteau had used them for filming whales, the decision to take them was as good as made. In the battles to come, Greenpeace would find many other uses for them. So too would the French: the Zodiac dinghy abandoned in Auckland was the first clue on the trail of the *Rainbow Warrior* bombers.

After two months wandering in the Pacific, the *Phyllis Cormack* came upon the Russian factory ship *Dalniy Vostok* and a whaling fleet off California. As one of the harpoon ships, the *Vlastny*, chased a family of whales, Greenpeace launched its Zodiac rubber dinghies and sailed them between the *Vlastny* and the whales. The Russians first pointed their harpoon gun at the Greenpeace members, then eventually fired at the whales, unaware that the scene would later be shown on television throughout the United States and Canada. The sight of a few men in rubber dinghies confronting the Russians, surrounded by the floating bodies of whales in a bloodstained sea, instantly won over millions of Americans.

On its return, the Greenpeace team was fêted by the media. And, from the whales' point of view, it was a public relations coup. The tales of Moby Dick and Captain Ahab had depicted whales as menacing, dangerous beasts. Almost instantly they were transformed in popular mythology into lovable and threatened creatures. The photograph of one whale in particular joined Elvis Presley and Che Guevara in the list of best-selling posters. But the reaction from other anti-whaling and conservation groups was not universally warm. Hunter, who by this time was one of the leading figures in Greenpeace, recalls: 'Rather than being welcomed as brothers and sisters by our fellow conservationists, we were greeted with token smiles and congratulatory remarks that barely masked the underlying mood of resentment and suspicion.' Many of these other groups had been plugging away at the whale issue for some time with little success, and resented this brash newcomer encroaching on their patch. Some feared that Greenpeace would draw funds away from their own organizations. One of the most prominent groups, the California-based Project Jonah, accused Greenpeace of 'machismo' and questioned its methods. Greenpeace, on the other hand, believed that Project Jonah resented the fact that someone else had caught the Russians red-handed under its very nose – just off the Californian coast.

There was also division within Greenpeace itself. David McTaggart recalls: 'In 1973 I had a discussion with Bohlen and a friend and said I was going to take my court case about the *Vega* to France. There was no Greenpeace organization then – it was still the Don't Make a Wave Committee. Bohlen and his friend said they couldn't help; court cases were too long and drawn out. "It's all yours," they said. So I set up a bank account in north Vancouver in the name of Greenpeace. I think it was probably the first account set up in that name. I raised a little money and went to Paris with about two hundred dollars to start the case. I worked away in Paris and wrote about thirty letters a day back to Canada to build a pressure base on the Canadian government. In the meantime, people in Europe were pushing me to start a Greenpeace office there.

'Then around 1975 Bob Hunter called and said he would

like to leave his newspaper job and work on the whaling issue himself. We said OK and he proceeded with an office in Vancouver and I continued to work in Europe. We set up an office in Paris, then in London and Amsterdam. Vancouver worked with a US office in San Francisco.'

By early 1978 the Canadian and American offices were about $250,000 in debt. Then, towards the end of the year, Vancouver sued San Francisco for one million dollars over the use of the Greenpeace name. McTaggart says: 'It was a big battle. In Europe we had just bought the *Rainbow Warrior* and had done something like ten or twelve campaigns in our first year and their court case was very embarrassing to us. To make a very long story short, I settled the case between the US and Canada in a smoky basement in Vancouver in 1979. They cancelled all their court cases and we paid off their debt. Canada, the US and New Zealand and Australia joined Greenpeace Europe. I changed the name to Stichting Greenpeace Council (known as Greenpeace International) later in 1979.'

On the way back from their encounter with the Russians, the *Phyllis Cormack*'s crew members began talking about their next campaign. Two men, 'Walrus' Oakenbough and Paul Watson, were concerned about the annual seal hunt on the ice-floes off Labrador and Newfoundland. Two-week-old seal pups – chosen because of their pure white pelts – are beaten over the head and skinned, sometimes while still alive. Thinking of a way to impede the hunt, the pair hit on a bright idea: to spray the baby seals with indelible green dye. That way nobody would kill them for their skins.

The green dye plan was announced in advance, and as the Greenpeace team prepared for action the Canadian government issued an order-in-council making it illegal to spray or mark any living seal. The team reluctantly agreed not to use their dye but instead headed on to the ice by helicopter for a televised confrontation with Norwegian sealers.

Whales and seals quickly established themselves as the main-stays of the Greenpeace economy: while the organization's activists took the campaign against nuclear pollution very seriously, there was little doubt that the rescuing of sea-mammals was what pulled in most of the money. And the combination of whales and seals is not without its irony. Paul Spong, who started the whale campaign, was quick to point out that orca whales – the type hunted by the Russians off California – include seals as part of their diet. What should Greenpeace do, he asked jokingly, if it spotted a whale about to eat a seal?

These early campaigns set a pattern for the future as Greenpeace grew and embraced more and more issues – too many, some members thought. Whether the issue was acid rain, the dumping of chemical waste or the killing of kangaroos, the essential ingredients were always the same: people confronting states or huge corporations. These are what made Greenpeace the model of a modern protest movement. While others – especially on the political left – still think in terms of dreary marches and placards, then wonder why journalists find their activities too boring to report, Greenpeace has discovered the secret of getting its message into the newspapers and on to the television screens. It excels at the sort of image-building that a multinational company would pay advertising and public relations executives hundreds of thousands of dollars for doing less well. As for the Greenpeace rainbow logo, it is an adman's dream – a simple, powerful image with associations which are readily understood by all nations and by all cultures: a reminder of the beauty of nature, a sign that the earth has been cleansed, and a bearer of hope for the future.

Greenpeace today has 1,200,000 members, half of them in the United States. And, although the organization embraces seventeen countries, detractors are quick to point out that these are almost without exception the well off, predominantly Anglo-Saxon nations of northern Europe, North America and Australasia. The Latin countries of southern Europe figure only slightly in the membership, and the Third World scarcely at all. It is all too easy to dismiss Greenpeace as a plaything of the white, well-educated but bored middle classes. It is easy to argue

120

that in the Third World concern for the environment is a luxury; that Greenpeace does nothing for 'real' issues like poverty and starvation. On the other hand, Greenpeace can justly claim that its support is strongest in the countries whose technology does most damage to the environment.

Between the extremes of the Third World and the United States, there are many countries where Greenpeace has made little or no impact on public opinion. In France, for instance, there are only 7,000 paid-up members, compared with 75,000 in Britain, 80,000 in the Netherlands and 200,000 in West Germany. Greenpeace itself blames Mitterrand and the socialists for the relatively low French membership, arguing that there has been no effective environmental lobby since they came to power. 'In France our name works against us,' says Brian Fitzgerald of Greenpeace International. 'Any name with "peace" in it is labelled as Communist. They always felt there was a political motive behind our protest. In the UK and US there is a sense of environmentalism as a goal in itself, separate from politics.'

Although there are seventeen nations with Greenpeace offices, only ten – Germany, the United States, Canada, France, Britain, the Netherlands, Australia, New Zealand, Sweden and Denmark – have voting rights. The rest – Belgium, Spain, Austria, Switzerland, Argentina, Italy and Luxembourg – must wait until they are more firmly established. There is an annual meeting when representatives from all the nations gather in Britain to make decisions on things like establishing new offices, budgets, and campaign priorities or appraisals. Day-to-day decisions are in the hands of four board members, two of whom are elected from European countries and two from North America and Australasia. These four elect a chairman – the position David McTaggart has held since the present structure was set up in 1983. For the public, it's a matter of take it or leave it; supporters vote with their cheque books.

In Lewes, there are a dozen regular staff, and around 250 full-time employees worldwide. 'It's an organization full of headstrong people,' says Brian Fitzgerald. 'There is a lot of internal conflict because of it. But people do have a say in what issues are taken on. Staff are generally underpaid and overworked – they have to have a deep commitment if they are going to stick with it.' Pay varies from country to country. The director of Greenpeace France gets the equivalent of $8,000 a year. The top salary – $35,000 – goes to an American director, but the average Greenpeace salary is $12,000.

It is also a demanding job, especially in terms of time. Peter Wilkinson, a former lorry driver who is now a director of Greenpeace UK, ran into marriage problems soon after joining. 'Eventually I had to make a choice. It was either Greenpeace or my wife. Rightly or wrongly, Greenpeace won.'

Andrew Booth, a worker in the London office, eats, drinks and – for a while – even slept Greenpeace, spending his nights in a sleeping bag by his desk. He realized it had taken over his life when a letter arrived for him. It said:

> Dear Andrew. My name is John Booth and I'm your father. Your mother is called Pauline and you have three sisters. Their names are Melanie, Rachel and Vicki. You also have a dog. We all live in Dewsbury, near Leeds, and you might like to get in touch with us some time. Love, Dad.

He had not written or phoned for six months. Nowadays he tries to escape occasionally. 'At parties, I've given up telling people what I do. I say I work in the media, the oil industry, or I'm an accountant. Otherwise they ask so many questions that you find you're talking about Greenpeace all night.'

Running Greenpeace costs money – around ten million dollars in 1985. Secret service agents in several countries, notably the United States and France, have combed the accounts for evidence of Moscow gold, but without success. In fact about ninety per cent of Greenpeace's money comes in small amounts from members – an average of less than ten dollars a head. Companies also donate, but usually in the form of equipment rather than money: engines, Zodiacs, discounts on fuel, and so on. The rest comes from selling Greenpeace merchandise. Beside badges, stickers, posters, books and videos, there are Greenpeace jogging suits, ecologically sound cosmetics, recycled stationery and a green umbrella with the message 'Stop acid rain'. In the United States, the range includes an LP of singing whales and a digital clock powered not by batteries but by two potatoes connected to zinc and copper electrodes.

Around twenty per cent of the Greenpeace budget goes on fund-raising. In America there is a lot of door-to-door canvassing, but not in Europe where people tend to resent callers and assume they are selling insurance or religion. Generally, direct mail is preferred because leaflets have an educational value even when they bring in no money. In the United States the mail shots are handled by a specialist firm. In 1984, for instance, the firm sent leaflets about the protection of kangaroos to a small number of Americans chosen from the mailing lists of various environmental organizations. The reply envelopes were marked so that the firm could tell which mailing list produced the best response. Then it mailed everyone on the best list. For the seals campaign, it did marketing tests with three types of leaflet to see which worked best (it was one with a photograph of a baby seal). In America, these mail shots are aimed typically at middle-aged, middle-class couples with children, their own home, and a bias towards college education. In Europe, Greenpeace does not have such a rigidly-defined marketing profile, though its members are generally younger. 'In a way, we're an environmental marketing organization,' says Fitzgerald. 'We're looking to market disarmament in the States in the same way as Reagan markets star wars.'

Occasionally, Greenpeace becomes a victim of its own successful marketing. The campaign against seal culling, because of its emotional appeal, proved extremely popular – particularly in Britain where the 'animal rights' aspect of Greenpeace is strongest. But while the money poured in from supporters, the organization has been trying to put the brakes on. There were accusations that it was saving seals at the expense of starving Eskimos. Greenpeace argues that it never opposed the hunting of seals by Eskimos; what it did oppose was killings on an industrial scale – and on that front the battle has largely been won. So the seals campaign is being phased out.

123

All national Greenpeace organizations give part of their money towards maintaining the fleet, which takes up about a quarter of the entire budget. There are four boats: the *Vega*, McTaggart's old ketch; the *Sirius*; the *Beluga*; and the *Greenpeace*. The 190-foot *Greenpeace* was originally a Dutch salvage vessel and ocean-going tug before being bought by the Maryland Pilots Association in America. They donated it to Greenpeace in April 1985 because they had no further use for it. Captain Michael Watson, one of the pilots, says they gave it away because 'in our state we are very environmentally concerned. Our ships travel through Chesapeake Bay and we are working to preserve the water quality and the wildlife there.' Although Watson describes the ship as 'very strongly built and in excellent condition', she has been something of a mixed blessing for Greenpeace. The change of ownership cost $500,000 in brokerage fees. She was acquired in order to deliver prefabricated buildings for the campaign in Antarctica, and will almost certainly be sold as soon as possible because she is too large and expensive to run.

Although Greenpeace is usually seen as a maritime protest organization, several spectacular actions have taken place on land or in the air. In Canada, Greenpeace members parachuted into a nuclear plant to prove that security there was inadequate. Others climbed chimneys to protest at air pollution and acid rain. When the US Interior Secretary, James Watt, declared the entire United States coastline open to possible oil and gas exploration, Greenpeace decided that he must have lost his marbles. So they tipped 5,000 marbles on to his office floor. In Britain, they tipped radioactive mud on the steps of the Department of the Environment. When the first Cruise missiles were flight-tested in the United States, they attempted to catch a missile with a huge net suspended from balloons. Nets were also used – more successfully – to tie up the Japanese embassy in Canada in a protest over Japanese fishing practices. One of the principles in all Greenpeace action is that members should not resort to violence, even if their opponents do so. One of the organizers in the early days, Paul Watson, disagreed with this and was squeezed out. He went on to establish an organization called the Sea Shepherds, which has been known to ram an 'enemy' ship.

Greenpeace is sometimes accused of directing its attacks mainly towards western countries. The simple answer to that is that it is much easier to protest at Moruroa than at nuclear testing sites in the centre of Soviet or Chinese territory. Nevertheless, there have been several confrontations with the eastern bloc. In 1983 a Greenpeace ship entered Soviet territory en route for Alaska to photograph Russian whalers. 'Seven people were arrested and put in prison – that's the problem with the Russians,' says McTaggart. 'But we launched the operation on the day of the international meeting about whales. All the delegates saw the pictures of what was going on in Siberia.' In Berlin the following year they flew a balloon calling on all four powers there to stop nuclear tests – until the East Germans confiscated the balloon. On another occasion, the *Sirius* sailed to Leningrad, the crew wearing T-shirts printed in Russian. It released hundreds of balloons with messages addressed to President Brezhnev: 'Please stop nuclear testing.' The *Sirius* was then escorted unceremoniously out of the harbour.

Success, though, does not come immediately from such highly publicized actions. There is also a lot of work done behind the scenes. One ingredient of success is discreet lobbying. McTaggart explains: 'There was one country we wanted to do something about at an international whaling convention, but we couldn't get through the bureaucracy to lobby the head of state. Then we checked out the head of state's wife and found she liked orchids. We tracked down the two best orchid specialists in the world and they wrote her a letter about endangered orchids. Later in the letter they talked about endangered whales. We got her support.'

The second key to success lies in research. Each Greenpeace worker is allocated to a single campaign. In this way they are able to build up expertise – often getting help from top scientists – and become formidable walking encyclopedias on their subjects. This makes them remarkably effective in television interviews and debates when they are able to attack or scold so-called experts from the other side, apparently on equal terms.

The third golden rule is short, simple, and one of David McTaggart's favourites: 'Whether it's a government or a multinational, you must find the weakest link and go for that.' The Bayer chemical company – the target of many Greenpeace protests – is not the largest polluter of the North Sea. Few people would recognize the name of the company which does most damage there. But in Germany and the United States Bayer is a household name for its headache cures. That, says McTaggart, is why it is a weak link among the marine polluters. Its name makes it especially sensitive to bad publicity – which is why Greenpeace decided to give Bayer a headache.

CHAPTER NINE

South sea trouble

Few have come as close to experiencing the Pacific idyll as Bengt Danielsson, who has sailed across much of the ocean that covers one-third of our planet. He learned of the Pacific's violent nature during the famous Kon-Tiki expedition of 1947, when a balsa wood raft launched off Peru was carried by the swirling currents to Polynesia, proving that in ancient times the South American Indians could have settled the south sea islands. This Swedish anthropologist has tasted the Pacific's tranquillity, too; once he chanced on a remote coral atoll called Raroia and described in a book how he was welcomed by Polynesian girls dancing on the beach and offered a meal of roast suckling pig.

With his wild white beard, Danielsson, sixty-five, looks less like a scientist than a mystical seafarer, one of the navigators, perhaps, that Captain Ahab might have used to track down Moby Dick. He first arrived in Tahiti to do field studies in 1951 but postponed his anthropological work when, on a stroll through the jungle one day, he stumbled upon a library kept by a retired French school teacher. The shelves were filled with books about Paul Gauguin, the Impressionist artist who worked and died in Tahiti. All these books maintained that Gauguin had lived in the same vibrant paradise that he portrayed on canvas. Danielsson looked into the subject more deeply and found that few had been more miserable in the south seas than Gauguin, a witless dreamer who arrived with 'a shotgun, a French horn, two mandolins and a guitar' – and would have died of starvation if syphilis had not got him first.

Danielsson's research into Gauguin's grim sex life – his venereal disease frightened away all but the most impoverished whores and the good native girls refused even to pose for his pictures – proved useful on his next project. This was a study of the sexual habits of Polynesians who, because they were beautiful and had few possessions, worshipped physical beauty above all else. Intercourse for them was a game, to be practised to perfection, without the romanticism that Gauguin and many other Europeans sought so desperately in the Pacific.

For Danielsson, the romance has been replaced by tragedy. Today, some of the descendants of Gauguin's beauties are grotesquely deformed because they were caught unawares by an incandescent atomic cloud. Many others have died of cancers brought on by radiation. And hundreds more may also perish from diseases that take decades to manifest themselves. Elsewhere in the Pacific, whole islands were obliterated by American atomic tests in the 1950s, and some scientists believe that in a matter of decades serious contamination may seep into the ocean currents from the seventy underground blasts that France has carried out on Moruroa. The Pacific, and its people, may have become the first casualties of the nuclear arms race. That is why Danielsson has become one of the region's most relentless crusaders against its destruction.

The joyful welcome that Danielsson received from the islanders of Raroia was identical to the one given to the first European explorer, Samuel Wallis, who landed on Tahiti in 1767. Unfortunately for his crew, Wallis could not afford to linger. His ship was starting to fall apart because the sailors were pulling all the iron nails from the hull to buy the favours of Tahitian women. Also, Wallis was after a bigger prize. He and the later European navigators who chanced upon Polynesia in the eighteenth century were searching for something far grander than an island paradise: by their calculations, a continent lay out there greater in size and riches than Asia.

It has only been in the last fifty years that world powers – the United States, the Soviet Union, China, Britain, France and Japan – have come to realize that the watery mass of the Pacific is just as valuable as any lost continent. Its lures are rich fishing grounds, vast mineral deposits waiting to be scooped up from the ocean floor, and remote atolls that, as far as the superpowers are concerned, provide an ideal testing ground for military hardware. The Americans, the British and the French have all exploded nuclear weapons in the Pacific. The Russians, like the Americans, also test their missiles there.

The Pacific has become a militarized trench, the coral curtain. In 1984 a study by the Swedish peace foundation, SIPRI, revealed that the US has 517 military bases in the Pacific. France comes second with fifteen and the Soviet Union third with ten. Nuclear missiles have drawn the Soviet Union and America so close that, on a war-room computer board, the vast ocean has almost ceased to exist. Russian warheads launched from the Kamchatka peninsula could obliterate Los Angeles within twenty minutes of the button being pressed. A missile fired from a submarine could strike in half that time. If all the bombs exploded in the Pacific had been used in a war, every major city in western Europe and North America would have been obliterated. So far, more than 200 nuclear 'experiments' have been carried out.

France is not Greenpeace's only adversary in the Pacific. Apart from the weapons testing by the superpowers, America, Korea and Japan have used the region as a dumping ground for radioactive rubbish too 'hot' to keep on the mainland. For twenty years after the Second World War, when the United States took the Marshall Islands from the Japanese in a series of bloody battles, the Marshalls were used by the American military for nuclear tests.

In the 1960s the Americans stopped their nuclear tests in the Pacific, but only after erasing six atolls from the face of the planet. The United States has held all of Micronesia, including the Marshall Islands, as a 'strategic trust' since the end of the Second World War. At the moment, negotiations are under way which would end this trusteeship, the last of eleven trust territories set up by the United Nations after the war. Under the proposed new arrangement, called the 'Compact of Free Association', the Marshalls (as well as the other Micronesian states of Belau and the Federated States of Micronesia) would gain a measure of internal autonomy, but the US would retain the right to keep military bases in the islands, as well as control foreign policy and defence questions for the Marshallese. For the United States, the most important condition is to retain the use of the Kwajalein missile range as the bullseye for long-range test missiles, fired from the Vandenburg Air Force base in California. The most destructive weapons in the American arsenal – Polaris, Minuteman and Trident – have all rained down through the years on the Marshall Islands. These missiles are, of course, fired without their nuclear warheads, but some of the dummies still contain uranium-238 which is spilled out. As the missiles arc across the ocean they are tracked by radar stations dotted on islands across the Pacific. According to a study by the World Health Organization, these radar stations emit radiation that may account for the high number of cataracts among the islanders. China and the Soviet Union also unleash their test rockets out into the Pacific.

Evidence has also emerged from de-classified files of the US Defense Nuclear Agency (DNA) that the Marshall islanders might have been used as guinea pigs by scientists to study the effects of radioactive fallout. On March 1, 1954, a hydrogen bomb was exploded on Bikini that was 1,000 times more powerful than the Hiroshima blast. Rongelap is within a hundred miles of Bikini, and several hours after the blast the atoll was covered in two inches of radioactive fallout. The people of Rongelap have since been plagued by radiation-related diseases. The US government claimed at the time that the fallout was 'accidental'. But, according to the DNA, the night before the test – called Operation Bravo – officials had received weather reports of winds blowing towards Rongelap.. As one scientist assigned to study the fallout's effects on the islanders remarked at the time: 'Greater knowledge of [radiation] effects on human beings is badly needed ... The habitation of these people on the island will afford most valuable radiation data on human beings.'

The home where Danielsson lives with his French wife, Marie-Thérèse, is far from the smog cloud that now hangs over the traffic jams of Papeete, the capital of Tahiti, the largest island in the French Polynesian chain. Their house, in the traditional islander style, has a thatched palm roof and is built on stilts to catch the ocean breeze. A telephone line leads away from the house, and this, according to Danielsson, is occasionally bugged by the French colonial administrators who are concerned about his protest activities. The mail he receives from environmentalists around the world has often been slit open. And three times now French agents have searched his home.

Because of his Neptunian appearance and his obsessiveness, Danielsson has been ridiculed in the Polynesian state-backed press as an unscientific prophet of doom. The French intelligence service, however, takes Danielsson more seriously. In May 1985 Christine Cabon, the DGSE agent who had infiltrated Greenpeace headquarters in Auckland, was ordered to find out all she could on attempts by Danielsson to get Tahitian militants to join the protest voyage to Moruroa.

The nightmare of the Mitterrand government was not that Greenpeace's voyage to Moruroa could halt the testing of its new nuclear warheads for the long-range Hades missile and its new generation of submarine-launched rockets. This was impossible, as even the most militant Greenpeace strategists conceded during the planning of the *Rainbow Warrior*'s voyage. Moruroa is a long thin shepherd's crook of coral with a French Legionnaire posted every ten paces. At least four warships cruise the waters of the twenty-mile-long atoll, and any landing attempt by the Greenpeace flotilla could easily have led to bloodshed. What worried the French was that the emotive issue of nuclear testing might inflame the independence movement already spreading through their Pacific colonies. A few hundred islands flung about the ocean is all that remains of the French empire, and the Pacific region is the only one left on the globe where France can still proclaim itself, with any justice, a superpower.

It is likely that Mitterrand's men over-reacted to the *Rainbow Warrior*'s voyage because of troubles in the French colony of New Caledonia. There, a civil war was brewing between the white settlers – some are descendants of prisoners exiled to the island by Napoleon III in 1871 – and the native Melanesians, the Kanaks, who want independence.

Successive governments in Paris have feared that the Russians are trying to destabilize the French Pacific and, without convincing proof, have accused some of the environmentalist campaigns of being inspired by the Kremlin. Since the Russians were given a naval base by the Vietnamese they have certainly grown bolder in the Pacific. The Soviet fleet routinely shadows American war games off Hawaii, and their 'trawlers', which have been granted fishing facilities by the new Micronesian nation of Kiribati, tend to go fishing off Kwajalein whenever a new American missile flies. Kiribati, which became independent from Britain in 1979, was one of thirteen Pacific nations to agree to a proposal in 1985 by Australia's prime minister, Bob Hawke, that the south Pacific be declared a nuclear-free zone. But as the French well knew, the treaty was virtually unenforceable.

When the Pacific islands are viewed in terms of their historical, political and cultural ties, there is no reason to suppose they would ever willingly fall into the Soviet camp. The tiny nation of Kiribati is sometimes cited as an example of growing Soviet influence in the Pacific. Ever since Kiribati became independent it had pleaded with American tuna fishermen to acknowledge its sovereignty and observe its licensing requirements and its 200-mile fishing limit. The Americans refused, so Kiribati signed a deal with the Russians instead. Several studies of Pacific politics – including one by the US State Department – have suggested that the most likely way the Russians will get a foothold is through insensitive treatment of islanders by the Americans and the French.

At first sight, the Kanak rebellion in New Caledonia, which contains nickel deposits vital to the French arms industry, seemed to fit neatly into the French conspiracy theory of a Russian takeover. The leader of the Kanaks, a former primary school teacher named Elios Machoro, and a score of his militants had flown to Tripoli for an audience with Libya's Colonel Muammar Gaddafi. The CIA in Washington and the DGSE see the hand of Moscow behind Gaddafi's machinations, even though the volatile colonel has acted against Communist interests as often as he has against those of the West. Machoro made the trip because he knew that Gaddafi had a reputation for dipping into Libya's treasury, rich from oil revenues, for practically every guerrilla movement from Mindanao in the Philippines to Northern Ireland. No proof, however, has yet been uncovered that Gaddafi supplied the Kanak leader with arms or cash.

Machoro returned to New Caledonia and, in a ceremony which summoned the ancient Pacific gods, declared the island to be the independent state of Kanaky, meaning 'land of the people' in Melanesian. A provisional government was set up in Thio, centre of the nickel mining, and his bushy-haired supporters barricaded off the town. French troops were flown in but the Kanaks, armed with rifles and cutlasses, held Thio under siege for three weeks. Machoro escaped but was hunted down and killed by marksmen. On the day of his death, January 12, 1985, some Kanaks sought revenge by murdering the teenage son of a white plantation owner. This snapped the patience of the largely pro-Gaullist settlers who blamed Mitterrand for being too soft on the native rebels. The whites went on a rampage of racial violence, setting fire to government buildings and stoning the High Commission, symbol of the uncaring socialist government back in Paris.

A second riot broke out in May when a mob of settlers, opposed to independence, began shooting at the headquarters of the Kanak Socialist Liberation Front, with rifles they normally used to hunt wild pig in the jungle interior. When the tear gas lifted, one person lay dying in the bougainvillaea-lined street and another seventy were injured. It was the worst outbreak of violence since Machoro's death. On May 9 a curfew was clamped down and the same day the French defence minister, Charles Hernu, flew out to New Caledonia. Some 3,000 troops and gendarmes are stationed on the island and, ostensibly, the reason for Hernu's trip was to find out if this force could quell any future unrest. However, most of Hernu's activities in New Caledonia were kept from the press. He surfaced once only, at a navy base where he was photographed being lowered into the missile tube of the nuclear submarine *Rubis*.

*

133

News of the hurricane of unrest buffeting New Caledonia soon reached Tahiti. A separatist movement was also under way there. It was one in which the issues of independence and anti-nuclear protest had fused. Both of the islands used for atomic tests – Moruroa and Fangataufa – are in the Polynesian chain, and the local parliament, the thirty-man Territorial Assembly, has long been at odds with the colonial administrators over nuclear experiments.

Mitterrand's socialists did not face the same political restraints in Polynesia as in New Caledonia. While campaigning for election in 1981, they had promised independence to the Kanaks. But they had failed to gauge the fiercely anti-independence sentiments of New Caledonian whites, who came to regard Mitterrand as no less than a traitor. In Polynesia, however, Mitterrand was not bound by any inconvenient election promises. The anti-nuclear independence movement in Polynesia posed a direct threat to the French nuclear weapons programme and, therefore, to France herself.

On March 2, 1985, the local gendarmes rounded up seventeen Polynesian separatists – those who would be sailing in the peace armada to Moruroa – while they were attending a rally in Papeete. The militants were given prison sentences just long enough to ensure that they would remain behind bars until after the *Rainbow Warrior* embarked.

The French have taken pains to assure the islanders that Moruroa is a safe enough place to have a holiday and, indeed, admirals and defence officials will strip off their uniforms at the sight of a press camera and dive into its lagoon – even immediately after an underground test has set the atoll shuddering – as if this is proof that contamination is a myth. A brochure printed by the Centre d'Expérimentation Pacifique, which runs the island, has many photos of happy soldiers and Tahitians on Moruroa, playing tennis and windsurfing.

But Danielsson claims that Moruroa is far from the paradisical picture that the French authorities paint. Ever since the French were forced by Algerian independence to move their atomic testing range from the barren Tiblisi range – known by the Saharan nomads as the Place of Thirst and Hunger – to

Polynesia in the early 1960s, Danielsson has fought to have them move their nuclear explosions yet again. 'The French say the tests cause no harm. So, if that's true, let them explode their bombs in France,' he says.

It is likely that the French would have shifted their nuclear testing ground out to the Pacific even if the Algerians had not driven them from their last possession in North Africa. The explosions were too close to France for comfort. During one of the earliest atmospheric tests, a freak Saharan wind caught the radioactive debris and scattered it about Europe. Soon after, physicists began to arrive in Polynesia, scouting the uninhabited atolls. Their presence was enough to stir rumours that the military was up to something. The Territorial Assembly in 1961 placed an official inquiry before the French ministry for overseas territories. Danielsson remembers every word of it. 'I can quote it. The minister said: "No nuclear tests will ever be made by France in the Pacific Ocean."'

But a year later, the Polynesians were in for a shock. A delegation of assembly men, in Paris for a routine request for funds, found themselves summoned to the Elysée Palace. The Tahitians were ushered into de Gaulle's office. The president imperiously announced that Moruroa and Fangataufa – located halfway between Tahiti and Pitcairn Island (of *Mutiny on the Bounty* fame) – would be used as A-bomb test sites. One of the delegates, John Teariki, dared to object but was immediately dismissed by de Gaulle. 'Go tell that to Kennedy and Khrushchev.' The audience was over.

Opposition to de Gaulle's decision was so widespread in Polynesia that the government decided to fly out two Foreign Legion battalions in case trouble broke out. Teariki and the other assembly men had been appalled by the impact of the American tests in the Marshall Islands. The assembly men, even de Gaulle's own party, protested through the colonial governor and, when that failed, through the overseas ministry. They were told it was a matter for the defence ministry. The bureaucratic warfare continued. The defence ministry sent a terse note back to the Polynesian officials saying that their

135

complaint could not be answered because it pried into military secrets.

In the meantime, equipment that had been dismantled in the Algerian desert was beginning to be unloaded on to Moruroa and Fangataufa. President de Gaulle was desperate to keep the nuclear defence programme going at full velocity. According to de Gaulle, 'France could not be France without "la grandeur".' Subordination to the United States through the North Atlantic Treaty Organization (NATO) was not in keeping with this grandeur. The answer, as de Gaulle saw it, was to maintain an independent nuclear strike force, the 'force de frappe'. In 1958, before taking office later that year, he told the press: 'NATO is against our independence and interest. Our membership in NATO is said to be for the reason of protecting France against a Russian attack. But I don't believe the Russians will attack at this time.'

When de Gaulle became president, France's nuclear development was far behind that of the United States, the Soviet Union or even Great Britain. Despite his vehement criticism of American superiority within NATO, the president swallowed his pride and asked Washington for technical assistance in making a French A-bomb. Not surprisingly, the US Congress refused. It made de Gaulle all the more determined to forge ahead into nuclear weaponry when the Eisenhower administration granted such aid to France's rival in the nuclear race, Britain.

It was soon after Congress's refusal that de Gaulle unsheathed his force de frappe. At a speech to the cadets of the elite Ecole Militaire, de Gaulle said that the strike force would be based on atomic armament 'whether we manufacture it or buy it, but one that belongs to us'. Ironically, one of the most strident critics of the force de frappe was François Mitterrand. In parliamentary debates, he argued that France should sign the test ban treaty and embark on a policy of non-proliferation.

It was not until July 2, 1966 – five years after the last test in Algeria – that France exploded its first nuclear device on Fangataufa. Then the rhythm of nuclear blasts quickened to make up for time lost while moving the bomb-making laboratories across the globe. France's impatience to build a nuclear arsenal equal to those of the other superpowers is perfectly illustrated by a mishap that involved de Gaulle himself.

In September 1966, the French president flew to Polynesia to observe the test of a 120-kiloton bomb. Arrangements had been made for him to watch the mushroom cloud rise over Fangataufa from the safety of a warship cruising twenty-five miles off the atoll. A bad storm, however, was blowing in a direction that would carry fallout towards inhabited islands, and the test was postponed. After pacing the deck of the cruiser *De Grasse* for twenty-four hours, de Gaulle ordered the test to proceed even though the wind had not shifted. The bomb was tethered to a balloon, lifted 1,600 feet into the air and detonated. Sure enough, a shower of radioactivity fell as far away as Samoa, New Zealand and Australia.

New Zealand and Australia were outraged. For once, the Territorial Assembly of Polynesia was not alone in its protests against the atomic explosions. The two governments lodged formal protests against France, but these also went unheeded. Danielsson, Teariki and another assembly man, Jean Ceran Jerusalemy, organized opposition on Tahiti and on the outer islands. They tried to educate the Polynesians to the dangers radiating from the nuclear atolls. A protest letter sent by Teariki to President de Gaulle in 1967 suffered the same fate as the complaints from New Zealand and Australia. De Gaulle's contempt for anyone who tried to meddle with his force de frappe led many Polynesian politicians seriously to contemplate independence. Even those Polynesians who at first welcomed the nuclear scientists soon changed their opinion.

At first the islanders did benefit from the arrival of the bomb-makers. As Gauguin had found, living in paradise could be tough. Wild game had been chased into the densest jungle and took days to hunt. Fresh water was scarce on many islands. Fishing and the cultivation of small plots of copra was all that the islanders had for survival. The Polynesians sailed in droves from the outer islands to seek work on Moruroa and Tahiti. But once the building was finished, so was their work. More than 30,000 new jobs were created, as the CEP had promised, but most of these were filled by technicians flown in from France. Shantytowns sprang up around Papeete filled with Polynesians sacked by the CEP. However, the military still provides more jobs than anything else, even tourism, and a thriving middle class of Tahitians does exist which is opposed to independence and the departure of the French fleet.

By 1973, however, international opposition to the atmospheric testing had reached such a pitch that even the French could no longer ignore it. New Zealand and Australia took their protests to the International Court of Justice at The Hague. At the start of the proceedings, France made it clear that she would not accept any ruling that tampered with her sovereignty in the Pacific and national defence. The court did grant an injunction against the French tests, but there was no means of enforcing it.

French haughtiness goaded New Zealand into sending frigates along to accompany the fleet of small craft manned by protesters that sailed into the test zone. Dock workers in New Zealand's ports refused to handle French vessels. The dockers' action was supported by trade unions in Australia and, eventually, in France. In 1975, France reluctantly agreed to explode all its atomic bombs underground.

The method chosen by the French scientists for their tests was to drill a hole through the coral crust of the atoll into the harder volcanic rock beneath. The bomb is lowered to the bottom of the shaft, some 500 to 1,000 yards down. Then the hole is plugged and the bomb detonated. The French authorities claim that this technique contains the radioactive damage inside an impervious layer of volcanic rock. In theory, the heat of the blast melts the rock, forming a glassy cocoon that traps the plutonium inside for eternity. But according to some scientists this technique is flawed. The device explodes upwards, creating a chimney effect that pushes the radiation towards the surface. In addition, according to a study of Moruroa by a New Zealand-based group called Scientists Against Nuclear Arms, the force of the blasts has fractured the atoll and radiation is seeping upwards and, possibly, outwards into the ocean.

An army map of Moruroa obtained by Danielsson reveals

that the long and narrow atoll has become a pincushion for more than seventy underground tests. As a result of the blasts long cracks, some stretching more than half a mile, now scar the island. The latest tests have been conducted inside Moruroa's lagoon and, according to the army map, fishing is now forbidden. Swimming, however, is not. Rear-admirals may take their plunge for the photographers, but few technicians can be found bathing in Moruroa's blue waters. The technicians' trade union, the CFDT, cautions against it.

Relations between the socialist CFDT trade union for atomic workers and the defence ministry have been strained. In 1981, a cyclone raked loose a thin asphalt layer covering a contaminated rubbish heap of timber, iron and clothing and tossed it into the sea. Some of it was swept into the ocean currents, but most of the rubbish was washed back ashore. Technicians sent out with Geiger counters found that the radiation count was twice the normal level. Workers in protective gear scooped up what contaminated material they could but several technicians complained that more effective measures should be taken to dispose of waste material – which remains radioactive for 25,000 years. Their entreaties were ignored, even though defence minister Hernu himself promised to do something about it when he visited the island.

When nothing was done to improve conditions, the technicians threatened to strike. They compiled a confidential dossier of nuclear accidents and sent it back to the CFDT headquarters in Paris. It was then leaked to the press. Fearing arrest, the authors of the report deposited their evidence in a Swiss bank vault and vowed to make it public if they were picked up by the police.

The dissident technicians claimed that in 1979 a huge nuclear bomb, hundreds of times more powerful than the Hiroshima one, got caught in an underground shaft. It could not be pulled up, nor could it be pushed to the bottom. Instead of extricating the bomb or even sealing it in the shaft, a decision was taken to blow it up. The blast caused a tidal wave in the lagoon, injuring seven people and probably causing severe fractures in the atoll through which radiation may eventually seep out. In that same

139

year, according to the report, two technicians were killed in an underground laboratory when an experiment with plutonium went disastrously wrong.

Most alarming of all, the technicians claimed, is that the atoll sinks three-quarters of an inch every time it is hammered by an underground test. Over the years, Moruroa has subsided more than five feet, which raises doubts about the ability of the battered atoll to contain radioactivity. If radiation does not leak into the ocean immediately, this is bound to occur within the next 25,000 years before the radioactive matter decomposes. Despite the protests by the union, no adequate measures have yet been taken to dispose of the piles of nuclear waste on the island.

So far, there has been no direct evidence of islanders dying from radiation. But environmentalists claim that this is because the French authorities in Polynesia are suppressing the information. No independent inquiry has been allowed by the colonial authorities and all health matters in the islands are overseen by the military. The army doctors claim that Polynesia has fewer cancer cases than other parts of the world. Nor is there proof, the French argue, that any islanders have cancers caused by radioactivity. The health department in Tahiti went so far as to claim that heavy smoking is the only cause of cancer among the natives. However, investigations by Danielsson and concerned scientists show that this survey – blithely circulated by French embassies in New Zealand and Australia – was so incomplete as to be irresponsible. It did not, for example, take into account those cancer patients treated privately or by native healers. The survey also ignored those Polynesians living on remote islands with no doctors. Even more damaging to the French case was the fact that no information was provided by the only hospital on Moruroa. Its records are regarded as a military secret.

Danielsson believes that as many as 600 islanders in the Gambier group, east of Moruroa, may have been contaminated by plutonium which has seeped to the bottom of the ocean from the atoll and worked its way into the food chain. One of the *Rainbow Warrior*'s missions was to have been to gather evidence of such poisoning. 'The French have forbidden any independent investigation into the health hazards of their testing,' Danielsson says. Requests by both the Territorial Assembly and the World Health Organization in 1981 to examine islanders near the test zone have been ignored by the Mitterrand government.

Although the socialists had been critical of the atomic experiments during the decades of Gaullist power, their attitude changed swiftly after their 1981 election victory. Mitterrand went through the motions of suspending the underground tests – for just four days. This was long enough for the military to persuade the new government that the blasting was necessary if France was to press ahead with plans to make a new generation of nuclear warheads.

In 1983, France yielded to international pressure and allowed a team of scientists from New Zealand, Australia and New Guinea to spend four days on Moruroa. It was hardly enough time to let the scientists even check the radiation levels in the atoll's lagoon or around the bomb shafts, let alone carry out any useful analysis of the ocean. Nor were the French willing to supply data on the rate at which the island sank every time a bomb was let off in the volcanic heart of the atoll. Nevertheless, the French took the findings of the scientists, published as the Atkinson report in 1984, to vindicate their claim that the nuclear tests were harmless.

To Greenpeace, it seemed that the French had not bothered to read the Atkinson report carefully. The French claimed, for example, that the scientists had found no evidence that the explosions had cracked the outer shell of the atoll, letting radiation seep out into the ocean currents. The scientists, however, did not have time to take samples of coral from the ocean depths to check for contamination. Nevertheless, the report warned that the situation could be dangerous. The scientists found that the shell of 'highly impervious' rock had been weakened by the underground blasts. If the tests continued, the radiation could indeed leak out within five years – or take as long as 10,000 years.

The Pacific countries were less than enthusiastic over the Atkinson report. At a summit of Pacific heads of state in 1984 a communiqué was issued which stated that while the scientists had allayed fears over the short-term effects of the testing, 'they provided no reassurance about long-term consequences'.

Moruroa is not the only battle that Greenpeace has chosen to fight in the Pacific. Outside Hiroshima and Nagasaki, nowhere is the misery of atomic destruction more evident than among the survivors of Rongelap.

CHAPTER TEN

Snowstorm in paradise

As the *Rainbow Warrior* entered the lagoon, its mast could be seen from all over Majuro atoll. The island, a thirty-two-mile loop of coral round an old volcano crater, was never more than 200 yards wide, which meant that everyone on Majuro would know within minutes that the *Warrior* had arrived. It was Sunday, May 12, 1985, and the Greenpeace flagship was about to perform its last action for the environmentalists' cause.

Steve Sawyer, an American-born international director of Greenpeace, stood in the sun on the white concrete quay which served as the main harbour for Majuro, capital of the Marshall Islands. It was only 10.00 a.m. but the heat and light were so intense that it hurt to keep his eyes open and the sweat dropped off the end of his nose. Sawyer and the rest of the crew had come 6,000 miles to move the people living on Rongelap, a contaminated atoll in the Marshall group, to a safer island. Rongelap and its people had been in the path of the American Bravo atomic bomb test of 1954. Its people had been left in the fallout which drifted down like 'snow' for three days before everyone was evacuated by the US navy. Later, after recovering from the skin burns, hair loss and other immediate ailments, the people were returned to the atoll and told it was 'safe'. The allegation against the United States was that the people were used as guinea pigs in an experiment to discover the effects of fallout and the results of living in a land contaminated by radioactivity. The people of Rongelap had finally come to the conclusion that they were being consistently lied to by the Americans. Miscarriages, thyroid cancers, leukaemia, deformities and premature aging were all symptoms of continuing contamination. Their appeals for help fell on deaf ears until

143

their senator, Jeton Anjain, one of the few university-educated Rongelap people, wrote to Greenpeace as a last resort.

The request caused a lot of heartsearching. Greenpeace has always been sensitive to accusations of caring for animals and the environment more than people in subsistence economies. Now it would open itself to the charge of using the fears of primitive people for its own ends. As a precaution, Greenpeace sent Steve Sawyer to the Marshall Islands to study the political situation and to check on the wishes of the islanders. He discovered that there was no chance of anyone else coming to the aid of the islanders. The international directors of Greenpeace knew Sawyer was a cautious man. They knew, too, that he would not recommend moving the people unless he was sure the political risks were minimal. They decided that at all times the wishes of the islanders were paramount (to borrow Mrs Thatcher's edict when Argentina invaded the Falkland Islands). It was this concern that led to the Rongelap evacuation's being a low-key little-publicized campaign. During the move itself, Greenpeace was anxious to make sure that everyone on the island knew what was happening. Before the evacuation began a meeting of the entire population was held and the head of every family agreed – for a second time – to the move.

The arrival of the ship signalled an end to the months of planning, the political manoeuvring, the fears of American intervention, and Greenpeace's own worries about appearing to use a native people as pawns in its campaign against the nuclear arms race. The proud prow of the *Warrior* drew towards the land, its painted rainbow and the white dove of peace reflected in the bright blue water. Islanders began arriving on the quayside. Nothing like this had ever happened in the Marshalls – for years it had all been promises and talk. On that morning, however, seeing was believing. For the twelve members of the crew of the *Rainbow Warrior* this was an emotional moment too. Apart from a brief stopover in Hawaii for supplies they had been sailing for weeks across the empty ocean. Up to now Greenpeace had tried to save whales and seals, or confronted big corporations and governments trying to dump nuclear and other toxic substances at sea. Now they were moving a whole people from one island to another. The quay was filling with happy, smiling women with garlands of flowers to put round the crew's shoulders. They were ready with welcome songs, kisses and thanks for the people who had come halfway round the world to help them. There was a great deal of hand-shaking and laughing, then nosing round the boat and photographing each other. But suddenly it was time for church and the whole Marshallese welcome party, as well as a crowd of curious onlookers, disappeared as quickly as they had arrived. They had gone to give thanks for Greenpeace's arrival and to pray for success.

For Sawyer and the crew of the *Warrior* this was the opportunity for a meeting. The crew meeting is central to the Greenpeace campaigning style. On paper, Sawyer was leader and organizer of the expedition; Peter Willcox, another American, was the captain of the ship, and everyone in the crew had his job, from radio operator to engineer to deckhand. Although broad plans are agreed months in advance and timetables drawn up, what actually happens in the campaign always has to be agreed by the crew on the spot. A curious feature of the organization is that any journalists or other visitors sailing with Greenpeace automatically become members of the crew, with the right to speak and be listened to by everyone else. On this trip Paul Brown, a British journalist with the *Guardian*, had signed on from Majuro as crew-deckhand in order to report the story.

Everyone sat on the foredeck of the ship and listened to Sawyer. The immediate plan was to let the crew have a day off, a blow-out in the local restaurant, and perhaps acquire a hangover before setting sail for radioactive Rongelap, 500 miles to the north. The mission, as the crew already knew, was to move the 250 people and their personal belongings from their home atoll to an uncontaminated island 120 miles away. There they would rebuild their village and their ancient way of life away from the dangers of radioactivity. Sawyer began filling in the details. The people of Rongelap knew Greenpeace was coming, but since the Marshall Islands had no serviceable aircraft and no supply boat had been to the island for six months

145

nobody quite knew what they would find. That week the only contact had been over a bad radio telephone line.

Sawyer did his best to explain the politics of the situation. Senator Jeton Anjain, Rongelap's one member of the Marshall Islands parliament, would be joining them on the voyage. He had been called by his people to be their 'saviour' and in 1979 had become their first elected representative in the islands' government. Since then he had campaigned for the removal of the people by either the Marshallese government or the Americans (who had contaminated Rongelap in the first place). When these efforts failed, he had written to Greenpeace asking for help. Sawyer explained that, while in theory the islands' government was in favour of the evacuation, it was not lifting a finger to help for fear of upsetting the Americans.

As for the evacuation itself, Rongelap was three days' sail from Majuro. There was twelve to fourteen hours' sailing between Rongelap and the new island, Mejato. Several trips would be needed to transport all the people. It sounded deceptively simple. The multinational crew listened in silence. Brown, the visiting journalist, already knew two of them – the chief engineer, Davey Edwards, aged thirty-one, from Rotherham in Yorkshire, and Grace O'Sullivan, from Ireland, one of four women crew members on the ship. They had both been on another Greenpeace expedition he had covered: a trip up the Irish Sea aboard the *Cedarlea* to try and block the radioactive discharge pipe from Sellafield nuclear plant on the Cumbrian coast.

After Sawyer, it was the turn of the ship's doctor, Andy Biedermann, to speak. Before joining Greenpeace, Biedermann, a Swiss, had been with the rebels in Afghanistan treating their casualties, most of whom, he said, had been shot by each other. He explained to the *Rainbow Warrior*'s crew about the dangers of radiation on Rongelap, advising that coconuts and other local food, particularly crab and lobster, would be contaminated by plutonium. It was entirely a matter for individual crew members whether they ate them or not. Those who wanted to have children would be advised not to sleep on the beach. The contamination could affect the sex organs, though he emphasized that the risk was small if they were there for only a few days.

The meeting broke up and Brown was introduced to Fernando Pereira, the Portuguese photographer who would be working with him during the voyage. Three months later in Auckland, Pereira became the first person to be killed during a Greenpeace campaign. The pair went upstairs to the *Warrior*'s communication room where the radio operator, Lloyd Anderson, lived and slept. There was computer equipment for storing news reports ready for transmission, and better-than-average radio equipment for telephone calls. Then there was an Associated Press wire machine lent for the trip on a semi-official basis by the news agency's London bureau for transmitting pictures. It had never been done before from such an obscure part of the world and it was by no means certain that it would work at all.

Pereira told Brown he had joined the ship in Hawaii. He had left his native Portugal because he was a conscientious objector to military service. He had become a Dutch citizen, earning his living as a freelance photographer, but he had given up six months of his business – unpaid – for Greenpeace because they needed a professional photographer. Brown was dismayed. He knew that newspapers had short memories and during Pereira's absence they would learn to rely on someone else for their photographs. When he returned, how would he pick up the threads of his livelihood? Pereira shrugged. 'I will manage. I have my reputation. They will want my pictures.' He smiled and added: 'We will worry about that when we get home.'

Brown asked about sleeping arrangements. Sleep was a problem, Pereira said. Their cabins were below the waterline at the stern of the ship – the noisiest and hottest place. The *Rainbow Warrior* had been built as an Aberdeen-based trawler with ventilation designed for Icelandic waters where it was a crime to waste an ounce of heat. Conditions on board made Brown determined to spend one last night in his primitive hotel on the island despite its giant cockroaches and extremely noisy but effective air-conditioning.

In the meantime, everyone went for a picnic on a small island nearby. The white coral sands were covered in beautiful shells,

147

constantly on the move, all apparently occupied by hermit crabs. The island's owner shinned up the enormous trees and cut down green coconuts for his guests – always part of a traditional welcome in the Marshalls. The crew swam in the clear, luke-warm water. The Marshallese swam too, but fully clothed. This strange custom, totally contrary to the western dream of nubile brown girls dashing through the surf, was a product of the Calvinistic Christianity that European missionaries had brought to the islanders in the 1880s. As darkness fell some of the crew members swam across the lagoon back to the ship, causing great alarm among the locals. Sharks cross the reef at night from the ocean to hunt in the lagoon. Fortunately that evening they were slow off the mark.

Three days later Greenpeace sailed for Rongelap, pausing only to hoist the *Warrior*'s beautiful sails. The sails had been fitted in Florida only a few months earlier at a cost of $110,000. It had taken the crew and a couple of volunteers from mid-October to the first week in March to convert the former trawler into a yacht. In a way it was a public exhibition of Greenpeace's beliefs, and for captain Peter Willcox, a former Hudson river sailboat captain, it was a dream come true. He had refused to serve in Vietnam and as a punishment had been made to serve in sailing ships for two years. He had found it was the perfect life and ever after wanted to be captain of an ocean-going sail boat. For Greenpeace, the biggest single cost factor in any campaign is the fuel. Peter Willcox said that on the way to the Marshalls, with assistance from the sails, the *Warrior* had made a forty per cent fuel saving between Nassau and Panama. Previously the *Warrior* used fourteen gallons of fuel an hour to produce a cruising speed of ten knots. Now, with the sails up in a reasonable wind, it used twelve gallons an hour and made eleven knots. In a stronger wind it could make ten knots with the engines off.

As they left Majuro atoll in the heavy Pacific swell and turned north towards Rongelap, the ship looked majestic under full sail. It was even moderately cool in the breeze. Brown felt in very high spirits until he realized that his stomach was not sharing the exhilaration. He recalls: 'The sails made the ship

148

both pitch and roll at once. For the first time in my life I was seasick – and not just a bit. Andy, the ship's doctor, stuck a seasickness patch behind my ear – a new invention, he said. It would cure me and last for three days, by which time I would have got my sea legs. Unable to go below, I lay on the foredeck and groaned.'

On the way to Rongelap the *Warrior* had to pass near Kwajalein lagoon, the largest in the world. The lagoon, which is sixty miles long and surrounded by a necklace of ninety-three islands, is almost a sea in itself. After the Americans took over the Marshall Islands under a United Nations trusteeship, they turned Kwajalein into a missile range. It made an ideal splashdown area for rockets fired from California across the empty Pacific Ocean. Since the missiles hit the lagoon at 8,000 miles an hour it was found necessary to clear the people from a forty-mile corridor through the centre of the atoll. The people were put on one tiny island called Ebeye at the southern end of the necklace, outside the target area. On the biggest island, the Americans built their own quarters with all the facilities one would expect in Los Angeles. The local people, denied their traditional way of life, were housed in corrugated iron slums with no sanitation where tropical diseases were rife, fresh water was rationed and the sewage pumped straight into the lagoon, once their life support system. The contrast between the two islands in 'paradise' is a great shock.

In 1958 the lagoon became a practice target for incoming intercontinental ballistic missiles. By 1985 it was a key part of the United States' MX missile programme and was being updated as a tracking station for the star wars programme. Fifty miles north of Ebeye and the American headquarters is a missile tracking station named Roi-Namur. As the *Warrior* passed by, the crew saw for the first time how the Americans were prepared to pour millions of dollars into the islands for military purposes while apparently leaving the islanders of Rongelap to cope unaided with the results of earlier experiments. All that was visible of the tracking station from the sea was a giant golf ball three times as high as the coconut palms, and an even larger radar dish. When the *Warrior* approached, the giant dish turned on its side and focused on the ship. The crew had expected the Americans to be watching them, but this giant eye made everyone feel uneasy. They took some pictures and dallied long enough, the crew hoped, to make the Americans feel equally nervous, then pressed on to Rongelap.

The Marshall Islands rise no more than six feet above sea level, so Rongelap appeared on the *Rainbow Warrior*'s radar long before the coconut palms came over the horizon. All the people lived on the atoll's big southern island. The northern islands, with their population of giant coconut crabs, breadfruit and sweet pandanas, had been even more severely contaminated by the Bravo bomb and the islanders had been warned against going there and gathering food. Since this warning they had received periodic but inadequate deliveries of tinned food from the American government. They had all eaten contaminated food in any case, because the warning was not given until more than ten years after the bomb dropped. Greenpeace discovered that the inhabitants had been boycotting some of the islands anyway. In the north, mutant coconut palms had sprung up with double and sometimes triple heads. This was a phenomenon not previously known to the Marshallese nor recorded in science.

As the ship came into the lagoon a launch full of women, singing and carrying flags, came out to welcome the *Warrior*. There was no quay so they anchored half a mile off shore and launched the Greenpeace inflatables. The whole population was on the beach to meet them. They all had to pass through a wooden arch decked with native blooms to be kissed and garlanded with flowers. The women sang songs specially composed for their arrival. While Fernando Pereira took pictures, the rest of the crew drank milk from green coconuts, knowing that the plutonium they contained was the reason the islanders were leaving. Dozens of children, very beautiful with wonderful smiles, peered at the crew from every direction. They were the first visitors to the island for six months.

Although the heat was oppressive, nearly a hundred degrees in the shade, with ninety-five per cent humidity, the crew wandered round the village gauging the size of the task. The only concrete building was a tiny blue and white church. Everything else was built of plywood with corrugated roofs. Many of the people – interpreting the term 'personal belongings' liberally – had dismantled their houses and neatly stacked the walls and roofs for loading on to the *Rainbow Warrior*. The school house, once a large building, was already piled up on the beach.

Loading began at dawn. The islanders were ferrying their belongings to the ship in two clapped-out cabin cruisers called 'boom-booms' because of their noisy motors. Both broke down on the first morning. Davey Edwards and Henk Haazen, the ship's first and third engineers, were astonished that the engines had worked at all. Neither had been serviced and Davey doubted that one had ever seen an oil change.

The sheets of roofing were so large that they had to be balanced on top of a boom-boom and manhandled on to the *Rainbow Warrior*'s deck. The ship's crew worked all day with hardly a respite. After months at sea, heaving the ropes to get the sails up, they were fit and ready for action. But the two journalists, Pereira and Brown, were grateful for the excuse of having to file pictures and a story.

That night Greenpeace took the first group of seventy-five islanders. One of the cabin cruisers accompanied them across the open Pacific to help unload at the other end. The *Warrior*'s crew used the radar to keep in touch with the boom-boom and to steer round the storms. As dawn broke the islanders were within sight of their new home, Mejato. This uninhabited island was on the north-west tip of Kwajalein atoll, outside the missile range and thirty miles from Roi-Namur. The crew was relieved to see that there was no American reception party. The ship anchored a full mile and a half off the island and, even though it was inside the lagoon, the sea was quite rough. The trade winds blowing from the south had sixty miles to whip up the waves from the other end of the lagoon. First the crew decided to unload the people and their belongings. In a sizeable swell this was no easy task. One woman panicked and it took several people to pass her bodily into the boom-boom and then calm her while her baby was passed down to her.

151

The new island was surrounded by knee-deep water to a distance of 400 yards. It was teeming with fish and had clams of all sizes. The men, using three-pronged spears like Neptune's trident, immediately caught some white fish, and the women set about cooking the first meal in their new home. The swell increased and unloading proved much more difficult than expected, especially with only one boom-boom instead of two. Everyone was so tired that Sawyer decided to stay another day to finish this first stage of the job.

There were 304 people to be evacuated from Rongelap instead of the 250 originally estimated. Still, there was no doubt that the people wanted to go and saw Greenpeace as their deliverer. Senator Anjain was a quiet, undemonstrative man, but the ship and these young sailors from far away were a dream come true for his constituents. He said that his people believed that the ship had sailed all the way from England to save them. This was the end of his task. He was going to retire as senator at the next election in 1987 even though he could go on unopposed. He was going to sell his house in the capital and build a new home among his fellow islanders. 'If they go hungry, then I shall go hungry. We will build ourselves a new home together where we can live in peace and not have to survive on the hand-outs from the Americans. We will learn again to grow our own vegetables, food uncontaminated by other people's nuclear bombs. We still remember the old crafts and skills. We want to regain our independence and our dignity.'

This was the message that the Greenpeace volunteers had come so far to hear. The crew members were full of self-mocking good nature as an antidote to the deeply-held views that had driven them to give up a year of their lives to such a venture. Henk Haazen, thirty-one, was a carpenter by trade. Well over six feet tall, with shaggy hair and blue eyes, he had a quick sense of humour and worked continuously, lifting, loading, running the boats through the surf and mending broken machines. He was the third engineer on the *Warrior*, but had been a successful businessman with a carpet warehouse back in Holland; so successful that his accountant had despaired of finding ways to keep his tax at a reasonable level, and advised getting married

152

and taking out a big mortgage. The prospect so frightened Haazen that he decided to see a bit of the world first – and he has never stopped travelling since. Among other things, he has motorcycled from Tierra del Fuego in the far south of South America, where he worked as an oil prospector, to Alaska. On the way he did a variety of jobs, including tobacco picking, but found he was increasingly helping the Spanish peasants with such jobs as mending engines and repairing generators. He learned to speak Spanish because 'I wanted to understand'. On the deck of the *Rainbow Warrior* was a sixteen-foot dugout canoe belonging to Haazen which he had bought for thirty dollars from a Nicaraguan fisherman 12,000 miles away. He described it as his toy. It was one of his few possessions. In a spontaneous gesture he presented it to the people of Rongelap. They were short of transport and had nothing of small enough draught to skim the reef. With its six-inch clearance it would be ideal safe transport for any sick child or adult needing to be taken to a doctor on the nearest inhabited island.

Most Greenpeace volunteers live for the current campaign, but Haazen had a plan. With another crew member, his girl-friend, a New Zealander called Bunny McDiamid, he shared a dream. She was twenty-eight, a graduate in sociology and literature who found her academic training was of little use in the Third World. Her plan was to return to New Zealand and study to become a midwife or a doctor. Henk, meanwhile, was to build a forty-foot steel-hulled ocean-going boat with a mechanical workshop below. They would then marry and travel the Pacific. 'There are many people in the Third World who need us,' Haazen said. 'I can fix their engines and teach the owners the basics of mechanics. Bunny can help them with basic medicine. We could have our own children too. We all have a dream and that's mine.'

At twenty-three, Grace O'Sullivan, from the Irish village of Tramore in County Waterford, was already a Greenpeace vet-eran. In an emergency she is the best person to be with: the first lifeboat woman in Ireland and the first woman member of a cliff rescue team (highly valued once the team realized she was lighter than men on a rope). She gave up accountancy to be a lifeguard on her home beach and then became the all-Ireland surfboard champion in 1982. 'I am just a small-town girl who cares for the ocean,' she says. 'Being with Greenpeace has opened my eyes and ears to the world. I see what governments are doing to the earth and the oceans and Greenpeace gives me the chance to do something about it. I like Greenpeace because they don't back off. We keep going because eventually we know we have to win.'

The crew met after dinner that night in the *Warrior*'s old fish hold to assess progress. It was decided that at least three and possibly four journeys would be needed to bring all the people and their goods to Mejato. Senator Anjain agreed to speak to the people and put a limit on how much they would ask Greenpeace to do. There was some discussion about how to bring the pigs and chickens across. The problem was left in abeyance because the crew was assured that the islanders would have a feast before they left and solve the problem by eating most of the animals.

So the toil went on. The worst night was on the second trip to Mejato from Rongelap. A sudden hurry to leave meant that the boat was swamped with people. The captain had set a limit of eighty passengers but clearly there were many more. In fact when they were counted off the next day there were 142. They were mostly sleeping on the open deck when the first of the tropical rain came with attendant squalls. Then they crowded into the corridors below deck and were sick everywhere. When Paul Brown woke up in his double bunk he found four Marshallese squeezed in too. It was a long night and an even longer morning. When Brown consulted the crew list it was his turn for washing up, sweeping the corridors and cleaning the 'heads' – the lavatories, washbasins and showers. He says: 'It was a gut-wrenching job but afterwards the crew accepted me as a "real" person as opposed to the soft expense-account journalist they half-suspected I might turn out to be.'

In the end there was no need to take the pigs. The owners of the new island offered a gift of some uncontaminated animals. The only livestock carried were some chicks brought by an old lady in a cardboard box which she hugged under her arm all night. The islanders brought almost everything else, including some kitchen sinks. One item which reduced the Greenpeace crew to helpless laughter was the tins of salmon. American food was given to the islanders by the military because it was forbidden to use the northern islands, their traditional larder, because of the contamination. They were given rice, for which they had acquired a taste from the Japanese, and American tinned food. Because of a botulism scare in the United States the military had been able to buy up what appeared to be millions of cans of surplus salmon. The Rongelap people were sick of salmon but because the supply ship had not been for six months it was all they had left. They had been reduced to a choice between contaminated food and salmon. They opted for contaminated food but, not knowing what their new island was going to be like, had decided to bring along the salmon just in case. Every family seemed to have at least a dozen large cans among its personal possessions. As each boatload of goods was passed along the human chain from the boom-boom to the hold, the cardboard boxes full of cans would suddenly appear. After a long day of lifting in such heat they seemed unbelievably heavy. The islanders were mystified by the helpless laughter of the almost exhausted crew when yet another cache of salmon was discovered among the more normal debris of a south seas home.

Amid the laughter and the adventure of moving for the children of Rongelap, there were the tears of the old people leaving their homes. Some of them looked much older than they were. The radiation had prematurely aged them. Women who looked seventy were only fifty-five. One woman, clutching her granddaughter's hand, had tears running down her face as she gazed for the last time on the island's church and the white-stoned graveyard. She said she had agreed to leave only for her grandchildren's sake and because 'Senator Anjain has promised, when I die, to bring my body back and place me next to my parents'.

By the end of the fourth trip to Mejato the last of the people and most of their belongings had been brought to their new home. Senator Anjain had stayed behind to count the coconut

155

trees in order to prepare a claim for compensation against the American government. After three days of frantic radio telephone calls to the Majuro transport minister it was a relief to see the government supply ship at anchor off Mejato when the *Rainbow Warrior* arrived at the end of the fourth trip. At least the islanders would have enough food to survive for a few weeks while they established themselves in their new home.

The Rongelap people had decided to throw a party – no doubt to include considerable quantities of tinned salmon – to thank Greenpeace for moving them. That left the crew with a whole day off before the next stage of the voyage. Five of them – Steve Sawyer, Henk Haazen, Bunny McDiamid, Davey Edwards and Paul Brown – decided to visit a wreck two miles away on the reef. They launched one of the inflatables and set off in high spirits. Shoals of fish jumped in unison out of the shallow water in front of the dinghy. They clearly thought the inflatable was a shark. The wreck turned out to be a Peace Corps vessel twice as big as the *Warrior*. It must have hit the reef at full speed, for it stood right out of the water. The party climbed out of the inflatable and shinned up a twenty-foot rope which hung invitingly down the wreck's side. The ship was in far worse shape than they had imagined. It was very rusty, the tropical sea salt and the sun rotting the metal. Two of the party went aft and found some divers' helmets. Suddenly they heard shouts of alarm. In tying the inflatable to the prow of the wreck, Steve Sawyer had clutched on to a rail. It had given way, sending him plunging into the wreck's hold thirty feet below.

They could see him, bleeding, barely conscious and unable to stand. But they could not reach him because the stairs had rotted away. There was no way in and no way out. Then, with the calm resourcefulness that typifies Greenpeace, a plan was worked out. Henk was lowered into the hold on a rope, followed by his tool kit. Using his club hammer and great strength he smashed his way through the rotting hull just above the water line. Bunny and Paul went over the side to reach the inflatable. As they got in, the violent surf snapped the mooring rope, but as they were swept away from the wreck Bunny got the powerful engine to burst into life. Davey joined Henk in the hold while Bunny brought the inflatable under the hole.

As Davey and Paul stood up to their necks in the surf, holding the dinghy steady, Steve was passed through the hole. Only briefly did it cross Paul's mind that there were sharks in these waters and that Steve's blood had been draining into the sea for fifteen minutes. Steve's shoulder was dislocated, and he had deep cuts in his arms and a hole in his side. Back on the *Warrior*, it took Andy Biedermann five hours to patch him up, delicately picking the rust out of his wounds. Steve remained conscious throughout, without complaint. The spike that had made the hole in his side had touched the wall of his stomach, but not pierced it. He was lucky that only his collar bone was broken.

Next day the *Rainbow Warrior* was due to start the next leg of its Pacific voyage, sailing for Ebeye at the other end of the atoll. Brown decided to return to London. The crew wanted him to go on to Moruroa, but he could not justify staying away from the office any longer on journalistic grounds. Fernando Pereira agreed. 'We could not see Greenpeace confronting the French at Moruroa,' says Brown. 'It never crossed anyone's mind that the French would carry the fight to Greenpeace, and I made a date to have a drink with Fernando when he got home.'

PART THREE
Hatching the plot

Rainbow Warrior under full sail in the Pacific heads for the Marshall Islands to rescue islanders trapped on Rongelap, a coral island dusted with radioactivity.

Left: The exodus begins: Rongelap's inhabitants load their belongings in preparation for the journey to a new island uncontaminated by fallout.

Above: A sad end for ship and sailor in Auckland Harbour. Pereira was drowned in his cabin in the submerged stern.

Left: The *Warrior*'s crew. Fernando Pereira took this and the previous two pictures. Photographing the Rongelap exodus was his last assignment.

Right: Pereira pictured shortly before his death. He was a popular and cheerful shipmate.

Below: Greenpeace's buccaneering president, David McTaggart, points a finger at an old enemy – France.

FACING PAGE:

Dramatic evidence of French attitudes towards Greenpeace. These pictures taken in 1973 show how McTaggart was badly beaten by commandos while leading a protest.

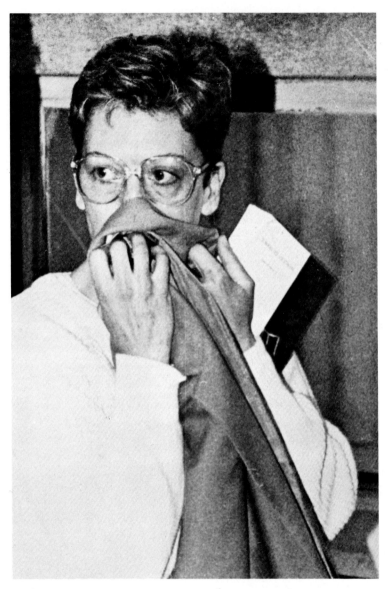

Captain Dominique Prieur, alias Sophie Turenge, France's most senior woman spy.

Right: Major Alain Mafart posed as Sophie's husband. Together they travelled to New Zealand on forged Swiss passports to aid the saboteurs but were caught and jailed.

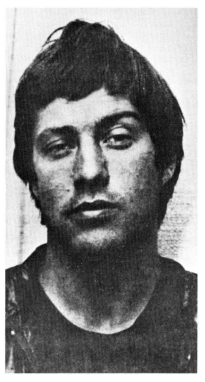

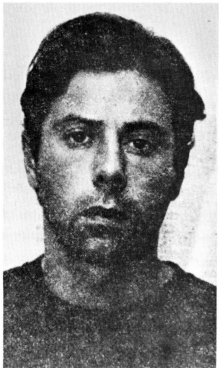

Above: Jean-Michel Bartelo, like Andreine a specialist in covert operations.

Above left: Eric Andreine, the French army sergeant expert in underwater sabotage.

Left: Roland Verge, skipper of the *Ouvéa*, delivered explosives and equipment.

FACING PAGE:

Top: French intelligence HQ in Paris where the bomb plot was hatched.

Bottom left: Christine Cabon, alias Frédérique Bonlieu, infiltrated Greenpeace.

Bottom right: Dillais, alias Dormand and Dubast, masterminded the bombing in Auckland.

* There is no known photograph of the fourth member of the *Ouvéa*'s crew, Dr Xavier Maniguet.

"**OUVEA**"

Nouméa. 28/6/85.

For a sailing initiation, Tasman Sea was a good one (...) "ParaRemGaRemGa" also with a 185 cm boat and 100 cm water deep (...) The main interesting lesson is that a 40 horse Power Engine on a sail boat is very very useful, very convenient, very efficient and in fact why to get a mast???

Xavier Baniquel (noble skipper of course)

(of course) Xavier n'est pas un fair lent man

Voilà France (Cevol.) the Skipper [signature]

Peut. Etre y a t'il autre chose en NZ?

The *Ouvéa* crew casually signed a restaurant visitors' book claiming their voyage was for pleasure. But one crewman hinted darkly at the end: 'Perhaps there is something else in New Zealand.'

Above right: The explosives were smuggled into New Zealand in the bilges of the *Ouvéa* which mysteriously disappeared with its crew.

Right: The French submarine *Rubis* on patrol north of New Zealand. Did the agents scuttle the *Ouvéa* and escape in the submarine?

OVERLEAF:

President Mitterrand with his close friend and confidant, defence minister Charles Hernu, who resigned soon after. Will the French premier follow?

Above left: In France, Prime Minister Fabius refused to apologize for the bombing.

Above: New Zealand's Prime Minister, David Lange, demanded retribution.

Left: Vice-Admiral Lacoste was sacked from command of French intelligence.

FACING PAGE:

Inset top: Bernard Tricot was asked to investigate French involvement in the bombing.

The Tricot report, a whitewash orchestrated by French intelligence.

Inset bottom: Superintendent Allan Galbraith, the Auckland detective who found fame and frustration.

OVERLEAF:

The dove of peace, a symbol of hope and success for Greenpeace.

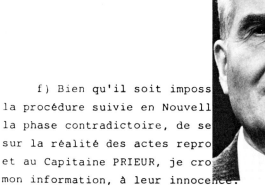

f) Bien qu'il soit imposs que
la procédure suivie en Nouvell tteint
la phase contradictoire, de se de
sur la réalité des actes repro RT
et au Capitaine PRIEUR, je cro de
mon information, à leur innocence.

g) C'est ce que je crois aussi, toujours dans l'état
actuel de mon information, pour ce qui est de l'Adjudant
Chef VERGE et des Adjudants ANDRIES et BARTELO. Une enquête
administrative nécessairemet rapide peut être difficilement
conclusive. Personnellement, je crois donc utile que ce
rapport soit suivi en France d'un examen plus détaillé.

Je vous prie, Monsieur le Premier Ministre, d'agréer
l'expression de ma haute considération.

Bernard TRICOT

CHAPTER ELEVEN
The pool of sharks

When Admiral Henri Fages met Charles Hernu, the French defence minister, on March 4, 1985, Greenpeace was item number five – last but one – on the agenda. For two summers France had continued its underground nuclear testing on Moruroa, unimpeded by the antics of environmentalists in their little boats. Now, according to intelligence reports, Greenpeace was planning to return in strength, possibly with five boats, including – for the first time – its largest vessel, the 417-tonne *Rainbow Warrior*. For Fages, in his last year as head of the nuclear testing centre, it was one problem he could do without.

What bothered Fages almost as much as the Greenpeace protest was the fact that France's external security service, the DGSE, seemed to be doing next to nothing about it. Some weeks earlier he had discussed the question with Pierre Lacoste, head of the DGSE. Lacoste, like Fages, was an admiral, a career naval man who had been dragged into the DGSE in 1982 to try and sort out its problems. But he was no spymaster, and had shown little initiative over Greenpeace. Fages had decided to go behind Lacoste's back and raise the matter with their joint boss, the defence minister. A complaint about a fellow admiral had to be discreet, however, and should not be at the top of the agenda. On the other hand, if it was the last item the minister might not judge it important. The last item but one seemed about right.

Three days before the March 4 meeting, in accordance with custom, Fages sent Hernu a file of documents covering the topics he wanted to raise. The Greenpeace dossier was brief but alarming. The group apparently planned to start its action in July, and would probably send five boats, including the *Rainbow Warrior* and the *Vega*, to Moruroa and the other testing site at Fangataufa. The crews would position themselves at the edge of territorial waters and launch small craft which would attempt to land protesters, including members of the Polynesian independence movement. The news that the *Warrior* and the *Vega* would be sailing for Moruroa had already been announced by Greenpeace in a press release from its Washington office on February 23. But the press release had not gone into details, so where had Fages got his information? The most likely source is Bengt Danielsson's mailbag. Danielsson is an inveterate letter-writer. From his native-style beach hut he engages in long, rambling and occasionally witty discussions with ecologists around the world. Tahiti is still under the thumb of France – which means that letters posted to Danielsson sometimes get a wider readership than their senders expect.

The French had, of course, faced similar threats from Greenpeace before. Apart from the protests around the atoll in the 1970s, the group had visited Moruroa in 1981 and 1982. On the last occasion the *Vega* had been arrested when she accidentally drifted inside the twelve-mile territorial limit. Even a single protest boat pottering around Moruroa for a week or two could tie up vast amounts of time, money and manpower. In order to prevent boats landing on the atoll, the French had to shadow them continuously. Keeping watch on one boat meant diverting two warships (each with a crew of forty or fifty) from other duties. Small wooden boats like the *Vega* are notoriously easy to lose on the radar screen, and whenever that happened the warships had to radio the atoll for a search helicopter.

That sort of disruption was bad enough, but to Fages and Hernu the scale of the 1985 campaign sounded far more ambitious. The *Rainbow Warrior* was the largest protest vessel ever to visit Moruroa. The good news was that it would be easier to track on radar. The bad news was that it was well enough equipped to stay in the area for a couple of months or more and to act as supply ship for a whole fleet of smaller boats. It was being fitted with sails which meant that it would be able to heave to off Moruroa just outside the twelve-mile limit. The object of heaving to is to maintain a more or less constant position. The sails are set so that the boat drifts extremely slowly – at about one knot – for several hours, then motors back to its original position. This would cause serious problems for the French warships shadowing the *Rainbow Warrior*. Without sails, they could not heave to without difficulty, and when they tried to move slowly to keep pace with the sailboat they would start to roll, making the crew very sick. Also, the *Warrior* could be used to launch inflatable dinghies which might attempt to land on the atoll at night. The dinghies would not show on radar, and could well reach the shore. If any protesters succeeded in landing the French would have to arrest them, check them for radioactivity, and then deport them. The prospect of deportees arriving at airports in Europe and the United States and describing their experiences to the world's press did not attract the French. Worse still, the rumour that Polynesians might take part in landings added a new – and alarming – political dimension.

Fages's complaint about Lacoste and the inactivity of the DGSE bore fruit immediately. Hernu needed little persuasion. As a fervent believer in France's independent nuclear strike force, he considered Greenpeace a threat. No sooner had the March 4 meeting with Fages ended than Hernu instructed the DGSE to step up its intelligence-gathering to 'forecast and anticipate the actions of Greenpeace'. The DGSE replied that sending several agents to the south Pacific and hiring a boat was beyond the scope of its current budget; it would need a special allocation of funds. A request for three million francs was passed straight to the president's military chief of staff at the Elysée Palace.

The headquarters of the French overseas intelligence service is a white concrete office block in a decidedly unfashionable arrondissement of north-east Paris. The building, some ten storeys high, stands inside the Caserne Mortier barracks complex at 128 boulevard Mortier, tightly guarded and surrounded by a high wall topped by long, sharp spikes. At one end of the V-shaped DGSE tower block is a round turret-like structure

163

with slits up and down its side. They may well serve as ventilation holes for a fire escape stairway, though in a different kind of emergency they would be equally useful as machine-gun posts. A few desks and telephones can be seen through the venetian blinds covering most of the windows in the building, but otherwise there is little clue to the activity within apart from a tall and complicated array of radio antennae on neighbouring buildings inside the fortress wall.

Just across a small side street – the rue de Tourelle – is the large and ugly municipal swimming bath, la Piscine de la Tourelle, that gives the secret service headquarters its nickname. Although the swimming bath is still open to the public, part of it appears to be off limits and the pool's roof is festooned with several sophisticated-looking radio masts whose connection with water sports seems obscure.

There is no sign to identify the Caserne Mortier as DGSE headquarters, but the buildings are well known to local café proprietors and shopkeepers as the home of France's famous – or infamous – 'barbouzes' ('spooks'). Although the French domestic counter-intelligence service, the DST, is listed in the Paris telephone directory under its own name, there is no official listing for the DGSE other than a number for the Caserne Mortier, 45559520.

The barracks block inside the compound is arranged so that visitors can enter and leave with discretion. Important guests from such exalted government departments as the Elysée Palace, office of the French president, are driven through the fortress's front gates and straight into an underground car park. The modest, typically bureaucratic office of the Piscine's director, where the walls and windows are covered with heavy curtains to keep eavesdroppers out and secrets in, is inside a chateau within the fortified garrison. Behind the director's desk is a large map of the world decorated with markers pointing out the spots French intelligence currently considers the hottest. In the waiting room the only reading material is the conservative newspaper *Le Figaro*, and the even more right-wing weekly *Minute*, which has produced a long string of scoops viciously critical of the policies and personalities of the socialist government. The magazine's scoops are frequently based on leaks supplied by disgruntled spies inside the Piscine's walls.

During the Second World War France established its first crude intelligence network in the Resistance movement. By its very nature the movement attracted people inspired by patriotic zeal and eager to perform acts of derring-do against the enemy. When it came to establishing a peacetime secret service the Resistance seemed the natural recruiting ground. Its members were the only people with any relevant experience.

By 1944 the three main strands of the Resistance had come together under the heading of the Direction Générale des Etudes et Recherches (DGER). At the end of the war de Gaulle was keen to set up a proper intelligence-gathering unit on the lines of the British MI6. He wanted it to focus on countries behind the iron curtain as well as on Africa and Indochina where the French had colonial interests. Unfortunately the characteristics which made good Resistance fighters did not necessarily correspond to the needs of the peacetime secret services. Many of the former Resistance workers were hooked on the romance and excitement of carrying out their clandestine wartime operations: many were left-wing sympathizers who did not recognize the Soviet bloc as enemies. Moreover they had no taste for the painstaking business of intelligence-gathering and did not comprehend that the rules for peacetime behaviour were stricter than those in war. Some simply took the law into their own hands. One DGER lieutenant attracted huge publicity for the supposedly secret service when he three times tried – and failed – to murder a woman.

When André Dewavrin, known as 'Colonel Passy', took charge of the DGER in 1945 he set about cleaning up its reputation. Passy wanted a more conventional secret service run through the foreign ministry and using embassies for cover, but he met great opposition from diplomats who did not fancy being under the same roof as the ruffians then employed by the DGER. As a result, the French foreign ministry made life very difficult: spies in embassies were given titles such as 'vice-consul' or 'assistant consul' which made them easily identifiable. One agent was sent to the Cameroon as joint press attaché to an embassy which had no press department. Passy also encountered resistance from the Communists, who saw the DGER as a Gaullist body. They caused a storm by revealing that Passy had built up three secret caches of money in England. Passy maintained that the funds were perfectly innocent – intended for use in an international crisis – but the affair nearly finished him.

The DGER was France's intelligence network from 1944 until the end of the war in 1945. From it, in 1946, Passy created the Service de Documentation Extérieure et de Contre-Espionnage (SDECE) which was to be France's answer to Britain's foreign intelligence service, MI6.

After de Gaulle returned to power during the Algerian war, he appointed Paul Grossin, a general, to investigate and overhaul the intelligence system. De Gaulle took personal charge of the SDECE and turned it into an extension of the government's forces, answering directly to the Elysée Palace. De Gaulle and his prime minister Michel Debre often acted behind the backs of the regular army, feigning ignorance when they were caught out. Despite repeated attempts to clean up the SDECE, by the late 1950s it was in a terrible state, bereft of finance, staff and expertise. Roger Faligot and Pascal Krop, authors of *La Piscine*, a history of the French secret services, say: 'The noble profession of spying, so cherished by the British, had a pretty awful reputation in France.' The French, unlike the British, could not recruit university graduates because of the service's loutish image.

Grossin discovered a secret dossier, to which only key cabinet members were privy, which revealed that the SDECE spent a million francs a month studying the political uses of cinematography. The research, which was receiving equal sponsorship from the tobacco industry, was based on an advertising idea from the United States. Normally a cinema film transmits twenty-four frames per second. The Americans had introduced a twenty-fifth frame which the viewer did not notice, but which registered subconsciously. Grossin ordered the SDECE psychiatrist to check on the project. The psychiatrist was unimpressed, so Grossin went to see for himself and found just a blank screen in the apartment he was funding. All the first experiments had been disastrous and the technique had proved useless for political purposes.

The SDECE also had a unit called Service 7 which opened the diplomatic bags of friendly countries. The Japanese found out what was happening and filled their diplomatic bags with memos about Communist China which were of no interest to the French. On one occasion the French opened a bag from the Egyptian embassy, only to find a note from the Egyptian head of intelligence in London congratulating himself on intercepting a French diplomatic bag there. Most of the information gathered in this way proved extremely trivial, including such astonishing secrets as the number of pencils and rubbers used by the Belgian ambassador in Paris.

The SDECE's pride and joy was its team of 'honourable correspondents', hundreds of men and women with ordinary jobs who undertook part-time work for French intelligence. Usually they were old-timers from the days of the Resistance who missed the excitement after the war. Many had jobs in sensitive areas of industry. For example, Air France pilots were recruited to re-route themselves over Communist countries and take photographs of sensitive areas. Service 7 recruited people from everywhere and even took on a gangster, Raymond Meunier, who went by the nickname the Big Wanker. Another correspondent was Antoine Lopez, the deputy head of passenger services at Orly airport near Paris. Two stars among the correspondents were a Dominican monk called Yves-Marie Dubois and a lawyer, Jean Violet, who wielded immense power in the secret services. They performed a double act at the United Nations and it was said of the monk that when he was not in his monastery in Paris he was looking for souls to convert in the corridors of the UN. Both men were briefed personally by Grossin before UN conferences. At the time France was coming under heavy fire for its Algerian policy, and it was only the efforts of these two that stopped the UN from coming down heavily on France.

Dubois and Violet used to get 500,000 francs a month to finance what was known as the church of silence. The money paid for intelligence operations behind the iron curtain under the cover of the Catholic church. So-called missionaries were trained in free-fighting, marksmanship and parachuting. They became known as the Black Paras.

During the late 1950s the SDECE set up its own terrorist organization, the Red Hand, which is known to have carried out twenty-two successful terrorist operations. Most of its actions were on German soil with the tacit approval of the German government. In Switzerland and Belgium they went down less well with the authorities. The targets were normally Algerian sympathizers or representatives of countries supporting Algeria. The Red Hand committed fourteen murders, three maimings and blew up five ships, usually those carrying arms to Algeria. They killed a trade union leader, an editor, two professors, students, lawyers and others. One of its members was Christian Durieux, a young Corsican maths teacher whose periods off sick from work corresponded with terrorist attacks by the Red Hand in Germany. The public and journalists were led to believe that the Red Hand was a fascist organization rather than an official government one. In an interview with the *Daily Mail*, Durieux said the Red Hand was set up in North Africa to give the terrorists there a taste of their own medicine. The name came from the hand of Fatima, the Muslim good luck charm, which was traditionally black or gold but was coloured red by the French to denote blood.

In 1965 the SDECE underwent more convulsions which centred on the Ben Barka affair. An Algerian leftist, Mehdi Ben Barka, was kidnapped by French agents in Paris and never seen again. At the time of his disappearance, the SDECE was a largely civilian force closely tied to such dubious elements as the gangster underworld and a private Gaullist political security force known as the SAC (Service d'Action Civique). Lines between the twilight world of official spies and the even darker world of the Gaullists' political interests were blurred indeed. But the Gaullist government was sufficiently shaken by the embarrassing disappearance of Ben Barka to launch a purge of some of the intelligence service's wild men.

*

168

From the moment in June 1981 when Mitterrand's top advisers learned that they would be taking control after more than twenty years of Gaullist rule, they recognized that one of the thorniest issues they faced was how to control the unruly and sometimes incorrigible spy agencies. During the years in the political wilderness Mitterrand and some of his closest associates were among the most frequent (and favourite) targets of the assorted barbouzes. One aide close to Mitterrand found that the secret service had concocted a fake dossier on him which linked him with Moscow and passed it on to the CIA station chief in Paris. The latter was so alarmed by the prospect that one of the top French security advisers was a possible Communist agent that the CIA threatened to stop sharing secrets unless Mitterrand had him sacked. An investigation was duly carried out and the adviser was exonerated.

The socialists soon realized that they were being sniped at by most government agencies and by unofficial spy networks loyal to the Gaullists and strongly anti-Communist. As they prepared for their ultimately successful 1981 election campaign, the socialists set up a committee to study how to gain control over the police and intelligence agencies. It included both socialist security experts and a few trusted former members of the intelligence agencies. The committee produced a series of papers for candidate Mitterrand on possible plans for shaking up the services, purging some of the most untrustworthy elements and bringing the services under stricter socialist control. Mitterrand's advisers also found several severe flaws in the intelligence system.

By the 1970s a service which before the Ben Barka affair had been composed of about sixty-five per cent civilians and thirty-five per cent military officers had been reversed. The unreliable and uncontrollable had been weeded out and the service was now dominated by a large contingent of new and less imaginative recruits from the military. But the dominance of the military in the reorganized SDECE had its drawbacks. According to one former government official, the soldiers had little idea how to handle the delicate spy networks that the French had set up in Russia and eastern Europe. Hamfisted incompetence by the new military managers had led to a severe deterioration in the agents' coverage of the eastern bloc, which should have been of prime concern to the conservative Gaullists. The combination of the ignominy which the SDECE attracted over its handling of the Ben Barka affair and the clumsy military way of its new staff made it difficult for the service to attract capable civilian recruits: academics and international business-men who in the past might have been willing to supply the government with information picked up during their studies and travels.

While in opposition the socialists had attempted to draw up detailed plans for reorganizing the services. But the papers were of little practical use, and once in power Mitterrand and his inner circle quickly tossed out the party's recommendations. During an all-night session at the Elysée Palace some of the president's most trusted aides hammered away at a new but very rough blueprint for bringing the spooks under control. Not trusting their secretaries, the advisers typed out the report themselves.

To take charge of this monumental reform of the secret service, Mitterrand called in two loyal outsiders – Pierre Marion, a former executive of Air France, the state-owned airline, and François Durant de Grossouvre. De Grossouvre is still little known to the French public. An elegant man, he is so adept at secret diplomacy and intrigue that one journalist who inter-viewed him remarked later that de Grossouvre would have been at home in the Medici palace or the court of Cardinal Richelieu. He and Mitterrand are in the habit of taking an evening stroll along the Seine or dining together. It was de Grossouvre who came to Mitterrand's aid after l'Affaire de l'Observatoire in the 1960s when the future president's career seemed finished. An assassin tried to kill Mitterrand by machine-gunning his car. Mitterrand survived and escaped into the gardens of l'Observa-toire. Later, a man told the press that Mitterrand himself had arranged the fake 'hit' for publicity. Mitterrand was never able to shake off the accusation completely. But de Grossouvre stayed loyal and, when the socialists finally came to power, was rewarded with the job of special adviser to the president on affairs of defence, foreign policy and intelligence. A keen sports-man, he was also put in charge of the president's many hunting preserves around France.

De Grossouvre was given an office on the ground floor of the west wing of the Elysée Palace and became the president's personal liaison with the intelligence service. In this capacity, he received one of the handful of top-secret intelligence briefing papers prepared by the security service each day for the president, the foreign and defence ministers and the military chief of staff. One insider said these briefings were of such poor quality that they usually contained less information than the Agence-France Presse wire dispatches.

Pierre Marion was appointed director of the foreign intelligence service, renamed Direction Générale de la Sécurité Extérieure (DGSE). A jovial and rotund man with a keen sense of adventure, he was known to have little enthusiasm for the socialist far left and considerable enthusiasm for bourgeois pleasures, including sailing his private yacht while wearing a cowboy hat. He had no apparent background in intelligence work. But some close friends believe that while working for Air France and later for Aerospatiale, the state-run aeronautical agency, he may have served as an 'honourable correspondent'. Marion, an engineer and amateur actor from Marseilles, had joined Air France in 1942 and had risen rather slowly. In 1963 he was made the airline's representative in East Asia and the Pacific, and began to help with intelligence work. Later he returned to Paris as joint director-general in charge of the airline's commercial operations. At this point he got to know Hernu; both were freemasons. Marion was in his sixties, tall and athletic but quick-tempered and given to theatrical gestures. His weakness was that he lacked friends in politics, apart from Hernu.

Mitterrand gave Marion several tasks: to direct intelligence work towards the East; to uncover Soviet moles; to dismantle terrorist groups; and to eliminate those at the top of the SDECE who might be tempted to put obstacles in the way of France's new policies. On April 4, 1982, a decree in the *Journal Officiel* published, for the first time, the powers and duties of the French secret service. The aim was mainly to clarify its field of operation in relation to other services such as the police.

In the shake-up that followed, the action service (the one responsible for the *Rainbow Warrior* bombing) became the 'Division Action', itself divided into three specialist sections: air support, commandos and maritime missions. Besides the diving school at Aspretto in Corsica (home of the *Ouvéa* crew), it has bases at Beuil (Alpes-Maritimes) and Noisy-le-Sec, on the outskirts of Paris. Aspretto, officially known as the Centre d'Instruction des Nageurs de Combat (CINC), draws its divers mostly from the army. Selection is extremely tough. Out of 500 applicants each year, only two or three are accepted. All active members are trained in very deep diving and very long swims. In one standard exercise they spend an entire night alone in the sea. First they leave a submarine through its torpedo tube, carrying an inflatable kayak. Once on the surface, they inflate the kayak and paddle for several hours. Then they deflate the kayak and half submerge it before swimming off to complete their 'mission'. Afterwards they return to the kayak and reflate it to complete their journey. Another exercise once involved planting dummy mines on Soviet civilian ships docked in La Rochelle Harbour. Besides diving, the men learn parachuting, sabotage, photography and 'neutralization' techniques.

On arriving at the Piscine, Marion found the intelligence service in a lamentable state. He quickly learned that even before the socialists had come to power, right-wing members of the DGSE – particularly in its action service – had held secret meetings to discuss resistance to the expected onslaught of the leftist government. Such was their suspicion that at several secret bases in France and Corsica officials burned files for fear the socialists would hand them over to the KGB. They also burned compromising documents, especially those concerning espionage on political parties or trade unions. More serious, they even destroyed important technical reports. Often the action service has to check the defences of sensitive installations by trying to break into them – places like the base at L'Isle Longue, Brest, headquarters of the French strategic force. Such

172

'attacks' have sometimes thrown up serious gaps in protection. But the benefits of these exercises were not to be made available to the socialists. As a final gesture of defiance, the chiefs at Aspretto kept portraits of the ousted president, Giscard d'Estaing, on their office walls for several months after Mitterrand had taken over.

The spooks of the Piscine wasted no time in intimidating their new boss. Marion was driven to the training camp at Noisy-le-Sec, taken from his car and surrounded by 400 men in knitted balaclavas – commandos of the action service. Marion was told that this was the initiation ceremony for DGSE directors. If so, it was a ritual practised only on the socialist appointees. Later, Marion was subjected to another unnerving prank: kidnap by his own spies. One Saturday afternoon four armed men burst into his first-floor office at the Piscine. They blindfolded him, shoved him into the boot of a car and kept him there for the long drive to the south of France. From there they took him by helicopter to a trawler in the Mediterranean, where the blindfolds were finally lifted from his eyes. It is doubtful whether Marion was much amused by such antics. During his short tenure at the Piscine he is believed to have been hospitalized with a nervous breakdown. Another incident was far more vicious. Pressure from the Elysée Palace was put on the DGSE to arrange special briefings for cabinet ministers. Marion delegated this chore to one of his colonels who immediately chose the four Communist ministers and tipped off a photographer at *L'Express* that they would be coming. The right-wing magazine then attacked Mitterrand for opening the Piscine's secret files to the Communists.

Marion started with good intentions. He decided it would demoralize the service to purge those elements regarded as potentially disloyal to the socialists. A house-cleaning was begun, but only a gentle one; notorious drunks and incompetents were prodded into retirement, but the purge went little further. Marion began recruiting new DGSE officials, most of them drawn from the gendarmerie, the one security agency which the socialists believed had some traditional sympathy for the left. (Charles Hernu, Mitterrand's new defence minister and overlord of the Piscine, was the son of a gendarme.) Marion also sought to weave new networks of civilian informants and part-time 'honourable correspondents'. His model was partly based on Britain's MI6, with its 'honourable schoolboy' tradition of seeking help from journalists and businessmen travelling abroad. However, because of the Piscine's terrible reputation, he found it difficult to launch this project. Meanwhile, right-wingers inside the service began to leak embarrassing stories to the conservative press about Marion's slow progress, and about his personal behaviour which, not surprisingly, became rather paranoid and erratic.

After only a year in the job, Marion and President Mitterrand agreed that he should resign, and he quietly departed the boulevard Mortier shark pool. He had tried and failed to set up an alternative spy network, bypassing his many adversaries in the Piscine. But he lacked the supporters to carry off his bold plan. Once the Elysée Palace realized that the security services could never be totally tamed to the political point of view, Mitterrand began to look to the military for a safer and less controversial replacement for Marion. It was Hernu's idea to replace him with Pierre Lacoste, a wiry admiral in his mid-fifties who was then commander of the navy's Mediterranean fleet. Lacoste is an intellectual, a naval strategist, with the look of a man accustomed to scanning far horizons for the enemy.

At the time Lacoste seemed a figure of political neutrality. But although his current posting involved strictly military activi-ties, his recent career had included high-level dealings with the political establishment. During the prime ministerial regime of the Gaullist Raymond Barre, Lacoste served as top military adviser. Operating from the prime minister's office at the Hôtel Matignon, Lacoste conducted a special study of anti-nuclear groups in Europe in an attempt to prevent such protesters from gaining influence in France. Lacoste's inquiries convinced him that the protest movements were heavily infiltrated by Commu-nists and influenced by agents of the Russian intelligence ser-vice, the KGB.

Earlier, as head of the national defence institute, Lacoste devised an innovative programme of seminars intended to unite

174

top military officials with influential civilians. Those invited to the seminars to explore the military point of view included journalists, businessmen and – at Lacoste's own request – a handful of prominent socialists, even though most of the military saw them as a lost cause. One of the socialists who seemed particularly interested in making friends with the military was Hernu, then mayor of Villeurbanne, an industrial suburb of Lyon, and a senior defence adviser to the would-be presidential candidate, François Mitterrand. Hernu, throughout his political career, made a point of cultivating the brightest young officers who would eventually become generals and admirals. During the seminars, Lacoste and other French officers succeeded in educating the socialists – who had initially opposed the nuclear weapons programme – in the value of France's force de frappe, or independent nuclear deterrent, composed of submarines and land-based ballistic missiles. Hernu was sufficiently impressed by the grey-haired admiral's political sophistication to remember him when the time came to pick a successor to Marion at the Piscine.

Lacoste was and is a strong advocate of the force de frappe which the French hold out as a threat of mass destruction against reckless acts of both superpowers. According to Lacoste, having the French on the scene as an unpredictable player in the nuclear poker game makes the world a safer place.

One essential element of maintaining France's credibility as a nuclear power, according to the admiral, is the need to keep up with the latest in nuclear weapons technology. In order to do so, he believes it is essential for France to be able to continue to test new atomic weapons at its south Pacific base on Moruroa atoll. Important weapons developments which need testing include the neutron bomb which France, without the reservations expressed elsewhere in the West, is developing to counter the overwhelming strength of Russian ground force in Europe. Also, Lacoste says that France needs to be able to try out the latest techniques for miniaturizing nuclear warheads using sophisticated computer microchips.

*

Admiral Lacoste agreed with Admiral Fages, head of nuclear testing, that the Greenpeace flotilla must not be allowed to reach Moruroa. But Lacoste thought the simplest solution was to tow the *Rainbow Warrior* away if it entered French territorial waters. He is understood to have opposed the sabotage plan until he was overruled by his superiors in the defence ministry and the Elysée Palace. Once the DGSE had been pushed into action, Lacoste sought funds for the operation from Mitterrand's military chief of staff, General Jean Saulnier. The plans for sinking Greenpeace landed on Saulnier's desk along with a stack of fifty other proposals that needed his approval. Saulnier, who always carried the president's top-secret nuclear trigger codes in his briefcase, would not risk the chance – however small – of Greenpeace imperilling France's bomb-making capability. 'He might have raised his eyebrows over the cost of the operation, but that's all,' says one former colleague.

After approval by Saulnier, the plan was sent to the office of Laurent 'Fabulous' Fabius, France's youthful prime minister. This was a matter of protocol, since the operation involved funds from the premier's office. Next it was passed to the defence minister's office. Hernu was concerned that the DGSE was still dragging its feet, so he asked Jean-François Dubos, the eminence grise of the defence ministry, to oversee the operation and ensure that Lacoste's team responded with alacrity. Dubos was Hernu's special adviser on affairs of the Piscine, and had an office in the ministry far grander than the minister himself. One visitor to Dubos's chambers recalls that in the space of one hour Lacoste telephoned him five times. 'See how much he relies on me?' Dubos boasted.

Once the plan was approved in principle, debate about the best way to carry it out continued in the hierarchy. According to inside sources, Lacoste of the DGSE and Dubos of the defence ministry disagreed over when the bomb should be planted. Dubos wanted to detonate the bomb when the *Rainbow Warrior* had sailed from Auckland Harbour and was on the open sea. This course would have left less evidence for the investigators afterwards. But Admiral Lacoste knew that it would also kill many of the Greenpeace crew, and his view eventually

176

held sway. Meanwhile Hernu is said to have given Saulnier a complete briefing on the sabotage plan, which was modelled on an attack French frogmen had successfully carried out on a Libyan ship anchored in Genoa Harbour.

But how far up the line of command did the discussions go? Was President Mitterrand personally involved? One former security adviser at the Elysée Palace doubts that the president would have been consulted beforehand. 'Mitterrand is capable of a very violent riposte – he sent troops into Chad, for instance – but he would have preferred not to know what was being planned for Greenpeace,' he says. 'Dirty tricks are not Mitterrand's style.'

On the other hand, whenever a risky operation is planned, whether in politics, the military, or even in business, everyone tends to cover his own back. Nobody wants to say 'Yes, go ahead' in case something goes wrong. Most people would rather say something like, 'It sounds all right to me, but I'll have to check with the boss first.' And so there is a natural tendency for everyone to pass the buck to the person above until eventually it stops – at the top. Of course, if someone lower down the ladder likes the idea but knows his boss will dislike it, he might do something slightly devious. He might choose his moment carefully, waiting until the boss is especially busy. Then he will mention the matter casually, making it sound as innocent as possible, hoping the boss will mutter 'Fine!' and return to the subject in hand. Whether that happened with the *Rainbow Warrior* operation will never be known unless someone who has kept silent until now decides to talk. Someone may – or may not – have mentioned it to Mitterrand. But certainly nobody was foolish enough to tell him in writing.

CHAPTER TWELVE
Parlez-vous français?

Monsieur le Président, nous sommes français et nous savons à quel point il est important pour le pays de conserver son indépendance économique et militaire...

The protest letter to President Mitterrand began diplomatically enough, with a gesture designed to establish ties and loyalties. 'We are French and we know how important it is for France to preserve its economic and military independence . . .' It had been Elaine Shaw's idea to write to the French president as a prelude to Greenpeace's Moruroa campaign – and to have the letter signed by as many French expatriates as could be mustered in New Zealand. For Shaw, who worked at the Greenpeace office in Courthouse Lane, Auckland, it was a quixotic tilt; nobody really expected the president to read it, let alone consider its contents, but it might win a few converts if the press showed some interest.

The new assistant in the office – a rather arrogant French woman who was helping, unpaid, with administration and clerical work – had volunteered to write the letter. Indeed, she had insisted on writing it, complaining that others had neither the linguistic ability nor the tact to ensure that the message would travel beyond the sorting office at the Elysée Palace. Elaine Shaw did not like the letter's opening. She thought it woolly-headed and would have preferred a hard-nosed, direct approach. But her new assistant was eager and she let it ride. Besides, it got to the point eventually, and improved as it progressed:

While living in the south Pacific by choice or necessity, we try to give the best impression of our country. But this impression is tarnished by measures taken by your government concerning

France's interests in this part of the world, measures which do not take into account local public opinion of which we French are an integral part. Like other ethnic populations we feel intellectually concerned and physically threatened by your attitude (the continuation of nuclear testing and French military reinforcements).

The letter raised the question of a European nation testing nuclear weapons thousands of miles from its own shores where others would have to live with the consequences. It also echoed the increasing fears of Pacific leaders that French reinforcements arriving in New Caledonia to put down the Kanak insurrection might destabilize the entire area. It asked the president to allow the people of the Pacific to live in peace, it called on him to find alternatives to nuclear testing and colonialism and it asked: 'Are we your enemies?'

With the benefit of hindsight, Elaine Shaw might have raised a chuckle on reading that question. But she did not know at the time of writing that the author, a woman she had welcomed into the organization and befriended when others tired of her incessant demands, sulks or arrogant pronouncements, was not really a travelling scientist sympathetic to Greenpeace. She was not even Frédérique Bonlieu, the name she gave when she arrived. By the time her true identity was known, the letter was not even remotely funny. Fernando Pereira was dead, the *Rainbow Warrior* was at the bottom of Auckland Harbour, the Moruroa campaign was in tatters and in the Greenpeace office there was a profound sense of anger that a French spy had easily infiltrated their ranks, read their files, learned their secrets and generally taken them all for fools.

There was also a deep, lasting guilt, irrational but wholly understandable. In New Zealand the Greenpeace office is run mainly by women who hold heartfelt convictions about other issues. The thrust of their movement is ecological but it is underpinned by personal dedication to two causes: feminism and Pacific independence. Perhaps this is because the office draws support from the radical well of the Auckland University campus nearby. There is a natural, even healthy, competition between the Auckland office and Greenpeace's mostly male leadership which comprises the international board of directors. The discovery of Frédérique Bonlieu's real identity touched raw nerves in the Auckland office. Though nobody said it, they felt they had lost face, had in some way been shown to be gullible. In the wake of the bombing, they thought that somehow the attack might have been the result of information culled from office discussions and the Greenpeace filing cabinets. They were right.

Her real name was Christine Huguette Cabon and, as spies go, she had the type of pedigree usually invented only by the most imaginative authors. Her family was steeped in military tradition. She was the daughter of a naval lieutenant-commander and the sister of an army helicopter pilot. Her grandfather had also served in the forces. She was born in 1951 at Fublaines south-east of Paris, but grew up in Pau, about twenty miles from Lourdes in the foothills of the Pyrenees. Despite its quiet, countrified appearance, Pau is an army town, lying close to the Spanish border and the troubles with Basque separatists. Until recently it was the home of the 3rd Parachute Regiment. Tragedy struck the town in 1983 when more than fifty members of the regiment died in a suicide bomb attack in Beirut.

Cabon's father came from Brittany and holidays were spent mostly on the beach at St Malo, where young Christine developed an interest in sailing, going for rides in the family dinghy. The happy days at St Malo ended abruptly when her father died while she was still quite young.

At the Marguérite de Navarre grammar school in Pau she seemed a normal pupil, bright but not exceptional. She passed the Baccalaureat exams at nineteen and went on to the local university, where her main subject was geography. It was there that she met the man who filled the gap in her life left by her father's death. Georges Laplace, now sixty-seven, a former Resistance fighter in the celebrated Maquis Vercors, was a lecturer in archaeology. Cabon joined his course on pre-history, where he found her 'one of my best students'. She took part in

180

several digs organized by Laplace's research centre. Such was the impression she made that in 1977 he put her in charge of an archaeological site at Arudy in the Ossau valley. But there was more to the relationship than that of a lecturer encouraging a promising student; Laplace began treating Cabon like a daughter, handing out fatherly advice and guiding her in the early steps of her career.

While studying she found work as a night supervisor in a boarding school. The work was not a proper teaching post – more a matter of seeing that the pupils behaved themselves. To become a fully-fledged teacher, Cabon would have had to complete a master's degree or, better still, a doctorate. Cabon was not sure she was good enough to take a higher degree and in any case her father's death had left her family short of money. She would have to start work after graduating, there was no question about that. But the boarding school job was unsatisfying and badly paid.

Then one day at the university, on a corridor wall, among offers of part-time jobs selling magazine subscriptions, calls to left-wing demonstrations on the campus, and leaflets offering second-hand Volkswagen vans, she saw a poster vaunting new army career opportunities for women. The pay was left tactfully unmentioned, but much was made of training and travel opportunities, and early job responsibility. She asked Laplace what he thought. The old Resistance man had no doubts and advised her to apply. 'Christine had all the qualities to become a good soldier. An unselfish character, a sense of duty, a lot of courage and tremendous loyalty. She was born for the service.'

The army is not a popular career for women in any country, especially well-educated women like Cabon, and the French army was only too eager to accept her. Now at last she would have a chance to use the skills she had acquired while studying geography – especially the art of map-making. There would also be opportunities to indulge her passion for archaeology. Not for long the humdrum tasks that armies usually give to women. Christine Cabon's duties would soon prove to be exciting, dangerous, and later very, very mysterious. She soon left other recruits trailing in her wake. Tough, disciplined and fiercely loyal to both the army and her country, she was promoted to captain before her thirtieth birthday, commanding her own parachute section in the elite special forces. In 1979 she went to Lebanon as one of the French uniformed observers during the civil war, and made close contacts with occupying Israeli forces. Then, as often happens, she made one parachute jump too many, badly injured her leg and was told by doctors that it would never again bear the stress her commission and active service might demand.

In such cases there is a natural progression for dedicated, talented officers forced into early retirement. Most nations would be loth to see the large investment in training go to waste, and the brightest are recruited into the intelligence agencies. Cabon was a perfect choice for the DGSE. A trained geographer and map-maker, an outstanding soldier with specialist skills and a very quick learner, she was overjoyed to be selected for training as a field agent in the foreign intelligence service. The change of job paralleled a physical change in Christine Cabon. Possibly through lack of exercise, she began to gain weight. Friends noticed that she no longer seemed to care about her appearance, and she became something of a loner.

When on leave, Cabon would return home to Pau to visit her aging mother, her sister and brother-in-law, and of course Georges Laplace. Probably to allay her mother's fears for her safety, she told acquaintants that she lived in Paris and worked in a research office at the ministry of defence. She never gave her office telephone number to anyone, not even her mother. Laplace probably guessed the true nature of her work but, in the best Resistance traditions, kept his suspicions to himself.

A test of her steel came soon after when she was sent to the Lebanon again – this time without her uniform. Her interest in archaeology gave her the perfect cover to sift through the political and military debris of that country for intelligence that might interest France and its allies. While ostensibly digging for information about ancient civilizations, she burrowed deep into the Palestine Liberation Organization in Beirut, convincing the militias that she was just another committed westerner of no great threat. Certainly she was never privy to PLO strategy or

182

intelligence, nor was she able to rub shoulders with anyone important. But she was a useful low-level mole and the time came when she proved to be of enormous help.

France has always enjoyed an exceptional relationship with Israel. Indeed, the Israeli air force jets which bomb and strafe its Arab neighbours are French-built Mirages or the home-grown Kfir fighters – modified Mirages built under licence in Israel. The goodwill resulting from the sale of technology and arms naturally extends to swopping intelligence. When the Israelis decided to start retaliatory bombing of PLO targets in Beirut it was Cabon who was able to provide pinpoint infor-mation, operating as a forward observer, identifying targets in the rubble-strewn city to limit civilian casualties and maximize the damage to PLO safe houses or covert administrative offices. It was a favour the Israelis would remember and return. The inevitable result of the Israeli raids, however, was suspicion. The PLO suspected westerners of providing the information and Cabon fled the Lebanon before she could be discovered and executed. The PLO put a price on her head and the DGSE sent her to a private clinic for plastic surgery, just in case the PLO spread its net and discovered her. Equally important was the possibility that she might have to return in another guise.

Early in 1985 Captain Cabon became 'Frédérique Bonlieu', a nice, enthusiastic, slightly girl-scoutish ecologist. At the Salon de Paris boat show in January she made contact with Jean-Marie Vidal, who runs a Mediterranean yacht company in the south of France and had been involved in anti-nuclear protests in New Zealand during the 1970s. Vidal recalls that Cabon said she was a geologist and was thinking of going to the Pacific. She asked him to put her in touch with various people he knew in the area.

Vidal says he wrote five letters on her behalf to contacts in Hawaii, Tahiti, Fiji and New Zealand, including one to Greenpeace in Auckland. That letter, handwritten in French and dated April 3, said:

Very soon one of my friends, Frédérique Bonlieu, will come to New Zealand. She is a young woman who will tour the country for geography studies. She is a scientist, an excellent navigator who shares our convictions. Accommodate her and make known to her your positions and actions, peoples of the south Pacific. She could send me information and we will try and get it in the French press.

Elaine Shaw of New Zealand Greenpeace says: 'No one here can read French but I got the gist of it. We get a lot of letters from people introducing someone passing through. They usually stay an hour or so and leave, so it wasn't out of the ordinary other than it was rare to have one from France. Then on April 24 Joan Cavaney, a former Greenpeace member who knew Vidal, got a telephone call from the woman saying she was Frédérique Bonlieu and she was in Auckland at the youth hostel. Joan called me and I told her to get Frédérique to contact us.'

Joan Cavaney left a message for the Frenchwoman on the hostel's answering machine. That same afternoon, Christine Cabon, alias Frédérique Bonlieu, phoned Greenpeace. Elaine Shaw took the call. 'She could hardly understand what I was saying. She was calling from the Central Post Office because she didn't know where the office was and asked me to go down to meet her. She described herself to me, saying she was wearing jeans and a navy blue top with white and red piping.'

Her first reaction on seeing the French spy was surprise. Cabon did not look the part of a travelling sympathizer. 'She looked so incongruous in jeans. She had very large thighs which were accentuated by the denims.' She was around five feet eight inches tall and weighed about ten stone. Her hair was mousy-coloured but more fashionably styled than in the photographs (dating from her student days) which later appeared in the press. She had high cheekbones and an extremely prominent nose. Shaw tried to joke with her, saying that her clothes – in the red, white and blue of the French tricolour – were very patriotic, but Cabon was not amused. 'She just talked and talked and talked, all afternoon. By seven p.m. everyone had gone home except Cabon and myself. I felt a little sorry for her. She didn't seem to fit in so I suggested we have something to eat before she went back to the hostel. I took her to the Hard To

Find café and we ate a Mexican meal. I remember her saying she had to be careful about her weight.'

The majority of Greenpeace workers in Auckland are self-supporting volunteers. At the time Shaw was on the dole so she was far from impressed when Cabon did not offer to help pay the fifteen-dollar bill. 'I remember feeling very angry at the time. It wasn't until we were outside and walking along the street that she said she was short of New Zealand dollars and could she pay her share when she had changed some francs. She said she could only stay at the hostel for three days and asked if I could help find her accommodation.'

The next morning Shaw collected Cabon and her bags from the hostel and drove her to the Greenpeace office. Cabon asked if she could help, translated the Vidal letter into English for the benefit of the office workers, and repeated her request for hints on where she might stay. Mischievously, Shaw turned to another Greenpeace member, Carole Stewart, knowing that she had room at her bungalow in Grey Lynn and would find it hard to refuse a request from a visiting sympathizer. 'It was a pretty broad hint. I have to admit I disliked her at first. She was very intense and tried too hard to be sincere. She had a very, very prominent nose which was good for looking down. I was not keen on her staying with me but I could not refuse.'

All day long Cabon sat around the office, asking anyone who walked in if they spoke French. She seemed to be constantly searching for someone to converse with. Shaw and Stewart put it down to loneliness and her difficulty in understanding English. Throughout her stay with Greenpeace it never became clear exactly how much English she knew; at times she seemed to have great difficulty, at other times she would volunteer to do translations. Later New Zealand police became convinced that she was actually fluent in English but feigned ignorance in order to discover who did or did not understand French. After that she was able to phone the DGSE openly from the Greenpeace office without fear of blowing her cover.

Greenpeace is normally sceptical about those who walk in off the street. They usually expect the life of an ecological campaigner to be exciting and glamorous, full of incident and

185

challenge. It's an image Greenpeace itself has created by its remarkable publicity stunts, but in the Auckland office the work is much more mundane. Had Cabon been truly willing to help she would have found herself licking envelopes for the mailing lists. 'Most of it is administration, fund-raising, answering telephones, public relations and letter-writing, but we do do the odd demonstration,' Stewart told her.

'We weren't sceptical about her because of the letter,' says Stewart. 'The moment she arrived she started talking about the nuclear issue. The first conversation we had was about independence. She argued that the Polynesian people had nothing more to complain about than any other people living in French provinces. The Pacific colonies were simply another province of France.'

Shaw recalls thinking that it was an interesting time for a French sympathizer to arrive in Auckland. France was building on its military garrison in New Caledonia after the threat of insurrection, and the 150-kiloton test was due at Moruroa.

In the evening of the second day, Shaw drove Cabon and her bags to Stewart's house. The French spy was to prove an unpleasant and ungrateful guest. 'She helped herself to food but never offered to help pay for it. She never helped us around the house or even did the dishes. My friend Renata, who lives with me and my daughter Rochelle, got quite fed up with her. Renata's German and Cabon kept on at her to speak to her in French. She was convinced Renata spoke French but Renata didn't want to know. They ended up having a row about it. My daughter Rochelle thought Cabon was just plain snotty. She slept on a camp bed in the lounge and kept complaining about how cold the house was and how it was always raining here.'

By the end of a week Stewart decided her guest had to go, but how? Conversations overheard in the Greenpeace office helped to solve that problem. 'She always seemed far more interested in our attitudes to the French colonies than the Moruroa campaign. She pretended to be shocked at the treatment meted out to islanders by the French,' says Judy Seaboyer, who also works at the Greenpeace office. 'She seemed to get depressed. She would sit in a corner. Once she said she found it difficult to come to terms with being French. We helped her get in touch with the Kanak Support Group here because she said she wanted to find out more.'

Carole Stewart grabbed the opportunity to manoeuvre Cabon in the direction of those who might feed her curiosity. 'I suggested she meet two people we knew, Jane Cooper and Karen Mangnall, a reporter on the *New Zealand Herald*, who lived together and were involved in the independence issues. Cabon met Jane, who did not like her at first. They talked about New Zealand and had a political disagreement – Cabon was fond of telling people that the issues were far too complex for them to understand. A few days after that she met Karen who was more keen and invited her to stay.' Two months later police officers searching the *Ouvéa* would find a map of Auckland with directions to an address written in the corner. When police called at that address, they discovered it was the home of Jane Cooper, who had innocently written the directions on the map for Cabon.

In the meantime the French visitor appeared to mellow. Her opinionated and patronizing attitude to anything anti-French slowly dissolved but she always remained secretive about her past. The Greenpeace office learned little more than the fact that she lived with friends in Paris (though she could not remember the address) and came from Pau in the south. She mentioned her interest in archaeology and her recent visit to Lebanon and told people she intended to go to a conference in Tahiti on coral reefs.

Soon she was in the thick of the office's administrative work. She was trusted to answer telephones, despite her apparent language problems, and staff the office on the odd day when everyone else went out to join a demonstration. But Cabon rarely put herself out. She wrote the letter to Mitterrand and helped translate a video film from French to English, but generally used the office for her own ends. She claimed to be writing about the organization and its motivation for French magazines and newspapers, arguing that the best way to stop nuclear testing and bring colonialism to an end was through internal public pressure. She made telephone calls to France

187

and received them in the office on many occasions. Her explanation was always the same. 'I am contacting friends who can promote the cause.'

In fact Cabon was brazenly contacting her superiors to give brief résumés of her work. She also pressed her 'colleagues' in the Greenpeace office to check the cost and availability of scuba diving gear for four friends who would be arriving soon for a holiday. She wanted to know how much it might cost to fill oxygen tanks, hire dinghies or boats. Seaboyer and Stewart both made calls for her. Then in May Cabon announced she was taking time off to travel around the island. She hired a small car for five days and disappeared.

Cabon visited Whangarei and the northernmost tip of New Zealand, the Aupori peninsula. Most tourists would have gone in the opposite direction for the more spectacular sights in the mountainous south. But Cabon was reconnoitring, taking with her the map later found by the police with Jane Cooper's directions written in a corner.

It was plain sailing for Cabon in Auckland. She had opportunities to search the office and discuss the movement, its personalities and tactics, freely. Part of her task was to find out details of the crew and equipment on board the *Rainbow Warrior*. Possibly the purpose was to discover whether – as the more paranoid members of the DGSE suspected – the ship would be carrying Soviet agents and mysterious scientific equipment to Moruroa. A more straightforward explanation is that, since Greenpeace had announced plans to keep the *Warrior* stationed off Moruroa for many weeks, the French wanted to know if this was really likely to happen – was the *Warrior* well enough equipped for a long stay, and how experienced was its crew?

Because Greenpeace has offices spread across the world, discussion about its operations and plans frequently takes the form of letters. The idea of using the *Rainbow Warrior* for the Moruroa campaign had been around since 1981, but planning had not got under way because the Greenpeace groups in Australia and New Zealand believed that it would be ineffective. The result of this dispute was a huge amount of correspondence discussing possible tactics. It was not until early in 1984 that the New Zealand group began to change its mind and planning began in earnest, with many documents circulating the Greenpeace offices. One of the New Zealand supporters of the plan was Elaine Shaw. A copy of a paper she had written, 'Outline for a Pacific peace cruise, 1985', had been lying around the Auckland office since May 1984. Part of this report proposed that the *Rainbow Warrior* should aim to arrive off Moruroa in time for Bastille Day, July 14. 'Meanwhile, from the east in the Caribbean, the *Fri* would sail for Moruroa, arriving at the same time as the *Rainbow Warrior* and the *Vega*.' It went on to discuss the possibility of using small boats or inflatables to land on the atoll. 'Such an invasion could take the French a little by surprise and would make it difficult for the French navy to cover all areas of the invasion. This might make it possible for at least one of the boats – or, more likely, a Zodiac from the *Rainbow Warrior* – to actually invade the lagoon and make a landing on Moruroa atoll . . . The publicity engendered by such an invasion would focus attention world-wide on the testing.'

Another letter in the file, dated October 11, 1984, must have caused even more consternation in Paris when Cabon reported its contents. The letter, from the New Zealand group to international headquarters in Lewes, said:

> We've had a windfall in Tahitian contact this week. One of the anti-nuke activists involved for about ten years was recently through Auckland, and he is very keen to have Tahitian boats go in to Moruroa while the *Rainbow Warrior* is there. Not the pirogues [a type of traditional canoe], but large, motor-powered boats – he knows about a dozen, with sympathetic owners . . . We discussed tactics, and he is very keen to take this further.

For Cabon, the only threat of discovery manifested itself late in May. Monique Ursem is a Dutch-born New Zealander studying at Auckland University who called in to the Greenpeace office from time to time to see her friends. During one such visit, on May 20, she was asked to help Cabon with translation – and immediately spoke to Cabon in fluent French. It shook Cabon, but not as much as the next surprise.

'I used to live in France, I studied at Pau University,' Ursem told Cabon. The French spy said nothing but the next day, concerned that someone in the office might remember that she had told them of her childhood in Pau, she told Ursem that she too had studied geography at the university there. They remembered the same professors, although Ursem had graduated six years later. It was enough to make Cabon revise her plans. It was clearly dangerous to remain while Ursem was around the office. On May 24 Cabon announced, casually, that she was leaving. The conference in Tahiti was due to start and she had to be there.

Nobody was sorry to see her go. She had always been difficult, an overpowering person who insisted on dominating conversations. Nobody suspected her real intentions. Nevertheless, Greenpeace had begun routine checks on the author of her letter of introduction. On April 25 – the day after Cabon turned up in New Zealand – Steve Sawyer, organizer of the Pacific campaign, telexed Greenpeace's international headquarters from Hawaii. 'Do you know a French guy called Jean-Marie Vidal, who was involved in anti-test campaign in early seventies? Apparently he has surfaced in New Zealand and would like your opinion of him.'

Back in England, David McTaggart thought the name clicked, but he could not be sure. So a reply was sent to Sawyer with no answers but more questions. 'Can you get any more info on Jean-Marie Vidal? Exactly when was he active? What did he do?'

Sawyer just shrugged. Those were precisely the questions he had hoped headquarters would be able to answer. He could have pursued the matter and discovered, perhaps, that Vidal actually knew very little about 'Frédérique Bonlieu'. But he decided to let it pass. He had made an inquiry and drawn a blank. And anyway, he was busy. The *Rainbow Warrior*'s campaign was hotting up.

Cabon arrived in Tahiti and quickly made contact with Bengt Danielsson, the anthropologist and anti-nuclear protester who was also a director of Greenpeace Sweden. Danielsson became suspicious almost immediately because Cabon knew almost nothing about coral reefs, even though she claimed to be an expert. Danielsson claims that at the conference and during the three visits she paid to his thatched hut she pumped him for details of Tahitian militants who would be sailing with Greenpeace. Danielsson remembers Cabon as humourless. At the coral reef conference she confided to him that she preferred the company of women to men. 'I replied that at least we had that in common,' he says. Despite his suspicions, Danielsson did not alert Greenpeace until after the bombing. On August 14 he wrote an open letter to the Tahitian and French press urging them to investigate her activities.

By the middle of June, Christine Cabon had resurfaced in Paris. Using her nom de guerre, she made several telephone calls to the Greenpeace office in rue de la Bucherie asking for an appointment with Louis Trussell, a New Zealand-born woman who had worked in the office since 1977. The pair eventually met on June 18. There was nothing immediately suspicious about her; nothing to suggest her military background. 'She didn't walk with a stiff back or anything like that,' Trussell recalls. 'She was wearing jeans and seemed quite relaxed.'

The women spent two and a half hours chatting on a sofa near the door, facing a wall covered with Greenpeace posters and shelves of literature. Cabon showed no signs of being nosy. 'She didn't go further than the reception desk. She didn't even ask to go to the toilet, which would have given her a chance to look around.'

Cabon began by saying that she brought greetings from the Auckland office and went on to describe her experiences as a French person in New Zealand and the cultural differences she had noticed. Trussell, as a New Zealander, naturally found this interesting and told Cabon about some of her own experiences living in France. Trussell formed the impression that Cabon was opposed to nuclear testing, though she insisted that the methods being adopted in New Zealand would not work in France. The petition to Mitterrand which she had drafted in Auckland was still well to the fore in Cabon's mind: New Zealanders simply did not understand how to write to a French president. Their style was wrong and they were trying to tell him things he already knew.

Trussell listened patiently. She found her visitor extremely self-opinionated, with some cosily bourgeois attitudes (not uncommon among Greenpeace supporters, especially in France). Nevertheless, she was obviously very perceptive and highly intelligent. Trussell asked for her address in Paris and Cabon obliged. Not until weeks later did Greenpeace discover that the address was false.

Immediately Cabon had finished her reports from New Zealand the chiefs in Paris met again. The plan was definitely on. All that remained now was to work out the details. At the DGSE frogmen's base in Aspretto, Corsica, Lieutenant-Colonel Louis-Pierre Dillais was assigning people to the team. First there was Dillais himself. As commanding officer, he would be going to keep an eye on things and make the decisions if anything went wrong and they had to vary the plan. His former deputy at Aspretto, Alain Mafart, would be more closely involved, servicing the sabotage team. Mafart, thirty-five, the son of an army doctor, loved adventure, no matter whether it was work or play. He had served the DGSE on secret missions in Africa, notably Chad, and later in Lebanon. For holidays he had travelled to Greenland and the Californian coast to photograph whales. Mafart would need transport in New Zealand, something larger than a car because of all the equipment ... a camper van perhaps. A Frenchman travelling alone in that would look a bit odd, so he needed a companion and a cover story. Enter Dominique Prieur. Thirty-six years old and married to a Paris fireman, she belonged to the new generation of intellectual spies. She had studied sociology and politics at Naterre University, where she developed a special interest in Libya and wrote a thesis on Colonel Gaddafi's Green Book. Prieur was a natural choice for the Greenpeace mission because she already had experience of spying on environmental groups in Europe. Finally there were the men who would be transporting the explosives to New Zealand and carrying out the operation: Verge, Andries

192

and Bartelo – plus Maniguet, travelling on a genuine passport as an innocent civilian and doctor (if needed).

It was Maniguet who called first at the Odyssée travel agency at 137 rue du Ranelagh, Paris. The agency is located in a ritzy arrondissement; the women passers-by are well furred and buy a better class of perfume. Walk-in customers, however, are rare and are treated warily. Perhaps they are put off by the agency's scruffy appearance. A few Polynesian figurines have been dumped in the window and decked with shell necklaces. The posters of palmed beaches are faded. The agency also advertises itself as a maritime library, though the two women at the desk seem at sea over any inquiry more difficult than a holiday on the Côte d'Azur. The manager is Charles Leroy, a tall, well-dressed man with a blond moustache. He sits in a separate office, whose panelled walls and military primness make it seem like the captain's quarters on a navy ship.

Odyssée is one of the few travel agents in France which offers cruises in the south Pacific aboard hired yachts. It was just such a cruise that Dr Maniguet was interested in. He was willing to pay 90,000 francs, he said, but did not want to sail alone. Perhaps Odyssée could find two or three other people to accompany him.

Requests for winter cruises in the Pacific are rare, and the chances of finding companions for Maniguet were, on the face of it, extremely slim. But as it turned out, the doctor did not have long to wait. A few days later Verge, using his alias Raymond Velche, phoned Odyssée. He described himself as a professional skipper. He already had two friends wanting to sail to the Pacific from Noumea and was looking for a fourth person to complete the crew. Odyssée was only too happy to oblige with the name of Dr Xavier Maniguet . . . and the yacht *Ouvéa*.

Today, Odyssée refuses to discuss the *Ouvéa* affair. Leroy, the manager, even shut down the office temporarily after it emerged that his travel agency had been used by the secret services. According to reports in the French press, Odyssée was chosen by the DGSE not only because it specializes in holidays for the avid sailor but also because of alleged links with extreme right-wing groups. The news magazine *Paris Match* ran a story quoting a Greek politician, Komimos Pyramoglu, saying that

193

Odyssée was used by a French political organization to send young fascist 'scouts' to train during the summers in the Eubee region.

On May 29, 1985, a man calling himself Eric Andreine arrived at terminal 2 of Heathrow airport on an Air France flight. It was a few minutes after 9.00 a.m. and he went straight to the desk of Hotel Booking International in the main arrival hall. There he asked the assistant, Kirti Shah, to find him a hotel room. Shah found him a room at the Vanderbilt Hotel in Cromwell Road, west London, and gave him a reservation slip to present to reception.

After checking in at the hotel, Andreine (who in reality was Petty Officer Gerald Andries of the DGSE) travelled to Barnet Marine Centre in Greenhill Parade, New Barnet, north London. Keith Chapman, who runs the store, says: 'All I can recall is that he did not speak one word of English. He spent an hour on the premises and finally chose a French-built grey inflatable dinghy and a low-power secondhand Yamaha outboard motor. It struck us as strange that a Frenchman should come all the way to London to buy a French-made dinghy and also that he should take such a low-powered engine to go with it, when the Zodiac is built to take outboards ten times as powerful.'

Andries handed the shopkeeper £1,400 in new £50 notes but did not want to have the VAT sales tax returned (which he was entitled to as a foreign visitor). Then he asked Barnet Marine to call a taxi. Back at the hotel, a porter helped Andries to carry the 180lb package from the taxi to his room. Andries spent that night in room 144 (decorated in pale pink) and in the morning left before 11.00 a.m., settling his bill for £64.90 in cash. One item on the bill was a telephone call to an ex-directory number in Paris – the DGSE. Andries apparently left London without the dinghy and its motor. Later, after the dinghy had been found in Auckland, New Zealand police, assisted by Scotland Yard and Special Branch, found that no packages answering their description had passed through British airports. They now believe that the Zodiac and the outboard left Britain by cross-Channel ferry, stowed on the roof of a car.

During his short stay in London, Gerald Andries could not

have attracted more attention if he had wandered the streets dressed as Napoleon. The chandler, the taxi driver and the hotel porter all noticed something odd about the Frenchman. But the oddest thing of all was why he bought the dinghy in London. In their planning, the French showed an almost pathological fear of being exposed by British intelligence. The French believed that the New Zealand authorities would be a pushover – unless Britain's MI6 tipped them off. Insiders at the DGSE claim that a decision was taken to throw the British off the track. Word was filtered back to MI6 that the French were planning a covert operation in their troubled Pacific colony of New Caledonia, and that New Zealand was to be used as a staging post.

This cover story seemed plausible enough. During the peak of the fighting between white settlers and the native Melanesians, who want independence for the island, French authorities intercepted an arms shipment aboard a vessel from New Zealand. The aim of the French operation in New Zealand, the DGSE is believed to have told its counterparts in British intelligence, was to crack the ring of gun-runners.

It is believed that the DGSE went so far as to inform the British that 'a couple' – presumably the Turenges – would be arriving in Auckland for that purpose. A DGSE agent then went through the charade of buying the Zodiac dinghy with great fanfare in London because the British had reportedly been told that the French wanted to camouflage their involvement in the New Caledonian mission. The Zodiac is made in France, and in the past, whenever the French secret services have wanted to use one of these dinghies for their clandestine operations, the manufacturer has willingly supplied a Zodiac without a serial number so that it could not be traced.

If the British secret services had been forewarned of the DGSE's plan, they seemed, at the start, willing to co-operate. But after the bombing of the *Rainbow Warrior* the French were stunned at how quickly the New Zealand police managed to trace back the mystery buyer of the Zodiac. Historical rivalries rumbled to the surface. In a fit of pique, the DGSE complained that the swift tracking job was evidence of Anglo-Saxon duplicity. In other words, the British had played along with the

French only to expose them at the point when it would do the most damage to French interests in the Pacific. After the Turenges were caught, an internal inquiry was launched in the Piscine to determine who had leaked details of the Greenpeace operation beforehand to British intelligence. The DGSE officers could not believe that it was their own incompetence and the quick response of the New Zealand police that had tripped them up.

CHAPTER THIRTEEN

Arrival

Landfall began with a blunder, the yacht almost foundering on the sandbar at the mouth of Parengarenga Harbour. The hazard was not immediately obvious to the crew of the *Ouvéa*, exhausted after their three-day voyage in rough seas. Heartened by the sight of New Zealand, even if it was the wild and barren north, they had gunned the forty-horsepower motor to take them past rocky Cape Reinga at the end of the Aupori peninsula. As the yacht rounded the grey-brown headland, white breakers thrashing at the mouth of the bay gave the first warning of danger lurking just below the surface.

Christine Cabon's reports had not mentioned the sandbar. She had visited the bay as part of her undercover mission, with instructions to find a sleepy haven that could be reached by car or van yet was as far from prying eyes, and officialdom, as the saboteurs could wish. The road maps she had brought back from New Zealand gave no hint that Parengarenga Harbour could be considered a hazardous port of call. Though the mouth was half a mile wide, it was all but closed by the sandbar, with a shallow channel no more than ten yards wide allowing access only to the most knowledgeable. The sandbar is not easily seen from the shore and possibly Cabon had visited on one of the days when barges come to dredge the pure white sand for glass factories in the south and had been misled by the apparent ease with which they navigated the bar. Raymond Velche, the skipper, cursed the planners now as he headed towards the foaming water. His three colleagues simply held on grimly, waiting for the grind of the hull as the *Ouvéa* beached herself. Three times she scraped the bottom, but Velche revved the engine each time the swell lifted the sloop and finally they bounced through.

Beyond lay a huge triangular harbour, unnervingly calm

197

behind its sandy battlements. It was framed by low, rolling hills which appeared to have been smothered under a blanket of teatree bushes much like giant heather. The Pacific winds keep them a uniform six feet high. But here and there bare rock walls indicated a dirt track winding down to the shoreline. Scarcely noticeable above the deserted white beaches were patches of grass and a few lonely bungalows with corrugated iron roofs. Bobbing at anchor were a handful of dinghies and rowing boats. A rickety wharf could just be seen but otherwise Parengarenga appeared lifeless, just as they had been told – and hoped.

The *Ouvéa* motored right up to the jetty. Two Maori children who were playing on the beach had watched the arrival open-mouthed. Their friends and neighbours regularly braved the bar in their dinghies on daily fishing trips but the sight of the white-hulled thirty-eight-foot sloop bouncing over the bar and motoring inshore astonished them. Three yachts – two of them French – had tried to enter in the past five years. All had run aground on the sandbar and been dashed to pieces by the waves within hours. The shattered bow of one, the *Drac II*, was still visible just above the surface. The four Frenchmen moored the yacht and climbed wearily up on to the track above them. Xavier Maniguet called to the children, Charlie Sucich, a tough little thirteen-year-old, and his sister Hope, just seven years old.

New Zealand holds many surprises for the uninitiated and the tiny settlement of Te Hapua where the *Ouvéa* had berthed has its fair share. It is the home of a Maori tribe, the Ngati Kuri, but only 150 members remain to live off their communally-owned 14,000 acres. More than 2,000 others have moved south to the towns and cities to work in factories and on construction sites. It is at first glance a poor hamlet. The nearest doctor is fifty miles away, the nearest hospital even further. Rusting cars and tractors spew their insides on to the ground around the houses and most people exist on state handouts. A meagre income is drawn from the pulp mills which leased 8,000 acres from the Maoris at fifty cents an acre more than forty years ago. The annual $NZ4,000 from this source is distributed among the entire tribe. But it is also a cheerful place. Visitors are warmly welcomed, meals gladly shared. Because mortgages,

198

insurance policies and other income-sapping demands are non-existent in Te Hapua, many homes have video recorders and colour televisions. The open-handed friendship displayed by its inhabitants, the pace and simplicity of life, is appealing enough to persuade others to settle there.

Jewel Sucich, mother of the two children who had first greeted the *Ouvéa*, was watching television in her home – which doubles as a very basic general store and post office – when her daughter ran into the room to announce the arrival of strangers. Jewel was married to the son of a Yugoslav immigrant who had arrived in New Zealand to dig for kauri gum – a fossilized sap similar to amber which is still found in large nuggets on the Aupori peninsula – and her house was the nearest to the wharf. Her first reaction was concern. The rarity of visitors from the sea and the drug trafficking that took place among North Island's more deserted inlets combined to strengthen her suspicion. A naturally shy woman, she did not offer the welcome normally given to tourists who arrived by the dirt track in their camper vans and hire cars.

Maniguet was the first to approach Mrs Sucich, followed by Velche. Berthelo and Audrenc stood back, scanning the shoreline. 'They asked me a lot of questions. First they wanted to know if they could get a shower somewhere, then they asked if they could buy charts of the harbour, because theirs had given no indication of the sandbar, and if there was anyone who could show them the way out of the harbour when they left.

'Then they asked for fuel for their boat. I was worried. All the men had gone away for the day to a rugby match and I felt nervous so I told them to go up to the school and ask there.'

Half a mile up the track on the hillside, the school house, with its tiny tarmac playground, was the next best building in Te Hapua after the small Maori meeting house with its hand-carved portals. Stephen and Marion Hovell had originally volunteered to teach in the Maori settlements for two years, a service which the education authorities encouraged by offering better jobs and pay in wealthier areas afterwards. But the Hovells liked Maoris and had worked on for sixteen years, the last three in Te Hapua. Stephen had even broken through the tribal taboos and won election to the council of elders. A happy couple with broad smiles and generous natures, the Hovells treat visitors like bosom friends. But Saturday June 22 was not the best of days. Stephen, Marion and their four children were all laid low by influenza. An epidemic had struck Te Hapua and they had closed the school house. 'It wasn't a good time to call, we were so sick,' Stephen says. 'Marion spoke to Maniguet. She went down in her dressing gown. We normally like to give visitors a big welcome but it just wasn't on, we were so crook at the time.'

'He asked us if we had any charts of the harbour and how they could get out again safely,' Marion says. 'I spoke to him in French. I asked him how they were and if they had had an enjoyable sail but he was not very talkative. I suggested they go and talk to Walter, our school bus driver. He fishes a lot in the harbour.'

The *Ouvéa* crew strode back down the track in search of Walter Murray and were almost run down. Paul Norman, one of the tribal leaders – a huge, handsome Maori with a beautiful blonde wife from Southend in England – came careering round the corner in his battered Morris. 'It's just a wreck really – it hasn't any brakes. I came bowling down the road and they had to jump for it.' He is as proud of the fact that he almost wiped out a team of saboteurs as he is of the meal his tribe gave a visiting dignitary a week before. It was no more than coincidence that the French ambassador to New Zealand had visited Cape Reinga earlier in June to unveil a plaque to a French explorer, Marion du Fresne, in Spirits Bay. Te Hapua, as the nearest Maori settlement, was called upon to welcome him with a hot lunch. Norman – who takes his name from a British soldier who married his great-great-grandmother – giggles infectiously as he recalls the stew of pig's cheek, tail and trotters. Though many might regard such a meal as a delicacy, Norman likes to think that the ambassador did not. Still, it was a better reception than the Maoris gave du Fresne 200 years ago: he was set upon and killed.

Back aboard the *Ouvéa*, now anchored ten yards off the wharf, all four men began to clean and tidy the boat. It surprised those

200

onshore who watched from their windows. The sailors looked exhausted, they were dishevelled and had obviously had a very rough crossing from Norfolk Island, yet they were denying themselves the obvious need for rest. They pulled the boat apart, piling up bundles on the deck. Then they stowed the sails, washed down the decks and carried out a hundred other chores that stretched their labours well past sundown. They had two dinghies on board, a grey Zodiac and another older and indistinguishable inflatable.

Hec Crene was tired himself when he steered his Land Rover off the track and up the bumpy drive to his home among the teatrees at Waitiki Landing, six miles along the road from Te Hapua. He is a tall, cheerful man, with snowy white hair above a face bronzed by years in the bush. At fifty-eight, his tenure as park ranger in charge of Te Paki Station was coming to an end. In eighteen months he would retire to the house he was building thirty miles south at Pukenui where there is the luxury of a tarmac road. He had been out most of the day on routine patrol and an equally routine rescue. As park ranger he was the nearest thing to a law enforcer that the peninsula had.

The single road which follows the spine of the Aupori peninsula to Cape Reinga is augmented by a spectacular alternative route along its west coast. It is called Ninety Mile Beach, though its uninterrupted expanse stretches for only forty-five. The Maoris call it One-roa-a-Tohea, which means Tohea's Long Run. The name honours a warrior who, legend has it, performed a remarkable athletic feat. When his chief asked for a meal of pigeons, Tohea ran the length of the beach, speared some plump birds, cooked them and ran back to deliver them, still warm, to his chief. Now the bus companies take tourists up the road to Cape Reinga and back along the beach through the surf when tide and weather permit. There is, unfortunately, only one way on to the beach at its northern limit: the pebble-strewn, shallow Kaueauparao river. Crene is used to winching the careless drivers of bogged-down Hertz rental cars out of the river bed, but that day it had been a tourist bus that had stuck fast. 'The secret is to keep moving. Some people say "But we only stopped to take a picture" – but that's all it takes to sink

201

up to your axles in mud. Sometimes in the summer it's as hard as rock but in winter it's a real problem. There's quicksand too. George 'Moby' Dick took his minibus down and got stuck. I went down there to winch him out at about three p.m. While I was out, Jewel Sucich called. We couldn't budge Moby and he got on the radio to find another bus to drag him out. I got back about six p.m. and Jewel called me again. She was a bit concerned because she was on her own with the kids and strangers had sailed into the harbour. It was strange. Three boats have tried to get in at Parengarenga in the past five years and they were all sunk. But there was nothing I could do about it that night. It was dark and they had been there since early afternoon. If they were smuggling anything or had anything to hide they would have done their business by then. I told Jewel I would pop down on Sunday morning to give them a look over, but I decided to call Lew Sabin to check with him.'

The nearest customs post to Parengarenga is more than 120 miles south in Whangarei, the northernmost official port of entry in New Zealand. Lew Sabin is a short, balding and muscular customs officer with an aura of authority developed during years of service as a petty officer in the Royal New Zealand Navy. He agreed immediately with Hec Crene. It was strange that a yacht should put into Parengarenga, but then the French were crazy sailors. Experience had taught both men that those French yachtsmen who did venture into New Zealand's waters were decidedly buccaneer with their boats and had to be humoured. Had the *Ouvéa* been crewed by Kiwis or Americans he might have acted immediately. 'But they were French and we all know here that they are damned stupid with their boats.' The crew's nationality decided it. There was nothing to be done that night. In any case it would have taken him five hours to drive north to Parengarenga. Sabin asked his friend to tell the *Ouvéa*'s crew to phone him. They must not bring any food or plants ashore, and must keep their rubbish on board. New Zealand, with its agricultural economy, lives in terror of imported pests and blight.

It was the fact that Parengarenga was so isolated that convinced Sabin he had little to worry about. If they had been smugglers they would certainly have chosen a better harbour with easier road access to make a quick getaway with the contraband. This was just a bunch of negligent French sailors who had been lucky to get across the bar.

Hec Crene went down to the *Ouvéa* at 10.00 the next morning. 'I met Jewel on the way down and we walked across the road to the jetty. The boat was a few yards off in midstream and I could see two men on deck, one in the cockpit and another sorting out some ropes. I called across to them and they started the engine and motored back to the wharf. They seemed surprised to see me and Maniguet asked me if I was from the customs office. I told him to come with me to Jewel's so we could talk to Lew Sabin on the telephone. I told him I was there on the customs' behalf and that they would have to speak to Lew. Velche came up to the house with us and I called Whangarei.'

Sabin vividly recalls the telephone conversation with Maniguet. The doctor complained that they had not known of the sandbar, and were exhausted and in need of rest. They had entered the harbour with all its risks, because they thought they could get customs clearance at Te Hapua. It was a lie neither the police nor the customs would register.

Normally the customs try to inspect a yacht as soon as it arrives. 'But there are hundreds of bays and only a few of us,' Sabin says. 'We have a coastal watch system where people dotted around the shore call us regularly to let us know what's happening near them and what new yachts have appeared in their area. Hec called us because it seemed unusual that the *Ouvéa* had come into Parengarenga.

'I suppose with hindsight we should have gone up and taken a long look, and we probably would have done so if it had been a Kiwi or American boat because they should know better than to try and get over the sandbar. Then again, what if I had gone up? I would probably have got my head blown off if I had found anything on board.

'It's impossible to form an opinion about a boat unless you are on board when it comes in. You get to know the crook skippers, and it's worth the effort pulling their boats out of the water and inspecting the keel for hidden compartments and pulling the inside apart. But we only do that if we have specific intelligence of a drugs run, or if there is something on board which makes us very uneasy indeed. The *Ouvéa* people had a plausible explanation that matched the reputation French sailors had.

'I told Maniguet to bring the boat down the coast to us. We are based in Whangarei but we have an office at Opua, further north, which we use mainly in the summer. I told the Frenchman I would see him at Opua in a few days.'

Maniguet replaced the receiver and turned to Velche. He smiled, nodded, then thanked the ranger for his help. Crene walked to his Land Rover and was about to climb into the driving seat when Maniguet and Velche called him back. They asked him if he would like to inspect their boat. Indeed, they insisted. They took him below and made a great show of the galley and the areas forward and aft, though he had not asked to see them. Then they sat him down and gave him a beer and talked – first about the *Ouvéa*'s vital statistics but quickly progressing to the mutual passion of New Zealand and France: rugby football.

'They stuck to black coffee, and Audrenc told Maniguet in French to ask me how the All Blacks were shaping up. They said they were the best team in the world and were always welcome in France. We had a nice long chat. Maniguet asked me a lot of questions about the area around the harbour and the cape. He wanted some maps and charts but I said I couldn't help him, and they wouldn't be any use in any case because the sandbar was always moving. I told them they'd best sit tight and wait for the sand barges, then motor over and ask one to show them the way out. That was the easiest way. I told him to tune his marine radio to the frequencies used by the barges, 2045 and 2480, and he could talk to the skippers direct.'

Crene became so engrossed with the newcomers, enjoying the conversation and the beer, that he forgot the time. Then someone called him from the shore. 'I recognized the voice straight away. It was Pakite Hau, one of the Te Hapua Maoris. He was yelling something about a pig-hunting permit but I knew he didn't really want one. He was just trying to wheedle his way on board – he's a nosy bloke. I just yelled back that I'd see him later.' Crene glanced at his watch and was surprised to see it was nearly noon already. It was not until later in the day, when he had left the *Ouvéa*, that he realized there was something out of the ordinary about the yacht. It was spotlessly clean; everything had been stowed tidily away. 'It didn't look like it had just been sailed across an ocean.'

New Zealand offers an irritating welcome to visitors from overseas. As incoming jets taxi to a halt on the airport apron, two officials from the ministry of agriculture board the aircraft, walk down the aisles to the rear and wait. A steward announces that according to regulations designed to ensure that no harmful bugs infiltrate the nation's crops, the aircraft's interior – and hence those still strapped in their seats – will be sprayed with a 'harmless' aerosol declared safe by the World Health Organization. Passengers have little chance to question the statement or protest against the intrusion. The only concession is an invitation to cover faces with handkerchiefs until the ordeal is over. While the *Ouvéa* crew had risked their necks entering the country, Alain and Sophie Turenge had only to endure the sickly mist of insecticide. The Turenges stepped off the Air New Zealand Boeing 747, Flight TE 1 from London via Los Angeles and Honolulu, which landed on time at 9.10 a.m. after a twenty-seven-hour flight, into the cool breeze whipping around Auckland's Mangere airport.

Their next ordeal was the thirty-minute wait to clear immigration and another thirty minutes to collect their baggage and pass through customs before they were free to hail a taxi from the rank outside. They had arranged in advance to hire a Toyota Hiace camper van from Newman's downtown Auckland branch, and it was there that they went first to collect the vehicle, registration number LB 9085. Becky Hayter was on the front desk when they arrived, paid $NZ860 in cash for three weeks' hire and drove off to start their 'honeymoon'. She liked them immediately. 'They were a lovely couple, really nice people.' They went straight to the Travelodge Hotel to sleep off the effects of jet-lag and checked in shortly before 11.30 a.m., just as the *Ouvéa* motored into the jaws of Parengarenga Harbour.

The Travelodge is an uninspiring building, but functional in the mode of all modern hotels. It was also the perfect base for the Turenges at the outset of their mission. It rises above Quay Street near the new shopping complex, just across the street from the main docks. From their room they could survey miles of waterfront and overlook the ferry terminal directly opposite. A hundred yards to the left was a dock framed by two wharves. To the right was the main dock area with Captain Cook and Marsden wharves where the smaller cruising yachts and visiting ships tied up. They were not quite sure yet where the *Rainbow Warrior* might berth when it arrived, but they knew the Greenpeace flagship was due in Auckland on July 7 and they had two weeks to reconnoitre.

A short walk down Quay Street provided invaluable information. Turning right out of the Travelodge and crossing the road, the Turenges would have realized immediately how easy it was to gain access to the docks. The ten-foot-high red Victorian railings, which stretched for 200 yards between two buildings, had two sets of gates at each end. At one, a dock security officer sat in a small kiosk guarding a turnstile through which pedestrians could gain access only by pass. At the other end the gates which had once opened to allow the trams through were not only unguarded but open most of the day and often during the night. At that stage no one could have suspected that a team of saboteurs would infiltrate the port area to plant explosives on the hull of a ship, though the security force must have been concerned about smugglers and thieves. Months after the bombing, it was much the same. Members of *The Sunday Times*'s Insight team walked and drove into the dock area many times, parked on the wharves and inspected the cargo sheds. They were challenged only once, half an hour after entering the docks. Opposite the red gates is the wharf police station, but that is manned by a single duty officer and closed at night. It was easy enough to approach by foot and, the Turenges observed, easier still by sea.

But there were other reasons why they should forgo the

206

dubious comforts of their camper van and install themselves in a hotel in central Auckland instead of staying in one of the city's hundreds of motels. The Travelodge was close to the Greenpeace office, just fifteen minutes' walk up Queen Street, turning left into Courthouse Lane. It was also a few minutes' walk from another, plusher hotel where, the next day, their controller would check in. It was perhaps fitting that the boss should choose the best-rated hotel in Auckland – the Hyatt. The man calling himself Jean Louis Dormand flew in on Sunday June 23 and hired a metallic blue Toyota Corolla for six days. He drove himself to the Hyatt and checked in for the duration of the mission. From the rooftop restaurant, he too could see the docks and the wharves where the *Rainbow Warrior* was likely to tie up.

Now the team was assembled. Major Alain Mafart and Captain Dominique Prieur were settled into the Travelodge posing as Alain and Sophie Turenge, a pair of Swiss newly-weds. Their camper van would give them the mobility needed in their role as back-up team, messengers and bag-carriers to the saboteurs themselves. At Parengarenga the three DGSE frogmen, Chief Petty Officer Roland Verge, Petty Officers Gerald Andries and Jean-Michel Bartelo, settled down for their second night at Te Hapua. They had deliberately chosen names that closely resembled their own so that any slip of the tongue in nosy New Zealand might easily be explained away by mispronunciation. The presence of the only man not travelling on false papers, Dr Xavier Maniguet, gave them respectability. His passport was smothered in immigration stamps to support their cover story that he was a rich travelling man and they were his crew. They could all afford to relax; indeed, they might as well treat their time in New Zealand as a vacation. Such was their arrogance, they did not contemplate the risk of discovery and took few steps to cover their tracks.

Nobody saw the *Ouvéa* leave Parengarenga and many wondered how it had managed to navigate the sandbar on the way out. It had been moored in midstream by the jetty on Sunday night,

June 23, but by 8.30 a.m. on Monday it was nowhere to be seen. It was in fact already sailing south down the Aupori peninsula. Velche had managed to guide the vessel through the narrow exit, following the 'keep left' instructions of Pakite Hau, the Maori, who had insinuated himself aboard the *Ouvéa* after Hec Crene's departure.

Through the vast Great Exhibition Bay, skirting Cape Karikari and on past Doubtless Bay, the *Ouvéa* sailed at a leisurely pace. Velche was in no hurry and the landscape to starboard was changing by the hour. The stunted, barren hills of the Aupori peninsula had given way to the lush foothills of the Maungataniwha mountain range which rolled down to the water. Instead of the panoramic bays there were now forested inlets with sandy coves and 150 picture-postcard islets, so many that the area had been named the Bay of Isles. It is a rich man's playground, where Auckland's wealthier citizens come to sail, dive or fish for big game. In the hills above the green, impenetrable bush has been pushed back to accommodate orange groves and pastureland. It wasn't always so. There was a time when it was a hell-hole of convicts, deserters and whaling crews. Even in recent years at least one of the world's most infamous drugs barons built his summer mansion there. (He died in a British prison in 1984.)

Opua lies at the southern end of the bay at the end of a winding road. Cresting the hill a motorist is presented with a breathtaking view of the tiny settlement. A long pier stretches out into the bay with timber buildings, some built on stilts, skirting the water on either side. Their front doors open on to the dusty road, their back doors open on to the water, and the inevitable boat is tied up outside. The bay is continually dotted with lavish yachts and ocean-going motor boats. Up in the hills there are landscaped motels for those who can't afford the $NZ250,000 required to buy their own small chalet home.

It is a peaceful hamlet with a post office, coastguard, harbourmaster's office and little else. The main attraction is the store, a many-faceted emporium. One room is a grocery, another a fast-food shop selling fish and chips or 'hambrudgers'. Next is the hardware shop with fishing tackle and bait and a row of petrol pumps outside. Round the side is the restaurant, and at the back the marina – a landing stage with connecting gangways and fuel pumps to replenish tanks. The store is run by Pat Colenso, a fresh-faced rector's daughter from Norfolk, England, who settled in Opua fifteen years ago.

'The Ouvéa came in about five p.m. on Tuesday and tied up by the fuel pumps,' she said. 'Usually we move boats from there as quickly as possible but as it was winter and we didn't have much custom I let them stay. They came in looking for some hot food and chatted for a while. They wanted to call customs in Whangarei to get the boat checked and cleared, so I sent them over to the post office.'

The customs man, Frank MacLean, had already received a call from the harbourmaster at Opua to announce the *Ouvéa*'s arrival when Maniguet called from the public telephone. Maniguet told the officer he was eager for customs to come and clear the yacht so the crew could complete the formalities and continue their holiday. MacLean called Gordon Grant of the ministry of agriculture's Port Quarantine branch and they drove up to Opua together.

'Everything was closed when we arrived so we had to climb over the gate at the side to get to the jetty where they were berthed,' said MacLean. 'We had seen the *Ouvéa* berthed when we drove down the hill. We don't get many yachts in June and July. They usually arrive in November and leave in May.

'We had a bit of a language problem. I'm not sure they understood us too well. Maniguet did all the talking. I still maintain he was the boss – he stood apart from the other three. He had a passport full of stamps and he talked about visiting South America, Costa Rica and Nicaragua. There's a lot in hindsight that should have alerted us. They filled in all the usual forms. The personal effects form of Audrenc had no cameras listed but he said he was a photographer. I said to Gordon how strange it was that four Frenchmen should come here on a sailing holiday in winter and three of the passports were brand new.

'We talked about Parengarenga and how dangerous it was but they just shrugged their shoulders, saying they thought they could find a customs office there. We were all sitting down on the bunks except Maniguet who stood to one side. Audrenc had been sleeping in the bunk when we arrived and he didn't bother himself too much when we sat down to go through the paperwork. You could tell it was a charter boat because it was clean. There were no snapshots or personal effects, it was as clean as a whistle. They reckoned they would stay on a month or so then sail up to Tahiti. It struck me at the time that they were military men – you know, clean, tidy short hair. They had the bearing of soldiers. They were pretty cool customers.'

MacLean's visit was vital to the *Ouvéa* crew. They needed witnesses who could, if necessary, testify later that the *Ouvéa* carried no suspicious equipment. It was for the same reason that they had insisted on inviting Hec Crene aboard during their second day at Parengarenga. When they set out from Noumea, of course, the boat had been crammed with the trappings of sabotage – plastic explosives and detonators hidden in the bilges; diving gear, oxygen cylinders, and the Zodiac dinghy and outboard motor purchased in London, stowed forward and aft. But under cover of darkness on that first night at Parengarenga they had carefully sanitized the *Ouvéa*, removing everything that they thought might incriminate them.

But the *Ouvéa*'s crew was not careful enough. They made one mistake at Opua which would provide the first link in the chain of clues once MacLean alerted Galbraith's detectives to his theory that the *Ouvéa* was connected with the bombing. The French agents, whether ignorant or simply forgetful, made the same mistake as the Turenges with the telephones. As in America, all New Zealand's long-distance internal calls as well as overseas calls are logged – a record is kept of the number dialled. On their second night at Opua, Velche went back to the post office call box and phoned Auckland. His call was to the Hyatt Hotel.

Alain and Sophie Turenge had moved out of the Travelodge as soon as their boss, Dormand, arrived. They checked into the Hyatt with him. They were seen chatting in the pastel pink and blue reception area on Wednesday June 25, just before the call came through from Opua. The *Ouvéa* crew members were

210

unaware that their immediate superior from Aspretto had arrived, expecting him later when the mission was nearing its climax, and were calling their back-up team. But Dormand had decided to travel to Auckland early and leave nothing to chance. He had already received reports that Maniguet was discontented with the rough sailing and that nerves were beginning to fray on board the boat. He ordered them to take their time – a necessary luxury to help establish their cover as vacationing sailors. Besides, the target was still more than a week's sailing away from New Zealand, and little preparation was needed for a task regarded as a walkover in Paris.

The *Ouvéa* left Opua early on Thursday June 27, so early that by 9.00 a.m. it was motoring into yet another quiet yacht haven, the sleepy Tutukaka inlet, two hours' sailing from Opua. The crew stayed on board for two hours before going ashore and walking up to the elongated bungalow which passes for a hotel and bar. In the deserted bar they asked Allan Stark for beer. On board the *Ouvéa* they had been used to the European brands shipped from France to New Caledonia, and had stocked up on Heineken. Now they wanted to taste a New Zealand brand. The barman brought out a selection of bottled lagers from which they were invited to choose. They drank slowly, stayed half an hour and left, returning to the *Ouvéa* where they remained until late the next morning, Friday. The hotel's owners, John and Glynis Daniels, saw them leave, lugging jerry cans to top up their fuel tanks. The harbourmaster was the last to see them, sitting on the deck of the yacht as its stern disappeared round the headland.

They were heading south again, to Whangarei, a short haul around yet another headland and thirty minutes' motoring up a bustling estuary to the very heart of a city. It had been nearly two weeks since they had last seen a town of any size, and now they would have an opportunity to let their hair down. There was still plenty of time before the climax of their mission – time to enjoy what Whangarei had to offer. For the Turenges, meanwhile, it was the end of their 'honeymoon'. Neither had acted out their cover story convincingly; they simply did not get on with each other. Dormand ordered them north. No more

211

duty-free shopping sprees for Sophie in downtown Auckland. No more nightclubbing for Alain in Queen Street. They were swopping the luxury of the city for the discomfort of the camper van. Cooped up in the van, their dislike for each other would grow more intense by the hour. But like it or not, there was work to be done. The strike force had assembled and now it must begin to deploy.

CHAPTER FOURTEEN
Deployment

WHANGAREI *Friday, June 28*

The Golden Palace Massage Parlour sits above a hairdresser's shop on Walton Street, midway between the Town Basin yacht marina and the Whangarei shopping centre. A used car lot and a patch of waste ground flank the timber-framed two-storey building. Up a steep, well-worn flight of stairs a shabby door opens into a deliberately darkened reception area. On the small front desk a cash register and credit card facility waits for customers. The charges are displayed on a handwritten poster. A half-hour's straight sauna and massage is forty New Zealand dollars for men – it is half price for women – but there are extras like saunas, hot spa baths and video movies. Tea, coffee or fruit juice is free, alcohol available at an extra cost. In Whangarei's Yellow Pages the parlour boasts a special welcome: 'There are no strangers, only friends who haven't met.'

The early caller is likely to catch the staff at 11.30 a.m. preparing for the busy day ahead. The masseurs are scrubbing down the jacuzzis, sofa cushions are being punched back into shape and video films are being rewound. The parlour closes again at 3.00 p.m. and opens for the evening trade three hours later. Behind the counter is a plump blonde in a black chiffon dress, on the wall a cheap mirror image of Marilyn Monroe. The woman, Lynette MacDonald, has time to cast an eye over strangers climbing the stairs before deciding whether an enthusiastic greeting or a suspicious growl is in order. She has fond memories of the French sailors who made a beeline for her parlour when they arrived. 'I wish we had more customers like those sailors. They were well behaved and very polite.'

The *Ouvéa* had first tied up at the boat hoist near the harbourmaster's office before moving across the Hatea river to

213

moorings by the road bridge which connects Quay Street with Riverside Drive. There were few boats there, apart from those of local residents, but one was the home of Simon Langer, a young, astute yachtsman who works in a local chandler's to support his love of the sea. He had greeted the *Ouvéa* on its arrival and chatted briefly to the Frenchmen.

'We get a lot of yachties here. Usually the Americans, the Germans or the French have plenty of bucks. The average New Zealand yachtie hasn't got a penny because he spends it all on his boat. You can tell the tourists as soon as they arrive. They hire expensive cars and go up town every night. The *Ouvéa* crew were nice guys, although only one spoke English.'

They had moored the yacht in mid-afternoon on Friday June 28 and immediately set off into town. They walked up Walton Street, past the closed massage parlour, and resolved to visit it that night. As they crossed into Cameron Street, nearing the town centre, the four-man crew spotted a Vietnamese restaurant in a sidestreet. The Shaolin offered oriental cuisine influenced by France's long (and eventually disastrous) colonial involvement in Indo-China. They made a mental note of that, too. In Cameron Street, Velche spotted the Strand shopping arcade and a bright, neon-lit shoe shop called the Athletic Attic. Maniguet was holding the cash but it was burning holes in the three divers' pockets. They wanted to spend.

Velche and Berthelo had already chosen the shoes they wanted when they walked into Kevin and Monica Johnson's shop – New Balance leather running shoes, imported from Canada and the most expensive in stock. They both wanted a pair. The shop was not busy so Kevin Johnson took his time with the French customers.

'They came in about four fifteen p.m. and said they liked the New Balance 700s which cost a hundred and thirty dollars. We only had the size eight and a half to fit the short guy, Berthelo, so they asked where else they might find a similar brand. I sent them across the road to Hannah's shoe shop but they didn't have any. About four forty p.m. they came back and bought the pair for the short guy. Velche had heaps of money in his wallet and he paid the bill. They asked for a receipt, which was strange

214

for tourists, and I told him that I could get the pair of shoes in his size within two or three days. Velche told me not to bother because they might be leaving before then.'

As the four men circled back towards the *Ouvéa*, they stopped for their first sit-down meal since leaving Norfolk Island. After drinking in a bar and befriending two women, the group – now six strong – chose a fast-food house on James Street, an ersatz pizzeria painted in the red, white and green of the Italian flag, with chintz tablecloths and empty raffia-covered Chianti bottles. It is owned by Reva Meredith, who turns out remarkably tasty de luxe and even Polynesian versions of the pizza. She also keeps a visitors' book behind the counter for Whangarei's visiting tourists and sailors. Among the casual references to her food, one entry stands out. It is dated June 28, 1985. At the top of the page the word *Ouvéa* appears, heavily overwritten to make it look prominent on the page. It refers to the yacht's port of embarkation, Noumea.

It was obviously the idea of the irrepressible Dr Maniguet to fill an entire page of the book with boastful references to their narrow escapes on the ocean. Maniguet retold the story of their 'heroic' voyage, embellishing his tale as usual to impress the two female guests. One was a hairdresser called Carole, who ironically turned out to be the wife of a Whangarei police officer. She was to see members of the *Ouvéa* crew again during their stay, though the detectives who investigated her connection insist it was 'a simple, innocent contact'. News of the *Ouvéa*'s brush with disaster at Parengarenga had already travelled before them to Whangarei on the North Island's bush telegraph, and they found little difficulty in cashing in on their fame now in the search for female companionship. The fact that they were French (and there were still some women in Whangarei who believed that that gave them a romantic edge over the competition) helped enormously.

Having regaled Carole and the other woman, one of her employees, with his exploits, the courageous, buccaneering Maniguet filled eight lines with adequate English. 'For a sailing initiation, the Tasman Sea was a good one ... ParengaRenga [sic] also with a 185cm boat and 100cm water depth [Maniguet here refers to the beam and draught] the main interesting lesson is that a 40 horsepower engine on a sail ship is very, very useful, very convenient, very sufficient and in fact why to get a mast???' He signed his entry 'Xavier Maniguet', adding in brackets 'not the skipper, of course'.

His bravado must have upset the other four men around the table. Velche, in an obvious attempt to deflate the braggart and perhaps curry favour himself with the two women, added: 'Of course. Xavier isn't a true yachtsman. Voilà France (Carol).' To emphasize his importance he signed it 'The skipper, Raymond'.

It was either Audrenc or Berthelo who added the final sentence. Not to be outdone by their English-speaking companions, one added a little mystery and asked Maniguet to translate. 'Perhaps there is something else in New Zealand??' Underneath, the author sketched a puzzling doodle. It shows what looks like a head and shoulders inside a television screen. To one side a clumsy matchstick man is lying down with his head in his hands, watching. His field of view is indicated by two straight lines, one to the top of the screen, the other to a point well below it. At the end of the lower line is a small triangular object with several dots rising from it.

There has been endless speculation as to the meaning of the sketch and nothing is certain. But one possible explanation is that Greenpeace, with its high public profile, is on television and it is the DGSE's undercover agents who are looking on. Whether the object underneath is a bomb or not should be left to the imagination.

The *Ouvéa* crew spent that night on the boat. They had tried to get rooms at the Grand Establishment hotel, but it was fully booked for the weekend.

WHANGAREI *Saturday, June 29*

They were up bright and early. At 9.40 a.m., after breakfast on board, all four men walked into the Avis car hire office near the dock. The general manager, Dave Cochrane, is a shrewd, sardonic man from Invercargill in the deep south of New Zealand where the weather is less kind than in Whangarei. Maniguet and Velche did the talking as usual. They asked for

216

a large car, possibly an estate car, for a day or two. They were not sure how long they would be staying. Cochrane explained that he had not got an estate car available but would reserve the next one to be returned. They got a Ford Telstar saloon instead, registration number LX 2824, and asked to be charged for their mileage as they did not expect to travel far. It was hired in Velche's name and he gave his address as 34, Place de la République, Bayonne, France. His false driving licence number was 25341 B and his date of birth July 10, 1950. (It had not yet been decided by Dormand precisely when the explosives would be planted, so it was no more than coincidence that Velche's assumed birthday was the same day as the bombing.) All three of his companions had their names added to the hire forms to enable them to drive the vehicle and, interestingly, Velche insisted on the optional personal accident insurance. It only cost two dollars a day, but did he really intend claiming if an accident befell them?

'Maniguet appeared to be the money man. He had a wad of notes half an inch thick. I noticed there was a distinct interrelationship between three of them, much like military people with one man in charge,' Cochrane later told the police. 'It was Velche who was obviously the boss and the others deferred to him. Maniguet was very matter of fact and didn't seem to fit into the pecking order. I didn't believe them when they said they were on holiday. I could tell because we look to see if customers are on business. If they are salesmen or something like that we try to find out by chatting to them, because obviously we would like to get all their company's business rather than the one passing hire. I certainly knew they weren't yachties. People who sail in here usually want to know all sorts of things – where to go, where to eat, where the action is. They want to be told what to do, where to go for a night out. They want to talk after days on a boat. But not these Frenchmen. It was strictly business with them – sign, seal and deliver.

'We tried to tap them a wee bit about what they were doing but they didn't give anything away. They didn't even attempt to chat up the rather nice young girls we have working here – most do. That was definitely unusual. Real yachties are always friendly when they come ashore and want to get to know people as quickly as possible.'

The *Ouvéa* crew continued to enjoy the weekend of leisure. That Saturday, June 29, having picked up their hire car, they made a short call to Dormand at the Hyatt Hotel in Auckland to announce their arrival. They explained that as yet they had no motel rooms booked and therefore no obvious telephone contact point. Dormand told them to call again when they had checked in to a motel, adding that their back-up team was moving north to meet them. There was still no hurry. The *Rainbow Warrior* was more than a week away and until the day of its destruction drew near Dormand did not want to risk his agents' being discovered in possession of incriminating evidence. The bags they had smuggled into New Zealand and hidden would have to remain where they were for a while. In the meantime they could stay in Whangarei and have fun.

Alain and Sophie Turenge had just checked out of the Hyatt on the morning of June 29. Their movements for the next two nights are unknown but on Monday, July 1, they arrived at Parakai on the west coast of North Island, just forty miles from Auckland. They had decided on a leisurely path north. Meandering off the main road to Whangarei, they chanced upon the Hinemoa Hotel at Parakai and decided to stay there. It was perfectly placed on a horn of land, with the Kaipara river on one side and the forested Pacific shore on the other. Though they did not know it at the time, another irony would strike them and their inquisitors – the hotel is part-owned by New Zealand's prime minister, David Lange.

Dormand had also checked out of the Hyatt. Driving a hired Holden station wagon, he had motored north to disappear for three days. Police still know little about his movements other than a brief overnight stay at Paihia, a few miles north of Opua, where the *Ouvéa* had docked to clear customs. It is possible that everyone was simply enjoying a few days off. Maniguet, meanwhile, flew to the South Island, where he pursued his two passions with varied success. In Christchurch the doctor attempted to hire an aircraft and fly it over the glaciers of the South Island's formidable mountain ranges. He was refused a permit on the grounds that it was too dangerous and too cold. He did manage to seduce the wife of an opossum trapper but had to escape through a window when the husband returned unexpectedly.

Dormand was less obsessed with sexual pursuit. Instead, he used Paihia as a base to check up on his team of divers forty minutes' drive to the south in Whangarei. They were disciplined but difficult – men who worked hard and played hard. There was also a communication problem: they still had not found a base with a telephone. He was also scouting out the east coast for an important rendezvous yet to be chosen.

WHANGAREI *Monday, July 1*

Raymond Velche had numerous logistical problems on his mind that day. He and his friends were tired of their bunks but they were still not properly prepared for the task ahead. Velche called again at Avis and asked Cochrane to extend the hire period of his Ford Telstar. Cochrane recalls: 'I told him there was an estate car available now, but he said he didn't need it just yet. He was expecting some equipment to arrive and asked if he could have one at the end of the week. He said they intended going further afield in the Telstar and asked for the hire agreement to be amended so that they would not be charged for mileage.'

The *Ouvéa* crew's next stop was Cater Marine, the chandlery where young Simon Langer worked when he was not on his boat. 'All three of them came in and looked around. They didn't look like real yachties, apart from Velche. He wore a battered pair of Docksiders, the sort of shoes worn by sailors who know their business. They made a beeline for the glass cabinet where we keep the expensive electrical stuff, near the counter.'

Velche was quite specific about his needs. Inside the glass case was a small plastic box with a digital display. It was a piece of equipment many ocean yachtsmen would regard as invaluable, a Harrier 6 log-speed timer made by Brooks and Gatehouse of England. It is linked to the satellite navigation equipment on board a boat and gives a constantly changing read-out of speed and course. In effect it saves long and tedious calculations, helping the helmsman to stay on course and estimate his time of arrival at the next port of call. It is, in fact, little more than a waterproof timing device with its own built-in battery. With minor modifications, someone with elementary knowledge of electronics and microcircuitry could easily convert it into a more sinister tool. It can be programmed to count in minutes and seconds up to a hundred hours. At any moment during its programmed time, the Harrier 6 can complete an electrical circuit, activating a switch on a device such as a household appliance, a lighting system – or even a bomb.

'We had one on board the *Ouvéa* but it was stolen from our car,' Velche explained to Langer who raised a quizzical eyebrow before reaching for the catalogue. He was surprised the log-speed timer had been stolen from their car, simply because there was no reason to take it off the boat; it normally stood on a shelf in the cabin which could be securely locked. Langer says: 'We all thought it was strange because we couldn't understand why they would go to the trouble of taking it off the boat. But we didn't bother saying anything at the time, because who knows why people do strange things?' When Langer quoted the price of the timer at $NZ700, all three men baulked. They conferred in French and then asked if it was possible to buy an electrical lead that would bypass the Harrier 6 facility and connect the other components of the satellite navigation equipment. 'It's a perfectly acceptable procedure,' Langer explained. 'But we couldn't make the lead on the premises. I had to ask Tutukaka Coastal Electrics to do it for us. I told them I'd give them a shout when it was ready – a few days at the most.'

The crew continued to look around the chandlery and ask Langer questions. 'They wanted to know what New Zealand's regulations were for lighting dinghies at night. I told them they just needed an all-round white light so that they could be seen in the water, and they chose the cheapest rubber torch – which was adequate but hardly the right thing. Then one of Velche's companions asked for a jacket. He liked the luminous blue Gulfstar jacket. It's an all-weather coat which sells for a hundred and five dollars. The only other thing they bought was a sea anchor for the Zodiac, which, they said, they wanted so they could do some fishing.' The sea anchor was little more than a drogue which can be thrown over the side in any depth of water and does not need to strike into the seabed to hold a boat steady. It fills like an empty bucket and keeps lightweight craft such as inflatables relatively stationary. The crew knew precisely what they were looking for: a metal anchor would be too heavy for the Zodiac and might rupture its skin.

Later that day, Velche revisited the Athletic Attic shoe shop. He double-parked his hire car outside and explained that there had been a change of plans. He and his friends would be staying a week and he wanted to order the pair of size nine or nine and a half shoes. 'He also wanted the New Balance shorts and singlet which we stock – the large size,' said Kevin Johnson.

Velche's final port of call was the Grand Establishment motel where, he discovered, there were rooms available at last, but for one night only. Velche checked into Number 48, which was memorable only for the presence of a double bed and a Renoir print. After so many cramped nights in the *Ouvéa*'s bunks it must have seemed like luxury. Berthelo booked into a single room nearby and, following the pecking order of military seniority, Audrenc drew the short straw and spent the night on watch aboard the boat.

WHANGAREI *Tuesday, July 2*

Velche was out shopping again. On Cameron Street, between the massage parlour and the Shaolin restaurant, he had spotted a fishing tackle shop, Leigh Distributors, and was greeted by the owner, Deyal MacKenzie. Again Velche knew precisely what he was looking for. He asked for a grappling iron, some 6mm rope and a tool for splicing. He told the shopkeeper that he wanted the grappling hook to use as an anchor for his dinghy. Not surprisingly, MacKenzie pointed out that his choice was unsuitable: what he needed was a sea anchor. Velche did not say he had already purchased one the previous day from Cater Marine. He merely repeated his story that he and his colleagues wished to fish in Whangarei Harbour and insisted upon the hook. Velche bought thirteen yards of rope and asked for a chart of Norfolk Island, which MacKenzie did not stock.

The crew had also made two pleasing discoveries. One was Motel Six, a short drive from the Town Basin but nicely placed on the outskirts of Whangarei by the side of the road going north to Opua, Paihia, and Parengarenga. It was quiet, it had plenty of rooms and they could stay as long as they liked. Unit 1A had its own kitchen and two bedrooms, both with a camp bed and sofa bed in case of extra guests. The owners, Barry and Joan George, were friendly, co-operative and left their guests in peace. The second discovery was good food and a beautiful French-speaking girl to cook it for them. The crew had been active in the pursuit of the opposite sex. Police reports would later record that they picked up women indiscriminately in bars, cafés and restaurants. They chalked up some successes, though the cook, Sandrine Skaya, was too clever for them. She took the precaution of bringing two inquisitive boys along when she was invited to inspect the *Ouvéa*. She also told her American boyfriend to keep an eye open.

The crew had begun treating the Shaolin restaurant as a home from home in Whangarei. Sandrine was managing it in the absence of her aunt, Sonya Skaya, who was visiting friends in Perth, Australia. The Skayas had fled war-torn Vietnam in 1965 and attempted to settle in Spain, North Africa, Greece and France before returning to the Pacific via New Caledonia. They had opened the restaurant and adopted the two boys, Truc and Thuy, who had escaped the Communist takeover in a boat-load of refugees. Perhaps it was because Sandrine was both beautiful and fluent in French that the *Ouvéa* crew visited so regularly. The restaurant sits at the back of an alley, but a garish hand-painted sign announces to passers-by that it is a 'martial arts diner'. This does not mean that karate or kung-fu is served with the noodles. The reference is based on an assumption that it might attract passing trade among the fighting cognoscenti. Indeed, inside all is peace and harmony – except for the cheap lacquered wood and flock wallpaper.

Velche and company were welcome to while away the hours on the raised dais above the tables which accommodated a sofa and a television set. Sandrine found them an entertaining change from the usual customers and they seemed to have plenty of money to spend on good food cooked in coconut oil. But the relaxed atmosphere did not last.

AUCKLAND *Thursday, July 4*

Xavier Maniguet was up to his old tricks again. Oblivious of the job in hand, he was still pursuing his chief interest. Undeterred by his narrow escape from the opossum hunter's bed – reputedly seconds before the cuckolded husband loaded a cartridge of buckshot in both barrels of his twelve-bore shotgun – he was seducing another man's wife. Maniguet was back in Auckland and seemed in little hurry to return north to Whangarei. He had flown back from the South Island, arriving at Mangere airport shortly before 6.00 p.m. on Thursday July 4. He had walked to the Avis desk in the arrivals lounge and rented the most expensive car they had left, a sporty red Colt Sygma. Then he drove into the city and checked into a room at the Sheraton Hotel. Detectives investigating the case later would marvel at his ability to find a bedmate at a moment's notice, though his success may have been due to his simple tastes and the fact that he just was not the fussy type. He so excited one woman in a bar that she took him to the Regent Hotel and picked up the bill. Later when the newly acquainted couple left the hotel they bumped into her cousin. Maniguet was introduced and the threesome went for a drink. The doctor had already agreed to another date with his latest conquest, but she was soon abandoned as the cousin succumbed to his charms. In a commendable act of sensitivity, detectives would later allow the first victim to tear up her statement describing their brief encounter and write another to avoid upsetting her husband. Her second testimony described only an innocent and casual meeting with Maniguet in the street which ended after a brief chat.

Though few might admire Maniguet's style, his stamina has to be conceded. The next day, Friday July 5, he returned to Whangarei and checked in at Motel Six with the *Ouvéa* crew. Maniguet's reappearance shattered the holiday atmosphere. Dormand had also returned to Auckland and checked back into the Hyatt. In between Maniguet's diverting romps, the two had met for a talk. It had been announced that the *Rainbow Warrior*

223

would dock within three days, and Maniguet was dispatched north to warn the *Ouvéa* crew to prepare.

The Turenges had also vacated their blissful room at the Hinemoa Hotel in Parakai and checked into another. That Friday morning they had arrived at the Beachcomber motel at Paihia in the Bay of Isles, just north of Whangarei. The owner, Jill Couch, remembers them well. They occupied Number 12, a self-contained second-floor studio with a double bed and a balcony overlooking the bay. They ordered bacon and eggs for breakfast. Only one side of the bed appeared to have been used when the maid cleaned up each morning, and the sofa pillows were crumpled – strange behaviour indeed for a honeymoon couple.

CHAPTER FIFTEEN

Execution

WHANGAREI *Saturday, July 6*

There was a sudden burst of activity in Unit 1A at Motel Six. Shortly before breakfast Raymond Velche made a long-distance telephone call to Auckland. It was 7.45 a.m. and the number he asked Barry George to get for him was 797220. Dormand, in his room at the Hyatt, picked up the telephone. The conversation was short and, to anyone who might have eavesdropped over a crossed line, completely innocent. An hour later the telephone in Unit 1A rang and Velche answered. It was Alain Turenge calling from Studio 12 at Paihia, forty-five miles to the north. He could not talk over the telephone. They would have to meet, preferably somewhere so far divorced from their present locations that no one would notice the French-speaking occupants of two vehicles drawn up by the side of the road. Dormand and the radio news bulletins had confirmed that the *Rainbow Warrior* would dock to a tumultuous welcome the next day. It was time to collect the gear they had hidden on arrival in New Zealand and begin the final phase of their mission.

Until now, it has been assumed by the police and the press that the first meeting in New Zealand between the Turenges and the *Ouvéa* crew took place that morning at Motel Six. This was because Liz McConnell, a Maori cleaner at the motel, told detectives that she came on duty at 9.00 a.m. and saw a Newman's camper van parked outside the *Ouvéa* crew's unit. She claimed that she poked her head around the door and saw five or six people, including a woman. She identified two of them as the Turenge couple arrested by the police. At the time it seemed a formidable piece of evidence, for it meant that detectives were able to prove contact between the Turenges and the *Ouvéa* crew. But that sighting must now be considered suspect. When McConnell was interviewed later by the Insight team, her story was so dramatically flawed that it could only be the result of an overactive imagination. She described a blue and white camper van. 'I didn't tell the police this because they would not believe me, but I saw the dinghy inside the van, on the floor.' Further questioning elicited a detailed description of the vehicle she had seen that morning. 'It was just a van, with windows in the side. There was nothing in the back, no seats or anything, just a floor and the dinghy.' What she was describing was not a camper van but an ordinary cargo van, for camper vans are fitted out with bench seats, a folding table, a cooker and a washbasin, with precious little floor space and certainly no room to take the half-inflated dinghy with an outboard motor. That in itself was a good reason to suspect McConnell's story, but there is another. The call from the Turenges in Paihia came through at around 8.30 a.m. They were still there fifteen minutes later. There was no time to drive forty-five miles to Motel Six in Whangarei in time for McConnell's alleged sighting shortly after 9.00 a.m. Besides, Velche, Berthelo and Audrenc were not there.

Velche and his colleagues left the motel at 9.00, drove the Telstar down to the Avis office and asked Dave Cochrane to exchange it. 'He said he wanted the station wagon now because their equipment was due to arrive,' says Cochrane. 'We had an ice blue Holden Commodore so they swopped the Telstar for it. There was a bit of a panic at first because they couldn't raise enough New Zealand dollars to meet the deposit. Maniguet asked if we would accept French francs and he produced a wad. I didn't know the exact exchange rate but I accepted fifteen hundred. He still had the Sygma and I asked if he could return it. We were getting low on cars. Another reason was that I was taking my family away for the weekend and I quite like the Sygma. But he wouldn't part with it. He said he needed it.'

Indeed he did. When the *Ouvéa* crew returned to the motel, Maniguet called Dormand in Auckland to inform him of their intentions. They had successfully hired the estate car and Maniguet himself was due to rendezvous with the Turenges to discuss the two teams' movements in the course of the next few days. The meeting took place around lunchtime that day in a lay-by off Route 12 in the mountains.

The details worked out at that meeting were carried back to Whangarei by Maniguet. The Turenges returned to Paihia for one more night. The plan was quite simple. The Turenges would meet Velche on the night of July 7 and they would travel together to the secret location where the explosives, diving gear, the Zodiac and the outboard motor had been hidden. They would retrieve the Zodiac first, inflate it and then use it to retrieve the heavier gear and return south. The Turenges would take charge of the inflatable, the engine, and the diving equipment. Packed in waterproof bags it would be easily stowed on the camper van. The *Ouvéa* crew members could not risk attracting attention to themselves by suddenly appearing in Whangarei with recognizable bags containing expensive equipment which they had not brought into New Zealand or registered with customs. They would, however, take charge of the explosives and detonators so that they could begin assembling their charges.

Berthelo and Audrenc now began to offload what little New Zealand cash they had left. Velche had not returned to the Athletic Attic to collect the New Balance shoes he had ordered, but his two non-English-speaking sidekicks called at midday. Kevin Johnson was upstairs eating his lunch and his wife, Monica, was serving in the shop. 'They came in and started buying T-shirts and sweat-shirts. It looked as if they were simply trying to get rid of all their cash, because when they discovered they had some change they went back and started to look for small, inexpensive items, like sweatbands and ear plugs, until all their dollars and cents were gone.'

They also booked a table at the Forum restaurant for the following Monday night. They said they had a special occasion to celebrate on Wednesday, July 10, but as they were sailing on the morning of Tuesday, July 9, and would be at sea, they wanted to hold the celebration on their last night ashore in Whangarei. They said it was Raymond Velche's birthday. But it was also the night they intended to bomb the *Rainbow Warrior*.

*

227

AUCKLAND *Sunday, July 7*

The *Rainbow Warrior* presented a dramatic face to the crowds packing the dockside along Quay Street. Other spectators had gathered in smaller groups at many vantage points along the shoreline of the Hauraki Gulf. In the numerous boat clubs on either side of the harbour, members packed the bars and watched from balconies and slipways as the twin-masted converted trawler sailed into Auckland Harbour, rust-streaked but still proudly displaying the bright rainbow-decked prow. A small armada of sail boats, motor launches, dinghies and speedboats jockeyed around the *Warrior* as she motored in towards her berth on Marsden Wharf.

It is hard to imagine why New Zealand should reserve such a greeting for the flagship of an organization that other countries variously regard as a nuisance, a hotbed of Soviet fifth columnists, a good cause to be supported with a small annual donation or just a bunch of do-gooders. In New Zealand at least, Greenpeace commands considerable public sympathy. In a country with all the geographic extremes of a carefully preserved landscape, a mild, often tropical climate and few natural resources, it is not surprising that conservation is highly regarded. New Zealanders even protest when local authorities rip out and burn the main natural hazard, a fast-disappearing poisonous weed. Industry is generally light, and hardly ever blights the landscape; agriculture rules, but only in harmony with its surroundings and a small, conservative population with deep-rooted – even old-fashioned – morals. From such a nation, Greenpeace can count on effective and friendly support.

It was the reason why a traditional Maori welcome was laid on at Marsden Wharf. It was a tumultuous greeting for a small converted trawler with fifteen anonymous crew members on board. Others, though, planned a different type of reception.

*

Trevor and Erna Rogers were still yawning when they went downstairs to open up their shop, the Highway Dairy, at 6.30 a.m. The store lies just outside Kaitaia on the main road north. Anyone travelling to the Aupori peninsula on Route One has to pass through the town, which is the biggest in a fifty-mile radius. The store opened at the crack of dawn seven days a week to catch the passing tourists and local workmen heading out of town. There is a brisk trade even at that time of day in milk, cigarettes and lunchbox snacks, and the Rogers are ambitious enough to grab any custom they can. 'We bought out the old owners for a hundred thousand dollars. That gives us a six-year lease to get our money back and make a decent profit. There are bad times coming in New Zealand and we want to make enough to set us up in Australia.'

Trevor was following his usual routine, opening the front door to go out and check that no one had attempted to break into or vandalize the cold store and stockroom, when he saw Alain and Sophie Turenge pull up in the camper van. He stared, shook his head, then stared again. Hitched to the back of the Toyota Hiace was a brand new Zodiac inflatable dinghy with a gleaming blue Yamaha outboard. It was perched at an acute angle, its prow chinning the rear door handles rather than sitting on a proper towing rig. 'It had its nose in the air. It had been jerry-rigged and tied to the door handles because those camper vans don't have tow bars. The hire companies hate people towing things in case of accidents or overworked engines. That's why I was surprised. The make of the dinghy surprised me, too. I've always wanted a Zodiac myself to go diving in – it's a top quality boat and you need that with the sort of rocks we have around here – but they are hard to find in New Zealand.

'Sophie Turenge walked up and asked me if there was a coffee shop anywhere nearby that was open at that time of the morning. She did all the talking, he just stood to one side. I told her nowhere was open yet so she walked around the shop and picked up a few things, a sachet of instant coffee and a large tub of yoghurt.

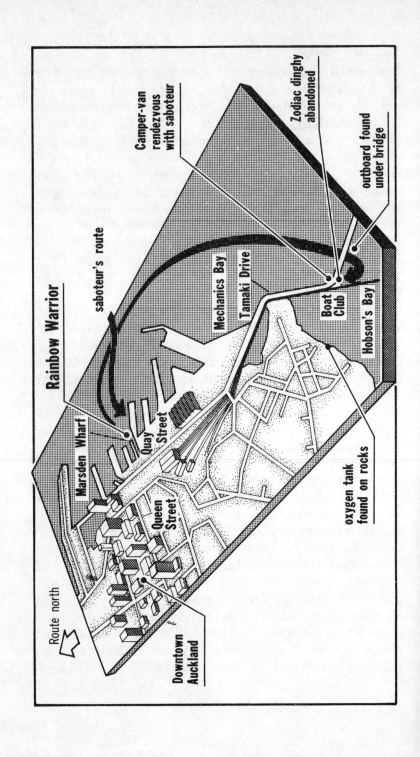

Rainbow Warrior

saboteur's route

Camper-van
rendezvous
with saboteur

Zodiac dinghy
abandoned

outboard found
under bridge

Marsden Wharf

Quay
Street

Mechanics Bay

Tamaki Drive

Boat
Club

Hobson's Bay

Queen
Street

oxygen tank
found on rocks

Route north

Downtown
Auckland

'He seemed like a hen-pecked husband, kept his mouth shut and sulked. They were both very heavily dressed against the cold and they looked very rough, as if they had been up all night long. He was pale and unshaven and they were both obviously very tired. She was a hard-looking woman, almost masculine, with a bony face, but that might just have been our impressions of them first thing in the morning because they did look as if they'd had a sleepless night. They didn't want to talk much and she spoke a few words to him in French or German. They weren't particularly friendly, either with us or each other. They paid their money, walked out to the van and drove off, heading south.'

When questioned by police officers two weeks later, the Rogers were unable to pinpoint the exact date of the Turenges' visit. They thought it was July 8 or 9 but could not be sure. After hours of deliberation with detectives they settled for July 9, which was then entered as a statement of fact in the evidence against the Turenges. (Later we shall explain why the Insight team has concluded that it was in fact July 8. We will show why the exact date is crucial – and how the police came to make a fundamental error. For now it is important to continue the sequence of events.)

AUCKLAND *Monday, July 8*

It had been raining hard all morning and the wind was high when the Turenges pulled up at the Newman's depot near Mangere airport at 11.55 a.m. Becky Hayter was on duty and recognized them immediately. The van's windscreen was shattered and Alain, the driver, explained what had happened. They had been driving on Route One between Whangarei and Auckland on Sunday when a stone was thrown up by a vehicle in front and hit the windscreen. It had happened in the Warkworth forest, a lush, hilly national park, famous for its thick vegetation and towering giant ferns. Certainly that road is littered with roadworks with long stretches of crushed grey rock awaiting a tarmac topping.

'They asked if we could repair the windscreen or give them a replacement van. They were anxious to be off, and it took a

231

little while before we realized we didn't have a windscreen available. So I arranged a new van for them. They were really quite pleasant. They got the same type, a Toyota Hiace. The number was LB 8945. I felt a little sorry for them and helped them swop their belongings over. They didn't have much, just a few items of food and some pieces of luggage.'

Becky Hayter is adamant that no bulky items were transferred. It meant that the Turenges had been able to rid themselves of the Zodiac and the outboard motor some time between 6.30 a.m. and midday that morning.

TOPUNI *Monday, July 8*

Logger Brendan Walton was working with a mate by the side of Route One, midway between Auckland and Whangarei, when they spotted the white Newman's camper van pull into the lay-by. It was 2.30 p.m. and the Turenges had had a leisurely hour and a half to cover the fifty miles from the Mangere depot. The van stood in the lay-by with its engine running for ten minutes or so then moved off, travelling north. The loggers' work was interrupted again at 2.50 p.m. when a grey Holden Commodore estate car turned into the muddy track. Two men inside were obviously looking for someone and they motored over to the spot where Walton was working. A small blond man in the passenger seat wound down his window and hailed the loggers. He did not know that Walton belonged to a religious sect called the Closed Brethren which restricts its members' contact with outsiders, so he asked if Walton or his mate had seen a camper van recently. Walton relaxed the Brethren's rules and responded. 'It just left, travelling north. If you hurry you can catch it,' he said. As the driver pushed his accelerator hard down, Walton gazed into the back of the estate car. There were two large bright blue bags, one bearing the name Zodiac. The other was lumpier and open; it seemed to contain something akin to an outboard motor.

Walton's curiosity might have ended there but for the driver's poor road sense. 'He didn't seem to understand our traffic regulations.' As they pulled out of the clearing they crossed into the right-hand lane, forcing a car coming up behind to overtake

232

on the inside. There was almost a nasty accident as the estate car accelerated hard out of trouble and Walton, for no particular reason except that he thought it might be useful, committed the registration number to memory and finger-painted it into the dirt on the side of his van. It was still there four days later when detectives called. Walton's foreman had informed the police of the incident after the *Rainbow Warrior* sinking and they walked over to the van to look for the now valuable graffiti. The rain had not washed it away. Clearly visible was the number of the Avis car rented to Velche – LR 8114. Later they identified his blond companion as the good doctor Maniguet.

In fact the Holden Commodore did catch the Toyota camper van, three miles further up the road. The Insight team established that the Turenges, realizing they must have missed their co-conspirators, stopped in another lay-by just short of a town called Kiawaka and waited. Velche caught up with them shortly after 3.00 p.m. and handed over the bagged Zodiac dinghy and the outboard motor.

WHANGAREI *Tuesday, July 9*

When Dave Cochrane arrived to open up the Avis office at 8.45 a.m. he found four Frenchmen, a Holden Commodore estate and Maniguet's Sygma waiting outside. They were leaving that morning, they said, and wished to settle their account. Few words were exchanged and by 9.00 a.m. all four were back on board the *Ouvéa*.

The *Ouvéa* crew had actually booked out of Motel Six the previous morning, July 8, but an hour or so later Maniguet had rushed back. There had been a change of plan, he explained, and they needed rooms for one more night. Unit 1A was still available and he gratefully accepted their old room, which they vacated at 8.30 a.m. on Tuesday. They had also called Lew Sabin, the customs man, to announce their intentions and request permission to leave.

It is easy to sail from New Zealand's shores without clearing the departure with the customs office. But it can cause problems. At a yacht's next port of call, immigration officials may be suspicious of passports that contain stamps authorizing entry to

233

a country but no sign of official approval for leaving. Such an omission might indicate people in a hurry to leave or anxious to avoid officialdom – and therefore indicate that they might have something to hide. The *Ouvéa* crew members knew they would need to call at Australian-controlled Norfolk Island on the voyage back to Noumea in New Caledonia, and they wanted no hitches in that plan.

Sabin boarded the *Ouvéa* just after 9.00 a.m. 'They had an old red dinghy on board but nothing else of note. I was on board for about thirty minutes. I took the immigration tickets out of their passports and that was it. They said they were returning to Noumea. I was aware of Frank MacLean's suspicions and it did strike me that there were four guys on the boat but no women. But they just seemed like four men who had come for a few weeks' sailing, maybe some skiing, and to play around. They waved me off the boat, untied it and motored out down the estuary. That was the last we saw of them.'

AUCKLAND *Tuesday, July 9*

At the Hyatt Hotel, the man calling himself Dormand could afford to relax. The *Ouvéa* was at sea and beyond detection, the Turenges had just checked into prime minister Lange's Hinemoa Hotel at Parakai again. Everything was set and he could now prepare his own departure from New Zealand. The Turenges were already booked on an Air New Zealand flight from Wellington to London via Los Angeles on July 23 – thirteen days after the date set for the destruction of the target. He himself would stay an extra two weeks, travelling to the South Island at a leisurely pace before boarding a jet at Christchurch for Sydney and on to Singapore and Paris. It was perfect. Immediately after the bombs were detonated the police would be ordering vigilance at all air and sea ports in the search for anyone remotely suspicious. It paid not to take chances or to rush their departure. Staying in New Zealand the extra days would only strengthen their cover stories of innocent honeymooners or holidaymakers. The *Ouvéa* was now out of the clutches of the police, officially outside territorial waters. Frankly, Dormand had not the slightest doubt that the operation

234

would be a resounding success. Steps had been taken to ensure that little forensic evidence would be found and none that could be attributed to France.

He felt confident enough to set his own embarkation plans in train. Dormand called the Horizon rental office in Auckland to confirm his booking: a Toyota Hiace camper van similar to that used by the Turenges. 'I want it today and I will leave it at your office in Christchurch on July 23,' he told the manager, Alan Struthers. In the event, Dormand delivered it on July 20 and flew out on July 23. There is a reason why both Dormand and the Turenges had chosen July 23 as their departure date. It was also the day the *Rainbow Warrior* was due to depart for Moruroa, and set the limit to the time they had to complete their mission if, for any reason, the first attempt to sink the *Warrior* failed.

AUCKLAND *Wednesday, July 10*

Dormand checked out of the Hyatt that morning shortly before lunch, stowed his luggage in the camper van and was not seen again until the next day. He was then 300 miles south, across the water, disembarking from the ferry that had taken him from the capital, Wellington, to Picton on the South Island. Alain and Sophie Turenge had booked out of Parakai's Hinemoa Hotel on the morning of the 10th and were not seen again until their encounter with 'Peter the fisherman' in Tamaki Drive, just two hours before the bombs exploded under the *Rainbow Warrior*. The *Ouvéa* was at sea on the morning of the 10th, but where precisely?

The movements of three other people that day would later exercise the minds of Superintendent Galbraith's detectives. One was François Régis Verlon, the young Frenchman who walked on to the *Rainbow Warrior* that night posing as a Greenpeace sympathizer. He chatted briefly and happily to members of the crew. One party member was Rien Achterburg, a Dutchman who worked in the Auckland office of Greenpeace. He was initially suspicious of the young visitor, though he did not know why. Dismissing the reaction as simple paranoia he introduced Verlon to Chris Robinson, the Australian who would be

235

skippering the ketch *Vega* in the Moruroa flotilla. Verlon, fresh-faced and in his early twenties, began the conversation with an offer to find friends in Tahiti who might help the campaign. It was an offer that both Achterburg and Robinson grabbed with both hands: they needed practical support and pushed him further. But Verlon's initial enthusiasm began to evaporate under pressure. His pronouncements suddenly became very vague and Robinson grew suspicious. Eventually both men were called to the skippers' meeting chaired by Steve Sawyer, the campaign co-ordinator, and Verlon was asked to leave.

That night Verlon flew out of Auckland, bound for Tahiti. His plane took off fifteen minutes before the blasts ripped into the *Warrior*'s hull. Verlon was interviewed at the request of Auckland detectives when he landed in Tahiti – by French police who naturally reported back to Auckland that the man could be safely eliminated from their inquiries. All efforts to trace Verlon since have failed and he appears to have disappeared completely. But one name that did crop up during further police inquiries was François Régis Verlet. He is a Singapore-based computer systems technician, and the son of a Frenchman who manages a company serving the oil industry in Abu Dhabi. That company once employed a doctor called Xavier Maniguet. Verlet flew out of Singapore's Changi airport on April 14, apparently to spend eleven weeks travelling the Pacific en route to Tahiti. It struck Auckland detectives as interesting that his departure was just a week before Cabon arrived in New Zealand, although he did not enter Auckland until two days before the bombing, and his eventual destination was the same as hers – Tahiti. Auckland police have so far failed to discover whether the links are anything more than coincidence.

They have also failed to find any connection with two other French nationals who were visiting Auckland at the time. They flew into Mangere airport on July 7, the day before Verlon/Verlet arrived. They had travelled from French Tahiti and appeared to follow a route south (similar to Dormand's) after the bombing. They too crossed to Picton on the ferry on July

11 and stayed at a ski resort until July 26 before flying out of New Zealand, three days after Dormand. All three remain the subject of continuing police inquiries, though it is important to stress that detectives still have an open mind about the latter two. After all, the route they took is popular with many tourists. 'They could well turn out to be innocent travellers. We have no reason to connect them with the bombing other than the fact that they were in the right place at the right time,' said a senior detective. 'We probably will never know. We have asked the French to confirm their passport details to check if they are genuine or false. Naturally we don't expect a reply we can trust.'

PART FOUR

The blasts backfire

CHAPTER SIXTEEN

Whodunit?

In the absence of a confession or a culprit caught red-handed, a successful police investigation requires three vital elements. The methodical accumulation of material evidence and corroborated facts, no matter how minor they might at first seem to be. Next, the ability to assemble those facts into a chronological reconstruction of events and cross-check additional information as it is uncovered. Finally, the detective's personal skills at analysing the evidence in order to construct the most rational theory that can be used as a framework on which to base further inquiries and complete the case. It is equally important to use that accumulated information to test the stories of suspects for obvious flaws. The end result is, with luck, an indication of *who* did *what, where, when* and *why*.

During their investigation, Auckland detectives accumulated 400 statements, many of them eye witness accounts covering the movements of the Turenges and the *Ouvéa* crew. They collected more than 1,000 exhibits – such as unidentified steel debris from the dock at Marsden Wharf, restaurant bills and motel receipts. They travelled around the globe, sending teams to Paris, London, Singapore, Sydney, Tahiti, Tonga, New Caledonia and Norfolk Island. It was the most exhaustive and ambitious investigation ever undertaken in New Zealand, with, at its peak, seventy detectives culled from every squad room in New Zealand working day and night. It cost over one million pounds in travel, administration and manpower. But Galbraith – who after the trial went on extended leave with other senior officers to recuperate from the stress of nearly six months' unremitting endeavour – still could not answer the crucial questions: *who* planted the bombs, *what* were the explosive devices used, *where* did the bombers hide the paraphernalia of sabotage when they entered New Zealand, *when* was the decision taken to sink the ship and *why?* Nine months after the bombing, those questions remained in the realm of speculation.

Perhaps only a dozen people know the answers: the *Ouvéa* crew has disappeared from the face of the earth, the Turenges are tightlipped still, and Dormand the team leader has been reassigned to other covert duties, leaving only the political and military hierarchy in Paris and they certainly are not talking. But there are vital indications which throw new light on the questions that remain.

Though the 'third team' theory remains a possibility, it is remote indeed. France, like Britain or New Zealand, is a great sailing nation with a history and tradition of excellence in sport and exploration at sea. Such interest is typified by the likes of yachtsman Eric Tabarle, by the myriad French yachts that line up in any great sailing adventure, transatlantic or round-the-world race. A visit to the Breton coast reveals a shoreline inundated with marinas, dotted with small boatyards. The western coast of Europe, the Mediterranean and Caribbean seas and both the Atlantic and Pacific oceans are all playgrounds for yachts flying the tricolour.

The French secret services have no shortage of highly competent sailors with first-hand knowledge of even the most distant backwater of the world. It has been suggested, even accepted in many quarters, that the *Ouvéa* crew was under orders simply to deliver the equipment to sink the *Rainbow Warrior*. That they were ordered to maintain a high profile in the north of New Zealand while the real bombers beavered away in Auckland, thus trampling the trail detectives might follow after the event. The truth is, any number of yachtsmen could have been culled from the DGSE's ranks of agents and sleepers around the world to perform that particular role.

Instead, three of Aspretto's most senior divers, two of whom had almost no yachting experience, were deployed to the south Pacific. It would have been an unnecessary expense and, given the weather, a stupid risk to send them, even with a doctor well versed in the health hazards of diving, unless they were required to carry out a specific task worthy of their underwater skills. Men trained to the highest degree in diving techniques, bomb

242

manufacture and ship sabotage, equipped with false passports and an apparently limitless expense account, are not sent halfway round the world to do the job of messenger boys. They were hand-picked professionals, chosen by the man who was the architect of the operation commissioned by his superiors, a man who knew not only how the order should be prosecuted but also knew, in person, the type of people he would need. Alain Mafart was an obvious choice as a second-in-command in New Zealand. He was already second-in-command to Lieutenant-Colonel Louis-Pierre Dillais, head of the Aspretto diving school, who had been chosen to pick the team and lead the attack on Greenpeace. Dillais knew personally the best men to carry out the bombing. He worked with them most days of the week in Corsica during the long, lean training periods between operational orders. Chief Petty Officer Roland Verge, alias Raymond Velche, was one of his most senior non-commissioned officers with fifteen years' military service and eleven with the DGSE at Aspretto. Petty Officer Jean-Michel Bartelo, alias Jean-Michel Berthelo, had ten years service with the armed forces, and four with the Action Division. Gerald Andries, alias Eric Audrenc, had been a military diver for ten years too, and six years with the DGSE.

In most armed services, it is the senior non-commissioned officers who provide the technical or operational skills. They are the best-trained men, simply because they tend to remain longer in their specialist roles than officers who progress up a regimented career ladder which takes them through various positions designed to test their talents for leadership, administration, man-management and tactical or technical flair. The non-commissioned officers prove the globally accepted adage that they comprise 'the backbone of an army'. Officers give orders; men like Verge, Andries and Bartelo carry them out – but they most certainly do not run errands.

But perhaps the most telling indication of the *Ouvéa* crew's purpose in New Zealand is the one fact which persuaded most people that the crew *did not* plant the explosive devices. They sailed from New Zealand at 9.15 a.m. on July 9, 1985, precisely thirty-eight hours and thirty minutes *before* the bombs exploded.

It was a remarkably good alibi. How could they bomb a boat

in a country they had left thirty-six hours earlier? But the alibi was also highly suspicious. Of all the French agents operating in New Zealand, the *Ouvéa* crew members were the only ones to weigh anchor and leave before the bombing. The Turenges and Dormand continued with their cover stories after July 10 following the pre-set plan to leave casually. If the *Ouvéa* crew really was a back-up team then its presence would have been required throughout the operation and beyond. Yet they left with indecent haste, made a great show of their departure by throwing a party at the restaurant, and made a fuss of Lew Sabin, the customs man who cleared them to leave New Zealand. They displayed all the signs of men who wanted people to notice not only that they were leaving, but precisely what time they would set sail. The *Ouvéa* crew *needed* an alibi.

They arrived in Norfolk Island late on July 13. The assumption was that the *Ouvéa* had made remarkably good time – so good that the crew could not possibly have sneaked back down the coast, hove to off Auckland and waited until darkness on the 10th before planting the bombs and sailing back to Norfolk Island in the less than three days remaining.

To the casual cruising yachtsman, a four-day sprint covering the 625 miles from Whangarei to Norfolk Island would be considered a good test of a crew's physical stamina and seamanship. It would rely heavily on a yacht's strength and seakeeping. To sail the same distance in, say, seventy-two hours, would be regarded by most as impossible. When detectives turned to knowledgeable local sailors for assessment, it *was* considered impossible. But the sailors, and in turn the police, had been assuming that the *Ouvéa* was crewed by people imbued with the etiquette of sail. The assessment was made by purists who would rely on the wind and not on expensive fuel, who would steer a course that kept discomfort to a minimum and who would not risk the safety of themselves or their craft simply for speed. But the men on board the *Ouvéa* were not typical yachtsmen; one was a highly competent mariner, the others desperate beginners. They were prepared, unlike most sailing enthusiasts, to get there quickly and safely at any cost. Velche had crammed the tanks to brimming point with diesel fuel in Whangarei and arrived in

Norfolk Island with his tanks almost empty. The *Ouvéa* had obviously been pushed to the limit – the tanks were hardly likely to be pumped dry by anything other than the engine – motorsailing all the way. Its forty-horsepower engines augmented the sails, cutting corners rather than tacking into the wind to limit discomfort in order to achieve a rapid passage. A rough analogy might be drawn with a racehorse and its jockey; the rider who thinks tactically, assesses his mount's potential and paces it accordingly. He may lose one race but at least the horse will be fit to run again. There is no guarantee, though, that he will outrun the reckless dash of an outsider who is willing to ride his horse into the ground, regardless of the consequences. Analogies apart, *expert* advice confirms that the *Ouvéa*, even with an inexperienced crew, could have uncomfortably completed the course.

Hugh Cudmore is the skipper of the British Americas Cup team, a sailor well versed in the essence of speed, sail and high seas. He has sailed out of Whangarei and Auckland once a year every year since 1978 and on the basis of his knowledge and New Zealand Weather Centre reports for the period July 9 to July 14 estimates that a thirty-eight-foot sloop like the *Ouvéa*, motorsailing from New Zealand to Norfolk Island could complete the voyage in between sixty-five and sixty-seven hours, perhaps in even less time, say sixty-two hours, if stretched.

For the knowledgeable, the Weather Centre reports make interesting reading:

DATE	TIME	WIND		WEATHER
9.7.85	00.00NZST	S. to Se.	10knots	Cloudy, showers
	12.00	S. to S.E.	10knots	Cold front, cloudy
10.7.85	00.00NZST	S. to S.W.	15knots	Showers
	12.00	S. to S.E.	10knots	Showers clearing
11.7.85	00.00NZST	N.E.	25knots	Rain and drizzle
	12.00	N.E.	25knots	Rain and drizzle
12.7.85	00.00NZST	N. to N.W.	20knots	Rain and drizzle
	12.00	N.W.	10–20knots	Rain and drizzle
13.7.85	00.00NZST	W. to N.W.	15–20knots	Showers
	12.00	W.	15–25knots	Few showers
14.7.85	00.00NZST	W. to S.W.	10–20knots	Few showers

'The crew would need to keep up an average speed of seven to eight knots and in the prevailing conditions that would be no problem,' said Cudmore. 'The toughest stretch would be along North Island's east coast, up to the North Cape of New Zealand, motorsailing up the coast with the wind on the vessel's starboard quarter. They would be riding into six-foot waves hitting the boat at a rate of five or six a minute, taking on water with every wave. It would be a very bumpy ride for about ten hours. Everyone on board would be soaked to the skin. They would be reduced to cold drinks and bars of chocolate or other cold snacks because they wouldn't have the time or the stability to cook.'

Once around the cape and into the Three Kings Basin and the open sea, the angle of the wind would become less acute and the motorsailing more effective. For the next 500 miles conditions would have been much improved, with a speed of eight knots easily sustained and often bettered for a large part of the voyage. The frequency of the waves would drop and perhaps only one wave in every half-dozen would wash over the decks and cockpit. 'It's a good, brisk sail – about the time I would expect the crew to make,' was Cudmore's final comment.

It is known that the bombs were planted between 8.00 p.m. and 9.00 p.m. on July 10. It is known that the man who abandoned the dinghy and climbed into the Turenges' camper van was driven off at speed between 9.00 p.m. and 9.30 p.m. The Turenges or Dormand had time to drive him north and he could have been back on board the *Ouvéa* by midnight. When the yacht docked at Norfolk Island on the 13th it was approximately 5.30 p.m. Sixty-five and a half hours had elapsed – the time calculated by Cudmore.

Under cover of darkness on the night of July 10, someone on board the *Ouvéa* sneaked ashore, to be picked up by co-conspirators and driven south to Auckland. There, at the end of a cul-de-sac on Stanley Point, on the northern shore of

Waitamata Harbour, the camper van pulled up. Jim and Barbara Titchener were eating dinner in their bungalow overlooking the harbour when Barbara saw through the French windows two men carrying a grey inflatable down the path to the muddy shore. At the back of the boat was a tall, slim man with thin fair hair. He lost his grip and dropped the boat, though he soon recovered. Barbara pointed and her husband turned to look out of the windows. He was too late. By then the two figures and the boat had disappeared in the darkness. The tall fair-haired figure was most certainly Alain Mafart – but who was the other man?

Of the nine people who saw a lone figure in a Zodiac in the harbour that night, one witness in particular remembered that the occupant of the dinghy was wearing a red woollen hat. Detectives hoped for a similar description from the other witnesses and were disappointed. But in the darkness along the waterfront it was not surprising that only one person saw the hunched figure so clearly that its headgear could be described. The Zodiac would have chugged through the odd patch of light from the neon glare along Tamaki Drive and the container port. It is interesting that the witness could be so certain that he saw a *red* woolly hat, not blue, black, white or yellow. Snapshots taken on board the *Ouvéa* by Maniguet and seized by the detectives who searched the yacht later at Norfolk Island clearly showed Berthelo and Audrenc posing for the camera. Berthelo was wearing a red woolly hat.

Raymond Velche was the only experienced sailor among the crew and, given the rough weather conditions, probably stayed on board to look after the *Ouvéa*, anchored out of sight of the sparsely populated shore. He would be unable to handle the boat alone and Maniguet was next to useless. If the operation went wrong and the alarm was set off, the *Ouvéa* would have to make good its escape at sea and two men would not be enough to handle it. Berthelo or Audrenc would have drawn straws to see who stayed behind and who went ashore to plant the explosives.

Berthelo is the best bet. New Zealand police think that he

was the man who went ashore. He was, in terms of his length of service, the junior agent on board and therefore lowest in the military pecking order. He might well have been the one to be given the dirty work. There was also another indication – a footprint in the Zodiac resembled the sole of a New Balance sports shoe. Berthelo had bought his pair at the Athletic Attic but Velche had never returned for the pair he had ordered. Galbraith's detectives were even more convinced when they read the reports of their colleagues returning from Norfolk Island. Velche and Audrenc had remained cool and aloof. But Berthelo was so nervous, so much on edge, that the detectives feared he might become violent. They decided to question him in pairs for their own safety. He remained volatile throughout the interview. It could have been the simple reaction of a highly strung individual – or the genuine fear of a guilty man facing exposure. The *Ouvéa* had been in Norfolk some hours, the crew had learned on the radio that a man had died, and the person whose hands set the timing device had had plenty of time to consider his predicament. Norfolk Island was Australian territory and the socialist government in Canberra has close ties with the Labour government of New Zealand. The two countries also have an uncomplicated extradition treaty. During questioning Berthelo must have feared the worst – until Galbraith was forced to admit that, as yet, there was not enough evidence to seek the crew's arrest.

It is one thing to believe you have the answer to a crucial question and quite another to prove it beyond reasonable doubt in a court of law. Galbraith and his squad believe that Berthelo was the bomber. But the theory was flawed and a cunning defence lawyer would expose it immediately. Although the evidence accumulated by police included suspicious sightings of the Turenges in many locations, their guilt would rest on the prosecution's ability to prove that the man they collected from Hobson's Bay on the night of the bombing was actively involved in the sabotage. One seemingly unarguable fact defeated the supposition that the Turenges had delivered the bomber back to the *Ouvéa* in their camper van – it appeared arithmetically impossible. The distance recorded on the camper van's dashboard was the key.

The crucial fact is that at midday on July 8 the Turenges changed their rented van for another one because of a cracked windscreen. They then drove north and were positively identified at Topuni by the loggers in the afternoon, and later by motorists at Kiawaka while meeting Velche and Maniguet. The next morning, July 9, they were believed to have been seen by Trev and Erna Rogers at the Kaitaia dairy further to the north and that night returned south and checked into the Parakai motel. On July 10 their camper van's registration number was noted by the outboard motor club vigilantes in Auckland, and the following morning they made a call to Paris from Hamilton. On the evening of the 11th they were back in Auckland and on the 12th they were arrested.

The distance covered between those positive sightings is more than 560 miles. But the records at Newman's hire office showed only 483 miles while the Turenges had it. It is always possible that dashboard milometers can be inaccurate. Allowing for a maximum ten per cent error either way on the van's clock, the Toyota could have covered between 504 and 616 miles. There is only one conclusion. The Turenges could not have visited all the places where they were supposedly sighted while they had the second camper van – let alone deliver Berthelo back to the *Ouvéa*.

Insight retraced the known sightings of the Turenges in New Zealand. The first camper van they hired was seen in Auckland, then Parakai, Paihia, and Waima before returning to Auckland. Such a journey is less than 375 miles. Yet the first van covered 518 miles and the Turenges did not indulge in sightseeing trips. Where did they go in the first van, between the time they hired it on June 22 and the day they exchanged it on July 8, that would account for the extra distance recorded? The answer is Kaitaia. The Rogers saw the Turenges not on July 9, but a day earlier. Adding Kaitaia to the itinerary of the first camper van puts an extra 112 miles on the clock, close enough to the recorded distance travelled.

The Rogers now admit they were unsure of the date. They could not pin it down beyond one of July 7, 8 or 9. By pre-dating the Kaitaia sighting by twenty-four hours everything falls into place. The Turenges' second van travelled 483 miles but was actually observed at points totalling less than 312 miles. They had over 170 miles to spare – enough to return Berthelo north. If they didn't, then Dormand most certainly could have.

The scenario that now fits the known facts is that the Turenges travelled north to meet Maniguet on July 6 to organize retrieval of the Zodiac, diving gear and explosives that had been hidden, probably underwater in one of the countless channels pouring into the Pacific through Parengarenga Harbour. Velche had switched the small hired saloon for the Holden Commodore station wagon on July 6, assuming that it would be needed to transport the heavy boat and equipment. But Alain Turenge preferred to take the camper van; it had cooking and sleeping facilities and there were few motels in the far north. They chose the next evening, the night of July 7, to collect the hidden gear. It was a Sunday and there would be few people on the roads late at night, and those who were would pay much less attention to a tourist's camper with a Zodiac inflatable and Yamaha outboard than they might to a new and expensive station wagon on the dirt tracks of the Aupori peninsula.

On July 7 the Turenges checked out of the Beachcomber at Paihia, picked up Velche and drove north. Under cover of darkness they stowed the gear on board the camper van and in the early hours of the 8th they drove south, through Kaitaia, where they arrived bleary-eyed and exhausted at the dairy. The Turenges had intended to stop at Whangarei while Velche and his comrades constructed the two explosive devices, and then drive south with the bombs, the dinghy and the other equipment. It was again easier to stow the bagged gear in a touring camper van and much less risky than keeping it on board the *Ouvéa* or in the back of the station wagon, for yachtsmen are nosy and the sudden acquisition of expensive equipment would not have gone unnoticed in Whangarei's Town Basin. Besides, it had to be kept somewhere away from the suspicious eyes of any customs officer who would come aboard to clear the *Ouvéa* when it departed on the morning of July 9.

But there was a hitch: the Turenges had cracked the windscreen of their camper van as they drove north on Sunday. It was obvious they would have to exchange vans, and they could not risk questions being asked at Newman's about their sudden acquisition of an inflatable boat, outboard engine and diving gear. The Turenges hurtled back to Auckland to exchange vehicles. It was then that they returned to Kiawaka via Topuni to retrieve the Zodiac, the outboard motor and the other equipment from Maniguet and Velche in the Holden Commodore. Where the Turenges slept on the night of the 8th no one knows. But it is possible that they stayed overnight at Motel Six with the *Ouvéa* crew and joined Velche's celebratory party at the crowded Forum restaurant. The next morning the honeymooners checked into the Hinemoa at Parakai, well off the beaten track where they could lie low until the time came to rendezvous with the bomber.

The modern limpet mine no longer resembles its wartime forebear, the discus-shaped steel dish of explosives with a heavy magnetic base and push-button timer. A standard design today is a light plastic tray with a D-shaped handle on either side. The flat frame has three compartments. Two contain foam buoyancy floats; the third, in the middle, carries an ingot of plastic explosive. A small plastic timing device no bigger than a packet of cigarettes sits on top and four small magnets at each corner provide the fixing method. It is light, easily stripped down and reassembled, and immensely powerful. But nothing like it was used to sink the *Rainbow Warrior.*

Galbraith had followed the familiar hope of all policemen: that forensic examination might reveal the telling clue. When it didn't, he asked his superiors to wire New Zealand House in London. It was a simple request. Though New Zealand is proud of its sleuthing and scientific expertise, the detectives needed an expert of another kind and hoped Britain could provide one.

251

Lieutenant-Commander Brian Braidwood RN is one of a recognizable breed; a stereotype Royal Navy officer, a stickler for rules and regulations but always ready with a warm and cheerful welcome for the newcomer in the mess. First impressions might bracket him as pen-pusher, deskbound in some thankless administrative role, for he lacks the weatherbeaten look of his sea-going peers.

Yellowing Admiralty memos and a collection of dog-eared photographs are the only decoration in his drab office on a shore-station near Weymouth on England's south coast. His desk is a functional battleship-grey affair with a glass top. The visitor's interest is maintained only by a couple of matching metal cabinets and a few unrecognizable steel relics dotted around the office. The strange objects, and the sign at the gates, betray the purpose of his commission. His office is in the Admiralty's Underwater Weapons Establishment at Portland and the relics are bombs, fortunately unprimed.

Despite his lacklustre surroundings, Braidwood is enthusiastic about his job as the Royal Navy's most knowledgeable bomb-builder. Among his many tasks is the design of special charges not only for navy divers but also for the covert purposes of the Special Boat Squadron (a small, select section of the Royal Marines and the waterborne equivalent of the army's SAS). His skills have been acquired over many years, from mine-clearance to mine-laying, from bomb-making to bomb-testing. It is his job to find the most effective way possible of destroying a particular target. It is natural, therefore, that he can also survey the damage done to any given hull and decide how it was done and by what.

In September Braidwood answered Galbraith's call and flew out to New Zealand. He was taken immediately to the naval docks in Devonport across the harbour from Marsden Wharf. The *Rainbow Warrior* had been raised. The gaping hole in its starboard side and the crack above the propeller shaft, together with the debris collected from the seabed around the site of the explosions, awaited his perusal.

American and European police forces have refined analysis of bomb fragments to such a degree that even the smallest remnant can reveal its method of construction, its size, and sometimes even the identity of the man who built it. Gauging the size of the device was easy enough. From the dimensions of the hole and the damage done, no more than forty pounds of plastic explosive was used, perhaps as little as twenty. But whoever had constructed the devices used to slash open the *Warrior*'s hull had intended that no clue to the origin of the bomb would remain.

Braidwood's first conclusion was that the bomb was, in naval jargon, an IED: an improvised explosive device. His next job was to assess the methods of construction and attachment to the hull. As Braidwood knows only too well, there are a hundred different ways of making a bomb and placing it. Limpet mines had already been ruled out. He knew that plastic explosives had been smuggled into New Zealand by the *Ouvéa* crew; he knew also that six strands of single-core wire, each about five to six feet long, had been found in the Holden Commodore after it was returned to Avis. It was safe to assume Velche and his comrades had smuggled in the detonators too. The rest was easy: any old alarm clock or the Harrier 6 log-speed timer from the *Ouvéa*'s SatNav equipment would be enough to time the device. That left only the method of attachment to decide.

Explosive devices are relatively simple to seal in an air-filled plastic bag. Tied to a given length of rope and anchored at the other end to the seabed by means of a weight, the bag containing the bomb floats upwards, until the rope pulls tight and it settles against the target. Similarly a heavier-than-water bomb can be hung at the end of a rope from a float on the surface. Another way is simply to attach a rope to a ship's rail and dangle it over the side. The *Ouvéa* crew had the wherewithal to do either. The drogue purchased in Whangarei could have been filled with sand from the seabed to anchor a bomb, or the grappling iron bought the same day – and used to fish for the equipment hidden at Parengarenga – could have been hung from the *Warrior*'s safety rail. But neither a drogue nor a grappling iron was found by divers after the explosion.

Most of the debris recovered from the seabed was rubbish. The most interesting finds, however, were some fresh and frayed lengths of rope and some strapping. They provide an indication of the method used to determine where to plant the bombs and the means of attachment. Some of the rope had knots tied at regular intervals. The bomber had approached the stern of the *Warrior* and simply tied the first bomb to the propeller shaft assembly. Then, using the knotted rope, he swam along the side, counting off the knots placed at pre-determined points until he reached the spot where, beyond the walls of the hull, the planners had estimated the engine room would be.

In the murky, silted waters, his hands felt for the bilge keel. It is an eight-inch-wide strake designed to help stabilize the ship in rough weather, like a long thin wing running the length of the hull below the water line. It provided the perfect anchoring point for the second bomb. Setting the timer, he swam back to the stern, set the second timer and disappeared into the darkness.

Now that Galbraith knew how the bombs were planted, he still wanted proof of who and why. The methods used by the saboteur convinced detectives they were not dealing with terrorists but with trained experts, men with the military know-how to improvise. A terrorist organization might have simply planted the bomb on board somewhere during the open-house party that night. A terrorist's aim would have been destruction, but not the type that was so coldly calculated that night. Whoever planted the bombs had wanted to do more than simply blast a hole in the ship. The bomber knew that in time a hole in the engine room could be patched up, the water pumped out, the engines repaired. So he planted a second bomb at the stern where the damage to the hull, rudder and propeller shaft would distort the structure so thoroughly that it would be unsalvageable. The bombers had intended to put the *Rainbow Warrior* out of action not temporarily, but permanently.

Ever since Galbraith had taken over the investigation on July 11, he had been sure of French involvement. Enough evidence had been amassed to put it beyond doubt. For the purposes of his case it did not matter who in the Elysée Palace gave the

254

order. Someone high up had stupidly decided to instigate an act of ludicrous state-terrorism against Greenpeace, and Galbraith, like millions of other people around the world, is still asking the question: *why?*

CHAPTER SEVENTEEN
Innocents abroad

August, 1985

Detective Inspector Bert Whyte, a slightly-built New Zealander in his early forties, happened to be the officer on duty the night the *Rainbow Warrior* sank. For that reason he was given a free trip to Paris on August 13. His colleagues in the Auckland police force may have envied his trip, but Whyte knew his task was impossible. The French had already snubbed New Zealand's prime minister himself, so they were hardly going to roll out the red carpet for a lowly cop. Whyte had never been to France before and did not speak enough French to hail a taxi cab from the Charles de Gaulle airport to the hotel near the interior ministry that had been chosen for him and his two detective colleagues. Whyte had a reputation for playing everything by the book. The problem, though, was that his book was very different from the one used by the French gendarmes who were supposed to be helping in the investigation. For a start, the French had bugged the two cramped hotel rooms used by the New Zealand detectives.

Whyte gave the gendarmes a list of people he wanted to interview. Mais oui, they said – and promptly wrapped every request in enough red tape to cover the Eiffel Tower. Mick Hall, the youngest of the three detectives, spoke a little French. He acted not only as translator for the other two detectives but also as their guide on the Paris Metro. The three detectives got to know the Metro well; they were forever riding to ministries and police stations where they were kept waiting for officers who never turned up – or, if they did, would courteously send them knocking on the door of some other bureaucrat. Hall at least had experienced the French talent for obfuscation before, when he was sent to chase after clues in New Caledonia – and came back empty-handed.

On their first day in Paris, the three jet-lagged detectives checked in with the New Zealand embassy, in a small modern building off avenue Foch – 'millionaires' row'. A telex had arrived from Wellington. The New Zealand government was demanding the extradition from France of those responsible for the sabotage. The demand was not just a wild stab. By then, the New Zealand police had been able to trace a telephone number that Dominique Prieur had called in Paris immediately after her arrest. The number, 846 8790, was on a 'red list' of secret telephone numbers allocated to the defence ministry. It belonged to an apartment in an ugly glass and cement block that was used by the DGSE. This 'safe house', at 11 avenue Faldherbe, had the advantage of being a short stroll away from the Piscine's headquarters on boulevard Mortier.

Naturally, Whyte wanted to talk to Admiral Lacoste, the chief of the DGSE. The gendarmerie seemed happy enough to oblige. But what Whyte had no way of knowing was that an internecine battle was being waged between the interior minister, Pierre Joxe, who controlled the gendarmes, and Charles Hernu who, as defence minister, was in charge of the DGSE. Any request regarding Greenpeace that came to the defence ministry via the gendarmerie was bound to end up in a waste-paper basket. It was Joxe who, with scarcely concealed glee, had informed President Mitterrand on July 16 that the Greenpeace operation – organized by the agents of Hernu, his detested rival – had been a spectacular failure. Joxe is a technocrat of the extreme left with little patience for the parochial socialism practised by Hernu.

According to the magazine *Le Point*, July 16 – the week after the Turenges' arrest – was the first time that Mitterrand had heard about the DGSE mission. But within a few days he had become personally involved in protecting the cover of his agents. *L'Express* magazine claims that on July 23, when the Turenges were charged with the murder, Mitterrand paid a surprise visit to Switzerland. Near Geneva he met Pierre Aubert, head of the Swiss department of foreign affairs, and Kurt Furgler. Asked by journalists about his impromptu visit, Mitterrand said he was in Switzerland 'to meet some friends – politicians – who have lots of things to say to me, just as I have things to tell them'. It is likely that this meeting was to clear up the matter of the forged Swiss passports used by the Turenges. It is also thought that Mitterrand requested – and obtained – the Swiss authorities' silence.

At the end of July, Lacoste – who had always been unhappy about the Greenpeace operation – sent Hernu a briefing document on the affair. The report, which ran to almost twenty pages, was a key document because of the amount of detail it contained and because it was Lacoste's official summary as head of the DGSE. It included all the information that the admiral thought the minister should be given. But Lacoste went even further: he asked Hernu if he should talk to Fabius and Mitterrand. No, said Hernu, that would not be necessary. Lacoste also wanted Mitterrand to see his report, though apparently it never reached the president. Hernu has since denied that Lacoste's report ever existed. Mitterrand, on the other hand, is convinced that it did exist. Whether it still exists now is a different matter.

The threat – real or imagined – that Greenpeace posed to France's nuclear weapons programme was enough to make the Gaullists close ranks with the socialists in an effort to contain the damage caused by the scandal. Discreet feelers were put out to Jacques Chirac, mayor of Paris and the leading opposition figure, to find someone impartial enough to conduct an independent investigation into the affair. The choice was Bernard Tricot, sixty-five, a high-ranking civil servant who had served as one of de Gaulle's closest aides. Tricot also had experience in spy inquiries. He had looked into the sordid Ben Barka affair in the 1960s. Because of his Gaullist credentials, Tricot could not be accused of doing the socialists the favour of burying 'l'affaire Greenpeace'.

It was one o'clock in the morning of August 8 when a messenger left the president's Elysée Palace carrying a letter for Laurent Fabius, the prime minister. The letter ordered Fabius to set up a 'rigorous investigation'. Simultaneously, Mitterrand sent a letter to the prime minister of New Zealand, David Lange, promising his 'full co-operation' with police inquiries. The timing of Mitterrand's move was interesting. Officially, the letters were written in the middle of the night out of consideration for the New Zealanders and the time difference between the two countries. A more plausible explanation is that two magazines were about to publish stories accusing the DGSE – for the first time – of sinking the *Rainbow Warrior*. By ordering the inquiry in the small hours, Mitterrand was able to eclipse the magazine articles on the morning news broadcasts.

Tricot began his inquiry on August 9 with an appointment to interview Lacoste. Unlike the three New Zealand detectives, he was at least permitted to see the admiral. But, as Tricot's hastily written report was to reveal, Lacoste was decidedly uncooperative when it came to discussing affairs of national security.

In the meantime, the French press was breaking one scoop after another, based on leaks from disgruntled officers at the Piscine. Mick Hall, the French-speaking New Zealand detective, was busy every morning with his dictionary translating the daily newspapers. The New Zealand embassy also obliged the detectives with a news digest that proved far more valuable than anything on offer from the gendarmerie. Following leads in the press, Whyte and his men charged down to Pau, near the Spanish border, to interview the mother of Christine Cabon. She was unable to tell the New Zealanders what they most wanted to know: where her daughter had been hidden by the DGSE. Next they paid a visit to the lair of Dr Xavier Maniguet in Dieppe. Since returning from his hasty trip to New Zealand, the doctor had spent much of his time in a luxurious hunter's blind he had built for himself in an artificial lake. There he spared a few minutes from his favourite pursuits – hunting, flying and chasing women – to talk to Whyte. It was the doctor who had chartered the *Ouvéa* through Odyssée travel, though he stuck by his improbable story that he had never met the other sailors before. The travel agency had simply brought them together to fill the yacht. No, he told the New Zealand detectives, he did not know where his former crewmen were holed up.

In fact the crew did surface briefly in Paris, though the French authorities did not bother to inform the New Zealanders until it was too late. It was on August 26, the day the Tricot report was published, clearing the French government and the secret service of sinking the *Rainbow Warrior.* The report suggested that the DGSE agents had only been spying on Greenpeace and that someone else – Tricot neglected to say who – blew up the ship. That day the three DGSE men identified in the report as the *Ouvéa*'s crew turned up at a police station in Paris. They did so on the advice of Tricot who said it would look suspicious if they did not come forward to declare their innocence. The three men were not detained, and by the time the New Zealand detectives located the police station their quarry had disappeared. The only good news that day was that Detective Cushla Watson, thirty-four, who had been sent to track down the mystery buyer of the Zodiac dinghy in London, had identified him as Petty Officer Gerald Andries of the *Ouvéa.*

The Tricot report contained few leads for the New Zealand detectives. In a long preamble to the twenty-nine-page document, Tricot explained that he might have spent longer than seventeen days on the investigation, but he believed he had already spoken to everyone useful. It was unlikely, he added, that he would be able to uncover 'new elements' without waiting a very long time.

Unfortunately, Tricot said, there were few documents which could cast light on the matter, but those which were available he had used to the full. He had also drawn on diplomatic and military dispatches, and newspaper articles had helped him to formulate his questions. He had interviewed several members of the government, in particular Charles Hernu, the defence minister (with ultimate responsibility for the DGSE). On the military side, apart from Lacoste, those interviewed included General Jean Saulnier, the president's military chief of staff during the planning stages of the Greenpeace operation, Admiral Henri Fages, in charge of nuclear testing until the end of June 1985, and Roger Emin, second-in-command at the DGSE.

Tricot emphasized that he had approached the investigation with an open mind. He was prepared to consider any hypothesis, no matter how implausible or how unpleasant for France.

Turning to the history of Greenpeace activities in the south Pacific, he said that the situation confronting the French government in 1985 was not particularly new. Greenpeace had organized protests at Moruroa since the 1970s. The main points of the government's policy were fourfold: (i) to obtain precise information about the intentions of Greenpeace, including the number and identity of boats likely to take part in an expedition; (ii) to prevent landings on the atoll with a minimum of incidents; (iii) to improve safety measures against the effects of nuclear tests on the people of the region; and (iv) to provide information for the public by inviting French and foreign experts to visit Moruroa. The announcement that Greenpeace was resuming demonstrations certainly irritated a lot of military and civilian personnel concerned with the testing. 'They were not alone in reproaching this movement for its lack of independence and impartiality.'

Tricot said that when Greenpeace originally announced it was resuming its anti-nuclear demonstrations it 'certainly irritated a large number of military and civilian personnel who are concerned . . . with the Pacific tests and who are not the only critics of the organization's lack of independence and impartiality. But proposals made by the services were all along the lines of what had been done previously to counter the demonstrations.'

Moruroa authorities were insisting on the need for more intelligence about Greenpeace's intentions and movements. This led to instructions being sent by Hernu to the head of the DGSE to intensify efforts to gather this information. 'Because this meant sending several agents to the south Pacific and . . . hiring a boat, expenses ran over the current budget and called for the allocation of exceptional funds. These were requested and obtained in normal conditions, i.e. with the agreement of the special chief of staff of the president of the republic.' This was the post held by General Saulnier who, Tricot reported, 'remembers that the matter had been put to him, that the sole purpose was to increase the intelligence effort, and that he gave his go-ahead'.

According to custom, the report continued, contact between the defence minister and the head of the DGSE was essentially by word of mouth. Hernu and Lacoste both said they had discussed the need for more intelligence-gathering. But while Hernu maintained that this was the exclusive subject of the talks, Lacoste said they had also talked about infiltrating agents into Greenpeace. Tricot added: 'These agents could be asked to consider ways and means to counter the action of this organization. I say "consider" and on no account to resort to action, even action which involved no violence.'

However, Tricot was concerned about the oral nature of the instructions. 'If any ambiguity, however slight, had got into transmission of orders from the top, where could this have led as orders were passed on down?' On the other hand, he was sure that DGSE officers would not have disobeyed their orders. 'When Lacoste took up his appointment in November 1982 he made a point of getting strict military discipline in the DGSE. That had not always been the case before . . . I am certain that the DGSE now acts according to more classical rules than during a certain previous period.'

The main role of the action service, Tricot explained, was to 'take part in the search for information in places where the DGSE does not have a permanent structure of surveillance. This is the case with New Zealand. This fact helps to rule out the theory, totally contrary to the internal discipline of the DGSE, but which did cross my mind once, that two different services of the DGSE, working on the same terrain, could have been led on by a feeling of rivalry to overstep their orders.' The DGSE officers whom Tricot met gave an account of their orders that fitted in with instructions received from their superiors. 'I am, of course, obliged not to exclude the theory that these officers banded together to keep from me a portion of the truth. I must also not forget the fact that the orders given to the agents, which have been shown to me, were not complete or were accompanied by verbal orders which altered their meaning. But this pessimistic hypothesis seems out of the question considering the training of these officers.'

Tricot was shown a defence ministry note calling for 'intensified intelligence-gathering on the positions and movements of the *Vega* and the *Rainbow Warrior* in order to predict and anticipate the actions of Greenpeace.' The word 'anticipate' had been underlined twice by Hernu. Tricot was anxious to know what exactly had been intended by the word. If it had meant the same as 'predict' there would have been no point in using both words. The French verb 'anticiper' could also mean to 'head off' or 'forestall'. Could forestalling Greenpeace include sinking one of its ships? Hernu said that 'anticipate' meant to find out things, though it could perhaps include infiltration. For Lacoste it meant a little more, but certainly not sabotage.

Tricot did not bother grilling the mole inside Greenpeace, Christine Cabon, although she would certainly have known the ultimate objective of the spying mission in its early stages. Tricot's reasoning was that she had left Auckland in May and, as a result, could not have been directly implicated in the sinking.

Nor could he interview the 'Turenge' couple – they were in jail. Staff orders dated June 14 to the Turenges said that their mission in New Zealand was to report on the boats planning to accompany the *Rainbow Warrior* to Moruroa, to identify the new crew of the *Warrior*, to identify the political, scientific and journalistic personalities involved in the campaign, and to report on its impact in New Zealand. Tricot said of the Turenges: 'It seems unlikely to me that they took part directly or indirectly in placing mines on the hull of the *Rainbow Warrior* . . . Mme Prieur never belonged to the naval divers and trouble with her back makes it difficult for her to make certain efforts.' Similarly, choosing Mafart would have been 'unreasonable' since he had not been in the underwater combat force since 1983. Less unlikely would have been indirect participation by the couple since they could have observed in detail the layout of Auckland Harbour, the habits of those frequenting it and the working methods of the New Zealand police. They could also (after July 7) have reported the exact position of the *Rainbow Warrior* and could have passed on their findings to other agents.

The only remaining French suspects, then, were the DGSE members of the *Ouvéa* crew. Their mission, said Tricot, involved navigation training in the Pacific, reporting on the Greenpeace ships and seeing if it would be possible to infiltrate future Greenpeace campaigns. The idea was to provide a boat themselves or alternatively get Velche chosen as skipper of a Green-peace boat. All this meant trying to get to know New Zealand (with the odd exception of Auckland). 'They were not to go to Auckland. Their superiors explained to me that in conformity with classical precautionary measures, the agents were not aware of the presence of the two officers at Auckland. Perhaps they suspected that others besides themselves were charged with getting to know this port, but they were not supposed to know the identities of the persons concerned.'

Tricot said the reasons to think the *Ouvéa* crew had carried out the attack on the *Rainbow Warrior* were 'not negligible'. The most worrying thing was the lack of evidence suggesting that the author or authors of the attack could have been anyone but them. There were, however, various possibilities: perhaps the bombing had been done by politically motivated individuals or by another nation's secret service. There was no lack of motives for this: to damage Greenpeace, a movement which does not upset only France; to damage the reputation of France; or to damage both Greenpeace and France by laying the blame on French shoulders.

There were reasons for suspecting the *Ouvéa* crew: their special navigation equipment, the very specialized training of the three men – experts in diving and mine-laying – and the many clues which according to the press were found by the New Zealand police. Even so, Tricot wondered if the clues were just a little too obvious. 'Why, for example, abandon oxygen bottles and why . . . bottles with a French brand name when equipment with a foreign brand name was in stock?'

There were also factors which pointed towards the innocence of the *Ouvéa* crew. For a start, there was only a limited timespan when the *Warrior* and the *Ouvéa* were together in New Zealand. 'The *Rainbow Warrior* arrived on July 7, the *Ouvéa* left on July 9 in the morning. To carry out the placement of mines in broad daylight in a very busy port hardly seems practicable, even with equipment which prevents bubbles coming to the water surface. That leaves two nights, that of July 7 to 8 and that of July 8 to 9. It is not much, even supposing preparations for the task were made by the "Turenges".'

Tricot recalled how the *Ouvéa* crew got to know local people. 'If, on the contrary, they were charged, or had charged themselves, with sinking the *Rainbow Warrior*, this behaviour would have been very imprudent.' Referring to the crew's activities between June 28 and July 7, he continued: 'Numerous photographs were taken by the three men during their trips. They [the photographs] remained on board the *Ouvéa* and have disappeared with it.

'The three companions maintained that they had spent the nights of the 7th to 8th and the 8th to 9th at the hotel in Whangarei or on the boat. That is also the recollection of Dr Maniguet. The evening of July 8 was occupied until 1.00 a.m. celebrating the thirty-fifth birthday of Velche, which fell, it is true, two days later, but which it was more pleasant to celebrate on land. After the customs formalities, which lasted from 9.00 a.m. till 10.00 a.m. of the morning of July 9, the *Ouvéa* left the port of Whangarei.'

Tricot thought that the *Ouvéa* crew members would have had great difficulty in combining their role as 'tourists' with an attack on the *Rainbow Warrior*. He said of the crew: 'Velche in particular appeared to me very thoughtful and prudent . . . I cannot see these men taking a decision contrary to the instructions they had received to the extent of sinking the *Rainbow Warrior*. Of course I raised the possibility with each of them and on each occasion they told me that such an act would have been beyond them and they had never thought of it.'

Throughout his investigation, Tricot was well aware that he was having to take a lot on trust. He added a note of caution: 'In my report, I did not exclude [the possibility] that I was deceived. I do not exclude that there may have been a kind of general agreement, or agreement at a certain level, not to tell me the truth.'

But he was certain about one thing. 'Everything which I have heard and seen gives me the certitude that at the government level no decision was taken to harm the *Rainbow Warrior*. There is no reason to think – and there are strong reasons to believe the contrary – that the DGSE gave its agents in New Zealand instructions other than those required to carry out government directives. Although until the court proceedings due in New Zealand it will be impossible to comment confidently on the reality or otherwise of the acts for which Major Mafart and Captain Prieur are accused, I believe, in the present state of my knowledge, in their innocence. The same I believe, in the present state of my knowledge, about Chief Petty Officer Verge and Petty Officers Andries and Bartelo. A necessarily rapid administrative inquiry can hardly be conclusive. Personally, I therefore believe it useful that this report be followed in France by a more detailed examination.'

Once the Turenge couple had been arrested, the political gloves came off in France. For more than a month, Mitterrand's right-wing opposition had kept silent; after all, it supported the French military and the nuclear tests. But on August 19 Jean Lecanuet, leader of a centre-right party, said that the socialist government had been caught in a blatant act of duplicity and was trying to pass the blame to scapegoats. It was obvious the secret service had sunk the boat. What he wanted to know was who ordered them to do so.

The secret service itself joined in the fray, rapidly developing more leaks than the shattered hull of the *Rainbow Warrior*. Certain high-ranking officials within the DGSE were convinced that the overriding interest of the socialist government was not to free the two agents trapped in a New Zealand prison, but to erase all evidence of its own responsibility. The many right-wingers within the secret services were determined that President Mitterrand and his cabinet ministers must take the brunt of the blame. Despite all of Hernu's efforts to win over the intelligence services through bonhomie, it soon became apparent that the DGSE's loyalty was not to the elected government but to itself.

There is also evidence that the right-wingers within the DGSE manipulated the internal inquiry into the leaks to purge agents sympathetic to the socialists. One of their victims was Richard Guillet. As a young officer, he had written directly to President Mitterrand in 1983 warning that the socialists were losing control of the intelligence services. He gave Mitterrand details of how the commanders of the underwater combat school in Aspretto had burned their files because of the socialist election victory in 1981. Alain Mafart, then second-in-command at Aspretto, was allegedly among those officers who were on the verge of mutinying after the socialists came to power. Mafart was swiftly transferred to the action service on the mainland.

Guillet's letter was ignored, probably because Mitterrand's advisers were afraid of angering the intelligence chiefs even more by conducting a purge. It was not until the Greenpeace affair that Guillet dared to try the Elysée Palace again, this time to alert the president to the harmful leaks flooding from the DGSE. Guillet also accused Mafart – with no proof – of deliberately sabotaging the mission to embarrass the socialists he so much despised. However, an acquaintance of Mafart said: 'Mafart was a good soldier. He was too disciplined to deliberately wreck an operation because he didn't agree with the government's politics.'

Guillet did not approach Mitterrand directly. In September, he and another dissident officer, Colonel Fourrier, the head of counter-espionage, contacted Paul Barril, who had worked in the Elysée Palace as the head of the gendarmes' anti-terrorist team, the GIGN. Even with Barril on their side, Mitterrand's advisers refused to take the complaints seriously. The Elysée made the mistake of notifying the Piscine of their accusations, and the three dissidents – along with five other socialist sympathizers – were arrested for having been the source of the leaks.

At the same time, the socialists engaged in their own half-hearted attempts to play the leaks game. Once it was proved that Mafart and Prieur were French spies, the improbable story was circulated to the left-wing establishment newspaper, *Le Monde*, that the sinking of Greenpeace had been a plan concocted by renegade rightists within the intelligence services who were in league with the white settlers of New Caledonia. How the plantation owners of New Caledonia would have benefited by scuttling a Greenpeace ship was never properly explained. Journalists at *Le Monde* unhappy with the report circulated the rumour that the interior minister himself, Pierre Joxe, had passed on this particular fable.

The damaging leaks were not stopped by the purge within the Piscine. Several journalists named in the arrest warrant swear they never received any information from Guillet and the others. In fact, the journalists claim that the true sources of the leaks were the DGSE officers who had led the purge. Those reportedly involved were General Roger Emin, who was second-in-command of the DGSE, and Colonel Jean-Claude Lascere, the head of the action service. It was reportedly Lascere who spread the rumour to his contacts at French radio on August 10 that the British had 'betrayed' the French spies to the New Zealanders. The dissident spooks were kept under house arrest for fifteen days, and it is believed that the charges against them will be quietly dropped.

Blocked at every turn, the three New Zealand detectives did not feel much like celebrating during their evenings in Paris. Besides, they did not have the money. Their superiors back in Auckland kept them on a tight budget. The detectives' meagre expenses hardly allowed for a night on the town. Occasionally they were taken to dinner by the embassy staff, but usually Whyte and his men turned in early. They read paperbacks and wrote homesick letters to their wives. Whyte and his beleaguered team stayed in France for ten weeks. They returned to New Zealand with three box files of documents. There was little in the stack of evidence other than newspaper clippings and interviews with French journalists.

CHAPTER EIGHTEEN
Underwatergate

It was Bernard Tricot's misfortune to be born with a surname which in French means 'knitting'. It gave the headline writers and cartoonists a field day. The left-wing daily, *Libération*, splashed its pun in huge letters: 'Tricot lave plus blanc' (Tricot washes whiter). Cartoonists everywhere had fun with tangled balls of wool and one even showed Hernu, the defence minister, half-naked as his knitted pullover unravelled. The normally ultra-serious *Le Monde* began illustrating its stories about 'l'affaire Greenpeace' with ironic drawings of a frogman wearing a halo.

The government's intention in calling for the Tricot report had been to quieten speculation. But now it began to have the opposite effect. Few people believed Tricot's conclusions and journalists in all sections of the French press set out to prove him wrong. Even the most soporific newspapers suddenly woke up.

The Tricot report was widely regarded as a whitewash. If so, it was a whitewash designed to peel off in the first shower of rain. Tricot had been set a near-impossible task: to discover the truth from a bunch of secret agents and officials who had obviously made sure beforehand that their stories would tally and who were prepared to fall back on the excuse of 'national security' if asked any embarrassing questions. Bernard Tricot, at first sight, appeared to have been taken in by them. In fact his report was far more subtle than that. It contained a number of time-bombs that were to prove every bit as devastating for France's socialist government as the bombs that sank the *Rainbow Warrior* were for Greenpeace.

For a start, not even Tricot himself was wholeheartedly convinced by his conclusions. He admitted openly that witnesses

269

might have conspired to mislead him and, at the end of his report, went so far as to propose that a more detailed investigation be set up. To the average French journalist it seemed too much of a coincidence that France had spent so much money on sending so many spies to 'observe' Greenpeace at a time when someone else just happened to blow up its flagship. In short, the Tricot report was the work of a dutiful civil servant who says 'Yes, Minister', when what he really means is 'No'.

The first time-bomb in the report was the admission that France had indeed been involved in an operation against Greenpeace, albeit a perfectly innocent one of intelligence-gathering. Before Tricot there had only been speculation. Now, at least, it was officially confirmed that something had been afoot. The report also established, for the first time, a link with the president's Elysée Palace.

The second time-bomb lay in what Tricot did not say. While denying formally that France had tried to sink Greenpeace, he uncovered no worthwhile evidence pointing to an alternative culprit. There were many other unanswered questions. Why had so many innocent information-gatherers, working in a friendly country, suddenly started using false passports? Why had the *Ouvéa* crew been allowed to scuttle such a valuable yacht without raising eyebrows back at the DGSE? Normally the secret service was so penny-pinching that its spies had to provide a receipt for every taxi ride.

But the third – and largest – time-bomb was that the Tricot report sealed off the most obvious escape holes for the Mitterrand government. Admiral Lacoste, proud of his efforts at cleaning up the DGSE, insisted that his officers would not disobey or overstep their orders. Tricot's own researches supported this view: the *Ouvéa* crew members were fine upstanding men and a credit to the republic. The inference from this was plain. Whatever the agents had done in New Zealand was no more and no less that what they had been told to do. Of course there was the possibility that a foul-up in the lines of communication had led to their instructions being garbled – but Tricot neatly closed that loophole, too. Everyone Tricot spoke to described the plans for the Greenpeace operation in more or less the same terms. True, there were slight differences in the accounts of Fages, Lacoste and Hernu, but broadly all agreed about the nature of the plan. The operation, then, was carried out to the letter – on the clearest possible instructions from above. Therein lay the trap. Everything would be fine so long as the government could sustain its 'intelligence mission' argument. But if proof later emerged that the operation was actually a sabotage mission, then everyone would know who to blame. Fages, Lacoste and Hernu would have been shown to be lying.

Back in New Zealand, much of the necessary proof had already emerged. The Turenges had given nothing away, but the evidence against the *Ouvéa* crew was increasingly damning. Tricot claimed that an important part of the yacht's mission had been to photograph the New Zealand coast – though even he was puzzled why divers trained in sabotage should be assigned such a task. One difficulty for Tricot was that the crew apparently failed to bring back any pictures – a lapse which he explained by saying they had left them aboard the *Ouvéa*. But the New Zealanders knew something Tricot did not know: when Frank MacLean, the customs man from Whangarei, checked the *Ouvéa* shortly after its arrival there were no cameras on board. And worse still, the search in Norfolk Island had produced traces of explosives in the *Ouvéa*'s bilges.

Throughout France's long August holiday the explosions that sank the *Rainbow Warrior* had rumbled on in the press, though the French public seemed relatively unconcerned. Despite the hostile reaction to the Tricot report, the government seemed to be succeeding in keeping the lid on the affair. One problem was that Noumea Yacht Charters of New Caledonia, the company which owned the *Ouvéa*, was suing the French government for the loss of its yacht and – worse still – threatening to subpoena the *Ouvéa* crewmen as witnesses. But on September 3 the company quietly dropped its case against France and opened private negotiations with the defence ministry, seeking 990,000 francs compensation. The dropping of the case eliminated one of the few chances of a court hearing in France on the *Rainbow Warrior* affair.

Another possible pitfall for the French government arose because the *Warrior* was a British-registered ship. Normally a Department of Trade inquiry would have been held to investigate the sinking. The French, hoping to put New Zealand off the scent, had earlier hinted that Britain might have sunk the Greenpeace ship. It was a foolish ploy, for France now needed Britain's co-operation. Discreet soundings were made by the two governments and on September 5 the foreign secretary, Sir Geoffrey Howe, reassured Parliament that neither the French nor the New Zealand authorities were taking seriously the suggestion of British involvement. A few weeks later the British government decided to spare the French further embarrassment: they announced that in the case of the *Rainbow Warrior* a Department of Trade inquiry would not be necessary.

Once the link with France became apparent, the world's press and television descended on the Paris office of Greenpeace. It is in an old narrow street on the left bank of the Seine, just out of sight of Notre Dame. The area, once run-down, is now rapidly becoming gentrified. Greenpeace's office is a double shop front and basement, with metal grilles that are lowered at night. On the opposite side of the road, appropriately, are a veterinary surgeon and a vegetarian restaurant. David McTaggart of Greenpeace International went to Paris to help keep the *Rainbow Warrior* story bubbling. On some days he would give as many as twenty interviews to journalists. 'At the press conferences reporters and photographers would be fighting and screaming. There were at least fourteen TV cameras and about thirty photographers in our small room.'

Immediately after the bombing, Greenpeace in Paris received several letters expressing shock and sympathy. But that soon changed as the evidence of France's involvement mounted and the French press began suggesting that Greenpeace was a Communist front or that it was going to Moruroa to spy for the Russians. The Paris staff waited anxiously for the postman, but only about twenty of the 7,000 fully paid-up members resigned. Elsewhere the attacks took a different form. Greenpeace has a campaign bus which travels around France. Several times it was pelted with stones and daubed with graffiti. Once someone tried to set it on fire. The mayors of Nice, Nîmes and several other places attempted to ban the bus from their towns – though they had no legal power to do so.

Weeks later, as the fuss died down, the long-term effects on Greenpeace France became clearer. The publicity certainly meant that the name was more widely known than before and there were far more inquiries about its organization and policies. But there was also another effect which worried the Paris staff. The *Rainbow Warrior* bombing had become an election issue and Greenpeace, against its will, had been dragged into party-political conflict.

For a while after publication of the Tricot report, Mitterrand continued the official line that, although the French secret service had carried out an infiltration and reconnaissance mission against Greenpeace, there was no involvement in the explosion. In a letter to the New Zealand premier, David Lange, on September 16, he wrote: 'It would be good if the accumulated grievances and unsubstantiated accusations of which France is the object could be avoided.'

But already Mitterrand's defences against the Greenpeace scandal were crumbling. By September 17, the president knew he was in deep trouble. André Fontaine, director of *Le Monde*, was about to publish a front-page story that a third French team – besides the Turenges and the *Ouvéa* crew – had been involved in the sinking. The story appearing in *Le Monde*, possibly leaked by the ministry of the interior, would blow apart whatever credibility was still attached to the Tricot report.

Fontaine let the Elysée know about the story in advance. He did so 'out of consideration', he says, though he may have been hoping for a reaction from Mitterrand. None came. At lunchtime on the 17th, *Le Monde* published. (It was a story which, incidentally, the satirical paper *Le Canard Enchaîné* had already reported on September 11, although it had caused little reaction.) By September 19, France's leading weekly news magazine, *L'Express*, was said to be on the point of naming members of the third team. There were many who doubted whether this third team existed; even the *Le Monde* report which started the furore had been worded very tentatively. Some suggested that the third team was an invention of the DGSE in order to help acquit the Turenges at their trial in New Zealand. But the effect of the story in Paris was to muddy the waters still further. Mitterrand decided he had had enough. On the afternoon of September 19 he telephoned his prime minister, Fabius, and followed up the call immediately with a letter. The letter referred to press revelations and concluded tartly: 'This situation cannot continue.'

The same day Charles Hernu, the defence minister, was making his last stand. At a press conference he reiterated the Tricot version of events: he conceded that Mafart, Prieur and the *Ouvéa* crew had been in New Zealand on a mission but he insisted that it was purely an intelligence mission. 'Make no mistake, however. Between intelligence and the attack of which they are wrongly accused there is an abyss.' He denied that he had given any orders to attack the *Warrior*. 'If I have been disobeyed or if I have been lied to, I will find out immediately . . . I will be merciless in punishing them.'

Hernu summoned top military figures, including Admiral Lacoste, and asked them to sign a statement that they had told him everything about the Greenpeace affair. Lacoste refused, arguing that he had a duty to protect subordinates. After that there was no alternative but to sack Lacoste. Hernu himself could no longer claim to be in control of his staff. By lunchtime on September 20, Fabius had recommended that Mitterrand accept Hernu's resignation.

Charles Hernu had known he was in trouble since September 17. What he did not know was that it would be bad enough to force his resignation as defence minister. He had been tipped off that *Le Monde* would be publishing a leak from his own secret services that a mysterious third team had participated in the disastrous mission. The leak turned out to be false; the idea was to convince the New Zealanders that the Turenges were bit-players in the plot and thus, it was hoped, get them out of prison sooner. But the September 17 article also put the blame squarely on Hernu for ordering the disaster.

Le Monde is an afternoon paper, but Hernu's worries did not stop him from enjoying a hearty lunch of lamb stuffed with olives in the officers' mess of the defence ministry on rue Saint-Dominique. Hernu is a rarity among Frenchmen; he does not drink wine with his meals – only champagne. That day the champagne happened to be pink. After the savage treatment he had received in both the left-wing and the right-wing press over the Greenpeace affair, it was a relief to descend to the officers' mess for the genuine camaraderie and support that awaited him. Some of the staff generals had been his friends since the Algerian war when, as a socialist deputy, he had toured the garrisons there on a commission of inquiry. Hernu did not share the aversion that many socialists have to the sight of a uniform. Indeed, when reviewing his troops on manoeuvres, he delighted in dressing up as a tank commander or a parachutist.

In between lunch courses, Hernu clasped his pudgy hands together. The gesture and his beard gave him the complacent look of a priest in a wealthy parish. He was jovial and demonstrative. As he spoke, his hands escaped upwards, as if charmed into flight by the power of his own words. He was wearing a thin gold watch on one wrist, a gold bracelet on the other. Photocopies of the *Le Monde* article were finally delivered. The press secretary who brought them hovered by the table. A journalist from the news agency AFP was on the telephone, waiting for a comment on the accusations. Hernu at first refused, then, with a sigh, agreed and began to draft a statement. For a brief period after fighting in the Resistance Hernu worked as a journalist in Lyon and he prides himself on his writing style. With a black fountain pen he drafted his reply. 'The Ministry affirms that it has always done and will continue to do the necessary to arrive at the truth,' he wrote with a grand flourish.

The article in *Le Monde* had not been as damaging as Hernu

had expected, but the pressure was mounting on Mitterrand to sack his defence minister. It was a tough decision for Mitterrand. Not only had Hernu succeeded in allaying the army's suspicions that all socialists were on Moscow's payroll, but he was also a close friend. During the years in political opposition, Mitterrand had relied on Hernu's knowledge of defence matters and, indeed, had been persuaded by Hernu to accept the concept of an independent nuclear force, first introduced by their Gaullist opponents. It was as a result of this that French leftists had nicknamed him 'Hernucléaire'. Hernu told *The Sunday Times* that his policy with the military had been to 'interfere as little as possible'. But, he added: 'The military are not to decide politics, only to obey the orders of the government.' While serving as defence minister, Hernu claims he was also able to convince the generals that the socialists were interested in 'carrying on the continuity of France's nuclear independence'.

The son of a gendarme, Hernu was born in Quimper in 1923 and has a loyalty to small-town institutions. He is an ardent Catholic and a member of a freemasons' grand lodge. This has made him more acceptable to the generals than the other socialists and Communists in Mitterrand's cabinet. The army viewed Hernu as an ally, one they could count on to lobby for giving the armed forces a bigger slice of the budget. Hernu also gained their respect for his handling of the Chad crisis, when France sent in paratroopers to defend the N'Djamena government against Libyan-backed rebels. The conflict was contained, France's ally remained in power and Colonel Gaddafi turned from the desert of Chad in retreat.

Although Hernu was forced to resign over 'l'affaire Greenpeace', his reputation has not sunk with it. He is being touted as the next socialist presidential candidate after Mitterrand. As one press commentator noted, the destruction of the *Rainbow Warrior* 'at last proves that the socialists have got balls'. Hernu was, in a sense, hoisted by Mitterrand's own caution. Opinion polls carried out in autumn 1985 showed that the French public did not blame the socialists for trying to rid themselves of the Greenpeace nuisance, nor were they all that upset with them for bungling the mission. But what the French, and the military in particular, could not forgive the socialists for was their clumsy attempts at a cover-up. Hernu still claims that Greenpeace has not damaged Mitterrand's personal popularity. But while Mitterrand's popularity has remained buoyant, the fortunes of his party have ebbed noticeably since the scandal.

Hernu has left his plush offices at the Hôtel de Brienne, with its world maps and many telephones connecting him instantly to other European defence ministers and to the Pentagon, and he now resides in the mayor's chambers at Villeurbanne, a rough industrial suburb of Lyon. He denied to *The Sunday Times* that Mitterrand still consults him on defence matters, but close aides claim otherwise. Since Hernu's resignation, there has been no change in France's basic defence policy: that world stability, in some measure, and France's own security depend on adding ever more powerful weapons to its nuclear arsenal. 'We are worried about seeing a world where the two superpowers both want to make it theirs.' For this reason, he says, France should never place its nuclear missiles on the bargaining table at the Geneva disarmament talks. 'We must maintain our independence.' He complains of the lack of political focus among western European nations, but seems unwilling to compromise France's maverick stance to that end.

The heads had rolled and it was time to put on a new – and cleaner – face. On Sunday, September 22, Laurent Fabius, the prime minister, appeared on television with his newly-appointed defence minister, Paul Quilès. Fabius admitted that the *Rainbow Warrior* had been sunk by French agents. What was more, those agents had been acting 'under orders'. He proposed a parliamentary inquiry to discover the full truth of the matter.

This new era of open government lasted rather less than twenty-four hours. The next day Quilès pointed out that it might be difficult to discover the truth because some essential parts of the Greenpeace dossier at the Piscine had disappeared. The news magazine *L'Express* attempted to come to the rescue a few days later by pointing out that 'all the service's documents are carefully preserved in duplicate at the impregnable fort of Noisy-le-Sec, in the Paris area'. Oddly enough, nobody in government seemed interested in this helpful suggestion.

CHAPTER NINETEEN
Aftermath

There was a surreal atmosphere at Auckland's High Court building on November 4, 1985. A murder trial was about to open. But it was no ordinary murder and no ordinary trial. Intense security measures had been taken after rumours that a commando operation was being mounted to free the two defendants. A submarine had been sighted in Hauraki Gulf and New Zealand's armed forces were on alert. Old wartime tunnels beneath the court house had been sealed up for fear they might be used by raiders to gain access. Weapon-detection equipment scanned the 150 journalists and a multitude of television crews from around the world who had gathered at the court house. Gun-toting police officers patrolled the grounds and the bomb squad stood by – just in case.

Auckland, a comparatively sleepy city rocked only by the occasional rape or drugs bust, was revelling in the attention now being paid to it by the rest of the world. As the 10.30 a.m. start approached, previously insignificant police officers and justice department officials groomed themselves in case the TV cameras panned in their direction. Restaurateurs begged people to book tables well in advance and vied for the expense account custom of the journalists. Hotels were booked solid and taxi drivers were doing a roaring trade. Outside the court, a comedian had dressed himself in the uniform of a French gendarme and offered 'genuine fake Swiss passports for sale'.

It had all the hallmarks of a carnival. Only the quiet band of Greenpeace supporters demonstrating in silence on the grass verge outside the court seemed to remember what the trial was about – the bombing of their flagship and the death of a comrade. Most people missed the white van, windowless and armour-plated, as it slipped through the sidestreets and into the back entrance of the High Court building. It carried Major Alain Mafart and Captain Dominique Prieur. Soon they would climb the stairs from the cells and take up their positions in the dock, facing Judge R. J. Gilbert.

The media circus, feeding on its own enthusiasm and lust for a story, had expected a six-week hearing. Some American television networks had already invested up to $US75,000 to ensure the trial's every twist and turn would infiltrate their viewers' homes. In fact it lasted just thirty minutes and displayed all the judicial drama of a traffic misdemeanour.

The humming court house had held its breath as the gavel hit the court clerk's desk. The sound of grating bolts and hushed footsteps on stairs heralded the ascent from the cells of the two defendants. Mafart was smartly dressed in jacket and trousers and maintained the arrogance that had irked his inquisitors. He appeared unimpressed by the attention he held, glanced once to either side, then sat down and stared straight ahead with his arms folded. Prieur looked frail and nervous, her face flushed as she darted looks at the press gallery and public benches in search of familiar faces. She smiled thinly in the direction of detective sergeants Batchelor and Morris.

The first significant sign that something unexpected was about to happen came when a silver-haired man got to his feet. It was not the Crown prosecutor opening the case but Paul Neazor QC, Solicitor General of New Zealand. He would not normally have been there. There had been rumours the day before, especially among the excitable French press corps, that the prosecution was prepared to strike a deal with the defendants' lawyers. But most had dismissed the gossip on the grounds that it would be political suicide for New Zealand's prime minister, David Lange, if the Turenges were allowed to escape the full wrath of the law.

Sitting in court was David McTaggart, the Greenpeace chairman, who had travelled to New Zealand especially for the trial. It was not retribution he wanted. The prospect of a six-week trial held out further embarrassment for the French; it would prolong the agony of the Mitterrand government and increase the pressure on France to compensate both the Pereira family

280

and Greenpeace for their respective losses. It might even force the French to think again about nuclear testing in the hope of re-establishing their tarnished reputation in the Pacific. McTaggart watched impassively as Neazor outlined the Crown's proposition. Slowly the colour drained from his face as he realized what was happening.

In essence, Neazor's statement confessed that the prosecution had failed to establish that Mafart and Prieur, the so-called Turenges, had intended to kill Fernando Pereira or anyone else on board. The charge of premeditated murder could not be supported, he said, but the defendants were willing to plead guilty to manslaughter.

Though the integrity of most judicial systems is enshrined in the belief that an accused person is presumed innocent until proved guilty, the truth is that few defendants are ever awarded such charitable status. The French daily, *Le Figaro*, summed up Neazor's statement perfectly. 'The presumption of innocence is contrary to reality.'

To many of the visiting journalists, Neazor's argument sounded flimsy. In most countries of the world, the placing of explosive charges is considered murderous. Bombs are indiscriminate. They cannot be pointed like a gun or aimed like a blow with the fist. The bomber has to accept that in placing the charge he risks killing an innocent bystander. No warning was given by the French agents, so surely they knew that the attack might kill. That thought was on the minds of many people that day in Auckland's High Court. David McTaggart was incensed; so too were the thwarted journalists. In accepting the manslaughter plea, Judge R. J. Gilbert had postponed the hearing for sentence until three weeks later. Outside, some Greenpeace supporters wept and wondered if anyone really cared that Fernando Pereira was dead.

A sell-out seemed the only possible explanation. In any other country the jury would have been allowed to decide the guilt or otherwise of the two French agents. At the very least it seemed proper that the evidence should be aired in public whatever the eventual verdict. The cover-up theory quickly grew. Newspapers around the world reported secret discussions between the New

Zealand government and that of France. It was claimed that France had agreed to help New Zealand's ailing economy by buying lamb and dairy produce in exchange for a lesser charge and no embarrassing court case.

'Alors! It's the great lamb chop spy swop,' the London *Daily Express* proclaimed on its front page.

France's new defence minister, Paul Quilès, confirmed on the day after the trial that the Turenge case had been raised by the foreign minister Roland Dumas during talks with the New Zealand prime minister's deputy, Geoffrey Palmer, in New York. Back in Auckland, Lange immediately denied the accusations that the trade deal had brought a promise to drop the murder charges and commute the manslaughter sentences to deportation. He admitted that the French had attempted to discuss the subject but insisted that Palmer and he had promptly refused to talk about it.

Nobody doubted that the Turenges had abetted the agents who planted the bombs which blew out the hull of the *Rainbow Warrior.* It had been front page news in New Zealand's press almost every day since July 10. By the time the Turenges took up their position in the dock on November 4 there was an air of certainty in New Zealand – and indeed elsewhere – a belief that they were guilty. There seemed to be little doubt that a jury would return a verdict of guilty on the murder charge, and Judge Gilbert would have little option but to impose life sentences on the pair.

But within the inner circle of knowledgeable detectives and lawyers there was a creeping uncertainty. Solicitor General Neazor had been aware that the world's press was preparing to descend on Auckland for the trial. New Zealand's judicial system would be under the microscope. As one source closely connected to the case later commented: 'We decided that justice had to be seen to be done.' The effect was that the prosecution lawyers examined the evidence in the minutest detail. They had to be seen to be scrupulously fair, just and honest.

It became obvious that there were serious flaws in the case. Though it was possible to prove that Mafart and Prieur had conspired and aided the operation mounted by the DGSE, the solicitor general concluded that the admissible evidence would not establish that the defendants were responsible for placing the explosives. Furthermore, there was no proof that either had intended to kill or injure or that either had known enough about the placement of the bombs to believe that they were likely to cause death. The fact that Pereira had drowned after being knocked unconscious and trapped by the explosions, and had not been killed by the blasts themselves, further weakened the murder case.

Moreover, the police could not prove that the explosives detected in the *Ouvéa*'s bilges matched those that sank the *Warrior*. The evidence was overwhelmingly circumstantial.

Someone else had spotted those flaws and had begun to work them to the advantage of his clients. Gerard Curry, a powerfully built lawyer with a reputation to match his stature, had been hired by the French government to defend Mafart and Prieur. Curry had approached Superintendent Galbraith and the Crown solicitor, Robert Fardell, five weeks before the trial was to begin. He followed the traditional lawyer's path before a court case and asked if they would consider negotiating a reduction in the charges. Curry had not yet been given the prosecution evidence and depositions. Nevertheless it was inconceivable that Curry, as one of New Zealand's top lawyers, had failed to hear on the grapevine that there were doubts in the prosecution camp.

On October 11 the evidence on which Curry would build his case arrived. He shut himself away in a beach house for the weekend and studied the dossier. The flaws convinced him that a deal was possible. He conferred with the lawyer sent from France, Daniel Soulez Lariviere, and his clients, Mafart and Prieur, outlining the options to them.

If they stuck with the murder charges there was a chance, perhaps a certainty, that they would get a jury already biased by the massive press coverage and prepared to convict in spite of the complex legal arguments he might muster. If they would consider pleading guilty to a manslaughter charge, he believed he could persuade the Crown prosecutor to accept it.

283

It was a difficult choice for Mafart and Prieur – to plead not guilty to murder and pray for a miracle or admit they were involved in the bombing and go to prison. They obviously felt they had no choice. They could no longer embarrass their masters back in Paris, for Fabius, the prime minister, had already conceded French responsibility; Charles Hernu, the defence minister, had resigned; and Admiral Lacoste, the DGSE boss, had been sacked. Not guilty pleas would only wash more French dirty linen in public. Anything less than life imprisonment would be a bonus. They decided to plead guilty to manslaughter.

There followed two weeks of negotiation. Curry hoped to persuade the Crown to concede even more ground but Neazor, by now directly involved in the negotiations, refused to budge. He too had weighed the evidence and had come to the same conclusion as Curry. But he could still have refused and allowed the murder charges to run their course. It was here that New Zealand's peculiar but commendable sense of fair play showed itself. It simply would not be just to allow Mafart and Prieur to face murder charges that could not be proved, in front of a jury that might be biased. It was a chivalrous but unpopular decision. Neazor agreed to reduce the murder charges to manslaughter but the lesser charges of conspiring to cause explosions and immigration offences would stick. Agreement was reached on Friday, November 1, just three days before the trial was to begin.

Three weeks later, on Friday November 22, Mafart and Prieur repeated their trek to the old High Court building to hear their fates. They sat impassively as Judge Gilbert laid the ghost of lamb and butter deals by sentencing them to ten years' imprisonment each. They were shocked by the judge's severity. They had expected much less, perhaps even deportation after a few months.

Mafart and Prieur were driven away to the old Mount Eden prison in central Auckland – the jail where David McTaggart had spent a few hours' imprisonment back in 1972. They each spent that weekend alone in a cell rather than sharing with other prisoners. 'It is politic to leave a lady on her own for the first weekend after she has been given a long prison sentence,' said the deputy superintendent of the prison, Russell Wood. 'If tears are appropriate then she can shed them in privacy into her own pillow.' Prieur was said to be handling the news 'not too badly' – but then she had been in a cell for nearly five months already. It would take time for the prospect of another ten years to sink in. Also, her husband, a Parisian fireman, had flown out to be near her during the trial, but soon he would fly back to France and she would be alone again.

The process of reconciliation was soon under way. In New Zealand and France Alain Mafart and Dominique Prieur are generally acknowledged respectively as poor dupes deserted by scheming generals and politicians or heroes of the republic. 'They were only following orders,' is the generally sympathetic judgement in Paris. Fan mail arrived at the prison by the bagful. Naturally the French government nurtured the public belief that they would be freed and deported to be welcomed back to the bosom of the DGSE. Word from within the walls of their prisons in the early weeks of 1986 suggested that the agents' fate was finally sinking in. The prospect of ten years in jail was only slightly worse than their realization that freedom has its drawbacks. Mafart remains cool, philosophical and arrogant. Prieur suffers – badly. Her days fluctuate between deep depression and hopeful optimism. Neither shows any sign of repentance, but the conceit that led them, their fellow saboteurs and their superiors to believe that they were somehow invulnerable and that New Zealand is nothing more than a Third World stage for their antics is cracking. Once back in Paris their lives must undergo dramatic change. Such an infamous pair can no longer work within the intelligence field, unless allocated some thoroughly boring desk job. The politicians are desperate to forget their existence – and those that might have protected

285

them have been sacked, or demoted in the DGSE shake-up that followed the sinking. Mafart and Prieur have good reason to feel bitter.

So too does the man whose orders they followed. Admiral Lacoste was too much of a good soldier to allow his right-wing political views to influence his relations with his boss, defence minister Charles Hernu. But after being sacked from the DGSE, Lacoste has no qualms about letting his sympathies show. He now acts as consultant for Raymond Barre, the Gaullist politician and political enemy of Mitterrand. There is no doubt that he is able to provide Barre with information that is highly damaging to the socialists.

However, Lacoste refuses to apportion blame for the abortive spy mission against Greenpeace. Instead, he makes his feelings known obliquely. He approvingly cites the reactions of Israeli leaders to an operation by their secret service, Mossad, which went wrong. Mossad assassinated a suspected Palestinian terrorist in Norway who turned out to be neither Palestinian nor a terrorist. After the Israelis confirmed that their victim was an innocent labourer from Morocco, the chief of Mossad offered his resignation to the prime minister, Golda Meir. She refused, saying: 'You're not to blame. I am.' Lacoste suggests that if French leaders – he refuses to mention names – had shown the same courage to own up to their mistakes, the socialist government would have come out of the Greenpeace affair looking like national heroes instead of buffoons.

The admiral has since published a study of French naval strategy on which he is willing to talk. He wears an academic's green tweed jacket which fits him too loosely, as though it were a garment that the admiral, now in his 60s, had not worn for many decades while in naval uniform. Lacoste believes that French nuclear weapons testing is far too important to be put off by protests from daredevil environmentalists like Greenpeace, which he is convinced is under the influence of Russian agents. Lacoste saw the protection of the atomic test programme as one of the navy's most important overseas assignments and therefore regarded the Greenpeace protest as a paramount threat.

He has some fond memories, however, and boasts of one in

particular. He believes that one of his main accomplishments during his brief stay in the Piscine was to rid the secret service of its gangsters. He says that in the past the intelligence network had exchanged favours with the criminal underworld, though he declines to give examples. Under his tenure, such practices were stopped.

The Greenpeace affair has clearly embittered the admiral towards the socialists in general and his former bosses, Mitterrand and Hernu, in particular. He says that in retrospect they were never well prepared to take on the awesome responsibilities of running a nuclear power. He says that they never shed their socialist paranoia and prejudice against the military (including the intelligence services) even after they were unquestionably in command of government machinery.

Lacoste is a strong supporter of the Gaullist policy of not aligning France's nuclear force directly with the command structure of NATO. He regards the NATO command as a nightmare of conflicting interests which pits Greeks against Turks, Germans against Belgians, and has Europeans squabbling with Americans in endless arguments over the most minor practical details of joint military manoeuvres. In these opinions Lacoste closely parallels the views of Mitterrand and Hernu, who turned out to have a distinctly nationalistic view of French military policy.

Four months after resigning as defence minister, Charles Hernu could be found seated in a bar filled with the swirling smoke of many Gauloise cigarettes. He was back on the political campaign trail in a working-class suburb of Lyon. Hernu had spent twenty years grooming himself to become the defence minister of a socialist government, and his days in office had been cut short by the Greenpeace scandal. Hernu had been sacrificed by Mitterrand, and also by the chiefs of the army and intelligence services whom he had tried so hard to cultivate. Of all those hit by the Greenpeace scandal, Hernu has fallen the hardest. He is mayor of Villeurbanne, on the unfashionable side of the Rhône river from Lyon, and in late January 1986 he was also

287

fighting hard for election as a deputy to the National Assembly. The socialists were trailing their right-wing opponents by thirty points in the opinion polls. Greenpeace was one reason for the decline in the socialist fortunes, and especially Hernu's.

It had not been an encouraging Saturday for Hernu's campaign. A meeting planned early that morning in an open market failed to attract more than a few dozen sleepy shoppers and taxi drivers who had wandered over from their rank. Many cabbies in Lyon had been driven off the streets by a new tax imposed by the socialists, and Hernu's reception was as chill as the winter air. The socialist caravan moved quickly on to a shopping centre and then to a café: La Boule in Montssuy. It was here, in this refuge crowded with loyal socialists, that Hernu's talents as a politician shone.

He even worked two Greenpeace jokes into his speech. 'Our campaign in the Rhône valley has attracted many foreign journalists but none, alas, from New Zealand.' And: 'We bear no grudges against New Zealand, especially their rugby players. In fact, Villeurbanne's team has just taken on two of them.' The socialists sitting around the long table chuckled appreciatively and drank their cassis. Hernu, as he always does, drank champagne. Admirers are willing to forgive Hernu his bourgeois habits, his hand-tailored shirts fròm Jermyn Street in London.

But even six months after the sinking of the *Rainbow Warrior*, the scandal was hardly a laughing matter for the socialists. The opposition had accused the Mitterrand government of abandoning its two loyal servants, Alain Mafart and Dominique Prieur, in New Zealand. The French press tended to portray New Zealand as one big Devil's Island. New Zealand's premier, David Lange, seemed unsusceptible to private threats of a French trade embargo. It looked likely that the two spies would not be allowed to serve the remainder of their ten-year sentence in France, as President Mitterrand had asked.

At first Hernu told the gathered journalists that he would only speak of local election issues. But soon he was referring wistfully to his days as a world statesman, to his good friends 'Michael' (Heseltine) and 'Caspar' (Weinberger). His mayoral office in Villeurbanne is too small to contain the ambitions and, after Greenpeace, the frustrations of an ex-defence minister.

Anonymity is a spy's greatest asset. Suddenly finding mugshots splashed across the pages of newspapers and magazines all over the globe, the DGSE might be expected to dispense with the services of its most celebrated post-war agents. It is doubtful whether Mafart and Prieur will be available for assignment even in the distant future; Lieutenant-Colonel Dillais can look forward to continuing in some administrative role; the skills of Christine Cabon, Roland Verge, Gerald Andries and Jean-Michel Bartelo will always be useful in training raw recruits.

But the DGSE's new bosses did not want them to surface for some time to come: there were still too many people waiting to interview them. Journalists with notepads and New Zealand policemen with arrest warrants formed an orderly queue to await the first sighting. It has been rumoured that all had been sent 'on vacation' after undergoing plastic surgery; the *Ouvéa* crew was 'in hiding', Cabon had reportedly lost herself in Gabon. The likely truth is that they were confined to barracks on some remote military base waiting for the dust to settle.

Even after the bombing, Christine Cabon continued to play the role of Greenpeace sympathizer. On July 19, using her Bonlieu pseudonym, she wrote to the Auckland office from an excavation site in Israel. 'The news about the sunk [sic] of the *Rainbow Warrior* has just reached me in the archaeological expedition in Pardes Hanna. What can I say after such news? I feel so choked. Why such a monstrosity?' By the time her note arrived in New Zealand Cabon had already been rumbled. Auckland police replied by asking the Israeli authorities to arrest her. That same day the DGSE cabled Cabon to say that her father was very ill. In fact her father had been dead for some years; the message was a coded instruction to return home urgently. By the time the Israelis moved to arrest Cabon she had already left the country. Back in Auckland, Superintendent Galbraith was furious. 'We know she was in Israel at the time of our communication to the Israeli authorities,' he said. Later, when her infiltration of the Palestine Liberation Organization became public knowledge, there were suspicions in New Zealand that Israel had allowed her to escape as a reward for earlier favours.

Xavier Maniguet remains his ebullient, boastful self, living in Normandy, chasing the ladies and boring people with exaggerated tales of his exploits. On a dismal February day in 1986, Maniguet could be found sitting in the restaurant of the Hôtel Présidence in Dieppe. A huge panoramic window looked out on to the deserted seafront and the grey English Channel which merged imperceptibly into grey sky. Unlike most residents of the Normandy port at that time of winter, Maniguet was looking fit and bronzed after a few days in the Alps. His dress was both casual and elegant: flannel trousers, pale pink shirt, cashmere pullover and a stylish blouson jacket in fine-quality leather. Over lunch he was careful to drink only one glass of wine.

Once again he denied any involvement in the Greenpeace affair. But he is worried, all the same. 'There is always the possibility of a fanatic or a madman . . . so I am armed. I am a hunter and I know how to use a weapon.'

Maniguet had been to the Alps indulging his second great passion – flying. He had been teaching take-off and landing techniques for light aircraft on glaciers. When he is not flying, Maniguet runs. His usual distance is ten miles – bare-chested – along the shore. 'The first mile or so is a bit tough. After that it's fine.'

But it did not take long to get round to his greatest passion of all. 'I love women very much. Too much to marry one woman. They have to understand that I may leave for the other side of the world tomorrow.' The residents of Dieppe take great interest in his 'love nest' (Maniguet himself prefers to call it his 'pussycat trap'). It is a warren of luxurious chalets beside a pond where he gives large parties.

'I am a patriot – even though that is not very fashionable – and a doctor in the naval reserve. I also consider myself a Catholic. If someone had asked me to join an operation which involved sinking a ship I would have refused. There were people on that ship.'

Maniguet plans to set himself up as a medical consultant for international companies. Not only is he an expert in curing divers with the bends, but he also claims to be a specialist in aeronautical and tropical diseases. He is at pains to point this out because of Greenpeace. Maniguet says the press only wants to hear about his underwater training because they think that ties in with the activities of the *Ouvéa* crew.

The doctor has quite a reputation in Dieppe. His physique apparently has attracted feminine attention, and according to Maniguet his 'pussycat trap' is seldom empty. Women opposed to blood sports would hardly be tempted to enter his trap. Maniguet bulldozed an artificial lake with an island in the middle. It is there that he built what appears to be a luxurious hunter's blind. With its low roof covered in grass and shrubs, it is almost impossible to see from across the lake. The inside of the 'pussycat trap' is like a warren of giant bedrooms, heaped high with cushions and pillows. When he is not bedding his lady visitors, Maniguet silently slides open the glass window and blasts away at the ducks that land on his lake. It is a nice life for an arrested adolescent.

But after Greenpeace Maniguet may find himself the hunted. He was afraid to drive his Porsche 911S to our interview for fear someone would note down his licence number. 'This precaution may throw off the journalists, but not,' he adds cryptically, 'the others.' And who are they? Maniguet refuses to answer, leaving one uncertain whether these precautions are those of a French spy or a boastful adventurer who has come to believe the tall tales he uses for his seductions. But in any event Maniguet, who says he earned his money not from the DGSE but from practising medicine overseas, may find that his sportsman's lair has turned into his own trap. New Zealand's prime minister, David Lange, has threatened that if Maniguet dares to leave France, he will be hit with an international warrant for arrest. 'France,' says Maniguet, 'has become a rather small and golden prison for me.'

*

291

Few mourn the death of a freelance photographer for long and Fernando Pereira, killed trying to save his cameras from the sinking *Rainbow Warrior*, was no exception. Pereira did not have the backing of any powerful newspaper to run the news of his murder in indignant headlines across the front page, or to throw weight behind a demand for an inquiry. While the political storm has raged in New Zealand and in France, the story of Fernando Pereira's short and unfulfilled life has sunk without a trace.

Born in 1950 in the village of Chavez, on the outskirts of Lisbon, Pereira seemed destined for a career in the armed services. His family had a long history of serving in the Portuguese military. Nobody doubted that Pereira would continue the tradition.

In 1970, during the Salazar dictatorship, Pereira was set to join the Portuguese air force to train as a pilot. Instead, to the horror and sadness of his parents, he fled to Spain. But Pereira was not welcome there under the Franco regime and moved on, to France and then Holland. There he was granted refugee status, married a Dutch woman and drifted from one job to another. He decided to become a photographer. The only newspaper that would use his photos was the Communist daily *De Waarheid*, which has a circulation of only 20,000. 'Sure,' Pereira once remarked to another photographer, Bert Verhoef, 'it's a Communist newspaper, but what do I care, I just want to take photos.'

Some French newspapers seized on the fact that Pereira had worked for a Communist newspaper before joining up with Greenpeace, as if his death were somehow excused by his alleged political affiliations. But one of his colleagues on the newspaper, Bert Zylma, said: 'Fernando was a great guy, friendly and without any political ideas. He certainly wasn't a member of the Communist Party.'

Fernando Pereira's body was flown from Auckland to Amsterdam. With the fall of the generals in Portugal, Pereira had been allowed back into his own country and had been reunited with his family. So Fernando's father flew to Amsterdam to attend his funeral.

The irony was that because of his journalistc experience, Pereira was probably the only man aboard the *Rainbow Warrior* who instantly identified the deep thudding sound on the night of July 10. He must have known that this was the scoop he had been waiting for, so he raced below deck for his cameras. He had no way of knowing that the French had planted a second bomb. He was found drowned with one camera already slung around his neck in preparation for taking the picture of a lifetime.

Authors' Note

The Sunday Times Insight team was in Birmingham investigating the September 1985 riots in an inner city ghetto when Greenpeace made its approach to us. Since the *Rainbow Warrior* was sunk in Auckland Harbour the organization had been inundated with requests for access to individual members and files by publishers in Britain, France, Australia and New Zealand. What concerned Greenpeace was the effort that would be committed to those books planned by an individual author or a team of two journalists, one working in France, the other in New Zealand. Greenpeace properly thought that the story demanded far greater resources both in time and journalistic skill; such was the immensity of what had happened at each end of the globe that a thorough investigation could only be carried out by an independent organization able to call on the specialist skills of its own staff, trusted correspondents and investigative reporters anywhere in the world.

The international directors of Greenpeace chose *The Sunday Times*. Its investigations and campaigns over the last twenty years are renowned. Insight books have probed wars from the Sinai desert to the Falkland Islands, international tragedies from Thalidomide to the Turkish Airlines DC10 crash outside Paris in 1974. The Greenpeace offer was, in effect, quite straightforward. Greenpeace would be willing to open its filing cabinets, to co-operate exclusively with us and provide us with unique access to its own researches if we took on the task of mounting the most searching investigation possible into the sinking of the *Rainbow Warrior*. There were no conditions; Greenpeace simply wanted a thorough and objective study to answer the important questions raised by the sabotage of its flagship, which would survive as an authoritative record.

The Sunday Times had already covered the sinking in its

news-pages and the investigative unit of *The Sunday Times* was in a period of transition. Its long-standing and highly regarded head, Paul Eddy, had just departed on a new career and a new team was in formation. It would have been perfectly understandable if Andrew Neil, editor of *The Sunday Times*, had insisted that the new team bed itself in and concentrate on issues closer to home. Instead he gave his full support to the project, knowing that it would consume much raw energy that should properly be channelled into the pages of *The Sunday Times*.

For that reason we are indebted to him and also to his deputy Ivan Fallon who urged us forward and kept the team on its toes. Others deserve our gratitude too. Peter Roberts, the newspaper's managing editor, smoothed our path through many obstacles. John Lovesey gave us enthusiastic support and valuable advice on the manuscript, as did *The Sunday Times*'s own libel lawyer, Antony Whitaker. Our design department artists, Phil Green, Gordon Beckett and Peter Sullivan, produced their usual high-quality graphics which are always worth a thousand words.

We are equally grateful to colleagues in France. Ann-Elisabeth Moutet of *The Sunday Times*, Roger Faligot, Pascal Krop, Jacques-Marie Bourget, Claude Angeli and Bernard Veillet-Lavalles provided valuable assistance.

We owe much to Greenpeace, to David McTaggart, Steve Sawyer and Brian Fitzgerald in particular. They worked patiently and tirelessly to aid our investigation. Though they disagreed with certain findings or observations they maintained their insistence that the book be an objective record and made no attempt to influence the result.

Finally we owe our thanks to Don Berry, Managing Editor, Features. For eighteen years he has been an inspiration to staff on *The Sunday Times*. His journalistic skills and his vision are assets he has gladly shared. If the reader judges *Rainbow Warrior* a success, then it is because it attempts to emulate his high standards.

Robin Morgan
Brian Whitaker
February, 1986

295

Index

Chatelain, Roger, 72
China, 128, 130, 167
Chirac, Jacques, 258
CIA, see Central Intelligence Agency
Claverie, Christian, 89, 93–5
Cochrane, David, 216–7, 219, 226, 233
Colenso, Pat, 209
Cooper, Bruce, 47–8
Cooper, Jane, 187–8
Cormack, John, 114
Corsica, 172, 192, 243
Cote, Paul, 113
Couch, Jill, 224
Cousteau, Jacques, 117
Crampton, Naomi, 36
Crene, Hec, 201–5, 208, 210
Cruise missiles, 124
Cudmore, Hugh, 295–6
Curry, Gerard, 283–4

Daily Express, London, 282
Dalniy Vostok, the, 117
Daniels, John and Glynis, 211
Danielsson, Bengt, 127–8, 130–1, 134–5, 137–8, 140–1, 162, 190–1
Danielsson, Marie-Thérèse, 130
Darnell, Bill, 114
Davidson, Grant, 84–5, 89
Debre, Michel, 116
De Gaulle, Charles, 135–7, 165–6
De Grasse, the, 87, 89, 92–3, 137
Denby, Senior Sergeant, 65
Denmark, 26, 121
Deodar, the, 27
Devonport, NZ, 27
DGSE, see General Directorate for External Security
Dick, George 'Moby', 202
Dillais, Louis-Pierre, 192, 207, 210–11, 217–9, 223, 225–6, 234–7, 242, 243, 244, 246, 250, 289
Django, the, 16
Don't Make a Wave, 113–14, 118
Dormand, Jean Louis, see Dillais, Louis-Pierre

Dubois, Yves-Marie, 167
Dubos, Jean François, 176
Du Fresne, Marion, 200
Dumas, Roland, 282
Dunkerquoise, La, 98–101
Durieux, Christian, 168

East Germany, 125
East-West Airlines, 65
Ebeye, 149, 157
Edwards, Davey, 22, 24, 29, 146, 151, 156–7
Emin, Roger, 260, 268
England, see Great Britain
Evans, Joy, 65
Explorer, MV, 9–10, 19, 21–4, 27
L'Express, 257, 274, 277

Fabius, Laurent, 258, 274, 277, 284
Fages, Henri, 161–3, 176, 260, 271
Falkland Islands, 35, 144
Fangataufa, 134–7, 162
Fardell, Robert, 283
Figaro, Le, 281
Fiji, 62, 67–8, 81, 183
Fitzgerald, Brian, 121–3
Fontaine, André, 273
Forum Restaurant, Whangarei, 227
Fourrier, Colonel, 267
France, 13, 15, 32–3, 40, 50, 61, 70, 74, 84, 103–7, 110, 112, 118, 121–2, 128–9, 134–8, 141, 161–7, 171–6, 178–9, 182–4, 186–7, 204, 211, 214, 222, 235, 242, 256–61, 264, 266, 268–73, 276–7, 281–3, 288, 291–3
French nuclear tests, 33, 81, 85, 88–9, 94, 96–8, 104, 110, 134–41, 175–6, 186, 258–60
Fri, the, 189
Furgler, Kurt, 257

Gaddafi, Colonel Muammar, 132–3, 192, 276
Galbraith, Allan, 37–8, 40, 42, 45–6, 48–53, 55–6, 65, 70–2, 74, 210, 235, 241, 248, 251–2, 254–5, 283

297

299

YOU'VE READ THE BOOK, NOW JOIN THE CAUSE...

GREENPEACE

SUBSCRIPTION RATES

Single Person £7.50 ☐ **Family £12** ☐ **Overseas £15** ☐
Unwaged, OAP, Students £4.50 ☐

Name_____ Address_____

_____

Cheque/Access   I enclose £_____ Date_____

please debit my Access No. ☐☐☐☐☐☐☐☐☐☐☐☐☐☐☐☐☐☐

TURN EVERY £1 INTO £1.43.

If you are a UK tax payer, please complete the Bankers Order and Covenant forms. **We can claim 43p from the Inland Revenue for every £1 donated.**

BANKERS ORDER

To the manager

(name & address of bank)_____

_____Postcode_____

Please pay Greenpeace £_____monthly/annually starting on_____

and debit my A/c No_____Signed_____

Address_____Postcode_____

For office use: Greenpeace Environmental Trust, A/c 05422043, NatWest Bank PLC, 31 New Bridge Street, London EC4V 6DA (50-41-02)

TAX RECOVERY FORM (DEED OF COVENANT)

I_____Mr/Mrs/Miss/Ms of (address)

_____Postcode_____

undertake to pay Greenpeace each year for four years (or during my lifetime if shorter) from today the sum that will after the deduction of income tax at the basic rate be £_____*pa   Date_____

Signed, sealed and delivered_____ LS

Witness's signature & address_____

_____Postcode_____

*just put here the amount you wish to pay annually.

ONLY COMPLETE THE TAX RECOVERY (DEED OF COVENANT) IF YOU PAY UK INCOME TAX. If you cannot pay by bankers order, please enclose cheque, PO or Access (sorry, no other credit card). Please complete and return to: **Greenpeace**, Subscriptions Dept., 29–35 Gladstone Rd., Croydon, Surrey CR9 3RP.

If you are not a UK resident, please contact an address below:
1/787 George St., Sydney NSW 2000, Australia.
2623 West 4th Avenue, Vancouver BC V6K 1P8, Canada.
Private Bag, Wellesley St., Auckland, New Zealand.